EVERY LETTER COUNTS

EVERY LETTER COUNTS

SUSAN HAMPSHIRE

BANTAM PRESS

LONDON · NEW YORK · TORONTO · SYDNEY · AUCKLAND

TRANSWORLD PUBLISHERS LTD
61-63 Uxbridge Road, London W5 5SA
TRANSWORLD PUBLISHERS (AUSTRALIA) PTY LTD
15-23 Helles Avenue, Moorebank, NSW 2170
TRANSWORLD PUBLISHERS (NZ) LTD
Cnr Moselle and Waipareira Aves,
Henderson, Auckland

Published 1990 by Bantam Press
a division of Transworld Publishers Ltd
Copyright © 1990 Susan Hampshire

This book set in Times

British Library Cataloguing in Publication Data
Hampshire, Susan, 1942–
    Every letter counts: winning in life despite
    dyslexia.
    1. Man. Dyslexia. Personal adjustment
    I. Title
    362.1'968553

    ISBN 0–593–01886–9

Printed in Great Britain by
Mackays of Chatham, plc, Chatham, Kent

This book is dedicated to all my fellow dyslexics.

Sadly, many dyslexics are still thought of as stupid or lazy. But dyslexics CAN be high flyers, remarkable achievers and, with their natural determination and compassion, do a job as well, if not better, than anyone else.

Author's Note

The author is donating eighty per cent of her royalties to two dyslexia charities. The majority will go to the Dyslexia Institute Bursary Fund to help provide specialist teaching for dyslexics of all ages, and the balance to the British Dyslexia Association for the sole purpose of paying for teacher training.

*   *   *

Over the past fifteen years I have travelled in England and America meeting many children who are dyslexic, but who have not yet had specialist teaching. At this stage these children have been withdrawn, lacking in confidence and too shy to talk. But six months or a year later I have met those same children after they have had special help and they have bounced up with smiling faces full of confidence. This proves to me that help provided by specially trained teachers is vital in order to give children with specific reading and spelling problems the start in life they deserve.

There are thousands of children who need help but who cannot afford it. The educational authorities in some areas are willing and do their best, but they do not have the resources to help. So, until there can be proper help provided in schools, many, many children will remain in the wilderness unless they are fortunate enough to have their lessons subsidized by a bursary fund.

Acknowledgements

Firstly I must thank Mary Atkinson, my editor, whose patience and perspective have made a tremendous contribution to this book.

COVER PHOTOGRAPH

The jacket cover photograph was taken by one of my favourite photographers, David Steen. Over the years David has taken many photographs of me (including the cover photographs for three of my books), but I didn't know he was dyslexic until a few months ago and that was only because Bantam Press told me!

CARTOONS

There are three very special thanks. To Ronald Searle who so generously drew and sent from France the brilliant cartoon on page xv. To Mel Calman and to Ralph Steadman for their witty contributions on page 38 and page 50.

Thanks also to *The Spectator* and *Punch* for permission to use the cartoons on pages 87, 122, 176 and 292 and to Nick for his cartoon on page 204.

I would like to thank some of the students of the Dyslexia Institute who wrote the jokes for the *Xceedingly Funny Joke*

Book (Walker Books) which the Dyslexia Institute have kindly allowed me to use.

RESEARCH

I am extremely grateful to my friends Dr Nata Goulandris and Diana Baring for their advice and encouragement. Susan Schulman who sent so much information regarding dyslexia from America, Susannah Sharp, my niece, who helped with administration, and my cousin, Don Pavey, who brought to my attention the eccentric spelling of past great writers.

Liz Brooks and Dr Harry Chasty at the Dyslexia Institute, as always, deserve a large thank you not only for their tireless work for dyslexics, but also for putting me in touch with several adult dyslexics and helping me compile reading lists. Thanks too to Jennifer Smith at the British Dyslexia Association who helped with addresses and information.

I am grateful to *Their World*, *Sports Illustrated for Kids*, *Red Book*, *Parade* and *Gentleman's Quarterly* for allowing me to use some of their quotes.

SECRETARIAL HELP

Not being able to type two words myself there is no way the book could have been written without the secretarial help of Sheila Hoad, Anne Marie McGarvey, Alex Hole, Susannah Sharp and, last but not least, Janine Fischer.

Bridget Garms, who transcribed nearly a hundred tapes and spent as much as four hundred hours doing this often tiring and difficult task, deserves a special thank you. And not forgetting Jennie Bull for correcting my grammar.

MOTHERS

I greatly appreciate the help from the mothers who talked to me and contributed from the parent's point of view: Jo Dance, Barbara Bush, Angharad Rees, Felicity Rudman, Mrs Linton Smith, et al.

Thanks too to the people who allowed me to quote from their letters, Anna Duke, Val Kearney, Lydia Jackson, Margaret Gilbert.

STATEMENTS

I am very grateful to Her Majesty Queen Anne-Marie of the Hellenes, His Majesty King Constantine of the Hellenes and His Majesty King Olav of Norway for giving their valuable time to talk to me and make statements for the book. And to Mrs George Bush for so kindly contributing. Also to Neil Allan, Jean Augur, Hamilton Bland, Donald D. Derrick, Jeremy Glyn, Jenny Goodsmith, Dr Nata Goulandris, Ron Grant and Lavinia Scott-Elliott who have helped with contacts and information.

THE CONTRIBUTORS

The biggest thank you of all goes to those who have told their story giving such positive encouragement and advice and without whom there would be no book: Ian Adam, 'Anna', 'Annette', Chris Augur, Nigel Augur, Jim Austin, Suzy Bailey, Charles Brooking, David Brown, Rosemary Burrows, Neil Bush, Lucy Butterwick, Sammy Chaudhry, Cher, Diane Clark, Paul Cotton, Richard Cotton, Wendy Craddock, Jo Dance, Susan Darby, Ian Davies, Peter Dazaley, Ian Duke, Barbara

Dunsford, Dr Dorothy Einon, Colin Fails, Tim Faulkner, Martin Feinstein, Judge Jeffrey H. Gallet, Sally Gardener, Clara Glynn, Whoopi Goldberg, Duncan Goodhew, Julia Green, Jane Henderson, Michael Heseltine MP, Gillian Howarth, John Howroyd, Dick James, Bruce Jenner, Felicity Kendal, 'Liza' Greg Louganis, David Malpass, Anne Micklethwaite, Alan Parker, Claire Pearce, Steven Redgrave, Angharad Rees, Beryl Reid, Richard Rogers, George Rolls, Ron Shaw, Geoff Sheard, Jackie Stewart, Andrew Stirling, Suzy, James Taylor, Diane Thomas, Hilary Thompson, John Tramper, The Earl of Yarmouth, Henry Winkler, Ray Weinberg.

Thanks to all the staff at the Colombe D'Or in St Paul de Vence for not disturbing me for days on end, except to bring me food, when I was finishing the first and second draft of the book.

And finally thank you to my son Christopher and his enthusiasm for reading the manuscript and finding the stories interesting and asking to read more and of course loving thanks to my husband Eddie who has lived with this book, and a dyslexic, for what must seem like an eternity!

CONTENTS

'Do you know, I can never remember whether to spell ⟨hieroglyphs⟩ with an ⟨bird⟩ or an ⟨bird⟩.'

Introduction

Compiling this book has been an extremely emotional experience, which on occasions has taken me to the depths of despair and back. Listening to and identifying with the conversations of people reliving their struggle has often been heart-breaking.

It is hard to believe that even when talking to the hundred and third person for this book, I can find myself fighting back the tears as a young woman describes her joy of getting all the words right in a spelling test as the happiest day of her childhood. Not her first doll, or Christmas or the first time she swam across the pool, but getting a spelling test right.

My own early days were so cushioned and protected by my family that my self-esteem and loss of confidence never reached the depths of many of my fellow sufferers. Getting a spelling test right was never more important or as important as life itself. So I was very lucky.

But even today it is still hard for me to accept that reading is such a major effort. Not writing, or reading the words that I have written myself, because I vaguely know what is there. But reading the unknown, that is an enormous effort and daunts me beyond all belief. Thank heaven for pictures, new paragraphs, capital letters, graphics or anything

1

else which helps to punctuate the sea of words and signpost comprehension.

Although I have lived with this handicap all my life, when I hear heart-rending stories of determination and courage I feel grateful that my own path has been comparatively easy.

But the question which keeps running through my head is why in this day and age are so many children having to suffer this torment? How wrong that a child should feel of less worth because at a given moment he or she does not come up to the required standards and read and spell when their friends can. He or she could be an Einstein, but if you don't read by your sixth birthday who cares about your potential! Underachieving at school can be a major blow to the confidence and leave its scars for the rest of your life.

HOW TO PRONOUNCE DYSLEXIC

Dis LEX ick

(not Dis lex tick)

WHAT IS DYSLEXIA?

Dyslexia was first recognized by two British doctors in 1896 and called Congenital Word Blindness. The word Dyslexia comes from the Greek *dys* meaning ill, and *lexis* meaning word.

Yet despite this early discovery, dyslexia was not medically recognized until nearly a hundred years later when in Britain the Kershaw Committee, headed by Doctor Kershaw, succeeded in getting dyslexia accepted as a neurological disorder in 1975. It was yet another six years before it was educationally recognized when the Warnock Report on education for children with special needs was published, which resulted in the Education Act 1981.

2

Meanwhile in Boston, USA, surgeons were performing autopsies and doing research on the brains of dyslexics, and noticed the presence of physical abnormalities in the language area of the dyslexic's brain. These abnormalities could possibly account for the problems dyslexics have with reading and spelling.

THE WORD

There has been continuing discussion over the years about the use of the word dyslexia and as to whether or not this handicap really exists. The main problem is that dyslexia is hidden. Unlike a broken leg or arm which anyone can see right away, only an autopsy can show the abnormalities in dyslexics' brains. But whatever the handicap is called, it is important that those with the disability are helped and not labelled 'stupid' and 'lazy'.

MISCONCEPTIONS

Dyslexia is not a disease you can catch and which then can be cured. 'You don't come out in spots', as Beryl Reid says. It is a condition you are born with. It can be handed down from the mother or father or can be caused by conditions at birth. *The difficulties can be greatly helped with special remedial teaching provided it is not discovered too late.* However I have heard of a man who developed all the characteristics of being dyslexic after the trauma of suffering head injuries in a car accident. This is known as acquired dyslexia.

TELL-TALE SIGNS

People who are dyslexic sometimes confuse their b's and d's, spell words with letters in the wrong order, misread words and find it hard to read the words of a sentence and comprehend the meaning at the same time. Some dyslexics are often clumsy and may not be good at kicking or hitting a ball accurately. Yet in other cases their manual dexterity and ability to work very precisely with their hands makes them great engineers, pianists, draughtsmen, dentists, painters, musicians, cabinet makers, drummers, and even brain surgeons.

Sequencing is a problem for dyslexics. Getting numbers in the correct order, the days of the week, the days of the month or the alphabet. Some dyslexics are only numerically dyslexic but that's not too good either if you send a cheque for £906.00 instead of £609.00!

THE EFFECTS OF DYSLEXIA AT SCHOOL

What happens to you at school whether you are dyslexic or not can have a profound effect on the rest of your life. Beating, bullying, teasing, being made to write lines, being kept in, put in a corner, called a dunce, rapped with a ruler, given extra homework, not allowed in the playground, are just a few from the long stream of punishments dyslexics remember from their school-days. Punishments for a crime you do not feel you have committed can have a long term psychological effect, and sometimes damage the confidence and self-esteem beyond repair.

But worse still is mistakenly being sent to a mental hospital, school for disturbed children, home for retarded children, remand home or being lumped with children who have learning and behavioural problems which have nothing to do with dyslexia.

MEMORABLE MISTAKES

Dyslexia can cause exasperating and sometimes expensive mistakes. One man thought he had booked a flight to Tasmania, Western Australia, and landed up in Tanzania, Africa. A friend of mine wanted to go on holiday in Dominica in the West Indies and was amazed when she arrived in the Dominican Republic.

I myself have made the mistake of misreading 500 kilometres for 50 kilometres, and booked to go to a water ski school that was not only three hundred odd miles from the hotel where I was staying but also from the airport. So I had carted my ski equipment halfway round the Continent for nothing!

No, being dyslexic isn't dull! In my late teens, early twenties, I flew all the way to New York for a film audition for which I had not only misread the date and instead of arriving on the fifth, I arrived on the fifteenth, but I had also misread the office block number, which in New York is really serious, so I got a taxi cab to a building twenty blocks the wrong way up or down Fifth Avenue and found myself in a pretty uninviting area, which was over three hundred or so numbers out from the building I was supposed to go to for the interview. The finer details I forget, but I certainly didn't get the film part!

A dyslexic photographer went to buy some carpet, the price was £800. But he couldn't write eight, so he went on buying carpet until it came to a number that he could write!

When a dyslexic boy was asked what he was reading he said 'The Growing PENIS of Adrian Mole' instead of 'The Growing PAINS of Adrian Mole'.

HELP STILL NEEDED

It is heart-breaking to know that there are over two million dyslexics in the United Kingdom. Countless youngsters are walking out into this increasingly overcrowded world without the helping hand they deserve. The need of any handicapped person, particularly one with a hidden handicap, is firstly moral support.

During the past four years I have spoken to about a thousand dyslexics and interviewed about a hundred, many of whose testimonies are here.

In some cases, some people are so used to their own dyslexia that when asked if there are any day to day difficulties, they answer 'No, not really'. Yet their spouse has shown me gadgets in every room to help with telephone numbers, messages, spelling and so on. I even met one wife who if she leaves the dinner in the oven for her husband who is dyslexic, rather than leave a note, which he would never notice, she puts a flower pot upside down on the stove, and on the top a tape recorder with a funny nose stuck on, and huge letters saying 'PRESS' in order to give the cooking instructions.

It is a fact that many dyslexics find it hard to talk about or admit their difficulties, often because they feel admitting their shortcomings will make them, in the eyes of the world, a lesser mortal. Certainly I too have reached the stage, after fifteen years of standing up and being counted, when I no longer feel able to talk about not reading until twelve or wetting the bed, with the same ease as I did years ago. So I can understand how this block can come about.

WHO IS DYSLEXIC?

An impressive number of people from all walks of life have been dyslexic and their contribution to the world of art, science, literature, engineering, politics and sport has been invaluable. Albert Einstein the scientist, Auguste Rodin the sculptor, and writers Gustave Flaubert, Lewis Carroll, and Hans Christian Andersen were dyslexic. Great statesmen like George Washington, Franklin Roosevelt, Woodrow Wilson, Winston Churchill, Nelson Rockefeller are also said to have suffered from this hidden handicap. Thomas Edison the inventor and Charles Darwin were dyslexic. Oscar winning actress Cher has not let this handicap hamper her brilliant career, nor have actresses Beryl Reid, Margaux Hemingway or Whoopi Goldberg.

The Royal Ballet's young ballet star Darcy Bussell who is dyslexic says luckily it only affects her writing not her steps! But Dexter Manley, the American Baseball Redskins' defensive end, said it has affected his adult life in that in his mid-twenties he had to humble himself to learn to read and write.

The writer Lord Ted Willis is dyslexic, so too is brain surgeon Harvey Cushing. Actors Ruth Madoc and Christopher Timothy, and film stars Tom Cruise and Henry Winkler all suffer from this handicap.

Sir Joshua Reynolds, first President of the Royal Academy and the most scholarly of artists, was bad at spelling and grammar. The romantic painter, Turner, who became Professor of Perspective Geometry at the Royal Academy, was quite impossible to understand. Students attended his lectures just for the fun of it. Napoleon never learned to spell correctly and his writing was terrible. There are samples of typically dyslexic spelling mistakes of poet Alexander Pope, playwright Ben Jonson and perhaps the greatest of all literary men, Sir Francis Bacon, as well as the mirror writing of Leonardo da Vinci the artist and inventor, at the back of the book.

Today there are many self-made millionaires, eminent architects, engineers, dentists, surgeons, authors, sportsmen, chefs, artists, actors, Nobel Prize winners, and even kings who are dyslexic. The interviewees in this book include Jackie Stewart, the racing driver, Olympic Gold Medallists Greg Louganis, Steven Redgrave, Bruce Jenner and Duncan Goodhew, as well as Michael Heseltine MP and Richard Rogers the architect.

From the parents' point of view, the King of Norway and Mrs Christopher Cazenove (Angharad Rees) give a special insight into dyslexia, as do Mrs George Bush, Mrs Michael Rudman (Felicity Kendal) and Mrs Charles Dance.

THE AIM OF THIS BOOK

The aim of this book is to show the positive side of being dyslexic. This hidden handicap has a very damaging effect on the self-esteem and confidence of the individual. So, showing the plus side of being dyslexic as well as relating the childhood traumas and teenage hurdles will, I hope, be comforting and inspiring to youngsters with this problem. It will show the jobs held by dyslexics, how they got them, how they cope with them, and also how they coped at school and with relationships in work and at home.

The irony is that this book which for me, a dyslexic, has been a gargantuan task to put together and write, will be an even more gargantuan task for the average dyslexic to read! So the comfort and inspiration that are intended may take a long time to reach my fellow sufferers.

Nevertheless I hope this book will give a clear understanding to those who are not dyslexic of what it is like to be born with this often misunderstood handicap.

THE BOOK LAYOUT

The main body of the book is interviews with dyslexics who have generously shared their early difficulties and go on to tell of their triumphs.

Many of the contributors have wished to remain anonymous so their names have been changed to protect their identity. But some dyslexics who are much in the public eye have felt strongly that they want to help their fellow dyslexics and are happy for the world to know about their handicap. These 'star' dyslexics, if you like, have their testimonies placed between the other contributors in the book. There are also a good many jokes from young dyslexics and cartoons, some of which have been specially drawn and generously donated to help the dyslexic cause. The cartoons and the jokes will, I hope, punctuate the chapters with a smile.

Taking into account that dyslexics will find small print extremely tiresome, the print is especially large. If you find reading tiring, take courage. Choose a profession you wish to know about and just dip into the book little by little and let the stories which have given me so much inspiration, do the same for you.

INSPIRATION FOR THIS BOOK

One of the first people I interviewed about four years ago before I really started to compile this book was a theatre lighting technician who I have worked with and who is now much in demand in New York. His traumatic start to life was in a way an inspiration for this book.

As a child 'Tom's' behaviour problems were so severe that between the ages of nine and fourteen, he landed up in no less than four institutions. His frustration manifested itself in outbursts of violence and constant truancy. Finally, in despair, the school advised that he should be sent to a home for disturbed children. When he had been there for some time, he became so frustrated and unhappy that after unsuccessfully trying to commit suicide, he ran away.

Still no one had recognized that his learning problems were the cause of this unrest, nor had they bothered to check his IQ, or have him assessed despite his parents' constant pleading with the authorities. They just said 'He's poor human material and will probably remain institutionalized for the rest of his life.'

Over the following years he stayed at a series of mental hospitals, where they gave him tests and brain scans (but nothing to do with dyslexia) and he was frequently drugged and given sedation to keep him calm. Again he managed to run away and this time he was put into a

9

remand home where he beat up two boys and assaulted a warden. Tom was now nearly fourteen and Borstal was the next stop.

It was only through the persistence of his mother battling with the educational psychologists to have him assessed for a possible learning disability that this story has a happy ending.

Before he was due to go to Borstal Tom broke his arm and was taken to hospital. While at the hospital his parents managed to arrange to have him assessed for dyslexia. He was confirmed as dyslexic, given specialist help and never known to be violent again. Obviously it wasn't quite as smooth as that, but the days of being in institutions were behind him. 'If I'd had to stay at Borstal that would have been it. But I was "rescued" in time. Otherwise I would have landed up robbing banks,' he says.

It is stories like this, of youngsters who have slipped through the net and landed up in institutions they have no business to be in, that make one feel the fight for dyslexics is so worthwhile.

PART ONE

Interviews

Beautician

ROSEMARY

Rosemary was one of the first people I interviewed on tape when I started to research this book. But it was my own dyslexia that put me in a tight spot when the recording was completed.

For some reason the words 'Rosemary' and 'Beautician' did not register as 'Rosemary Beautician' but as 'Robot Electrician'! Where, I wondered as I searched for months, was 'Rosemary the Beautician'?

In despair I wrote a long two page letter to Rosemary, asking could I please see her again. Then out of the blue my son picked up one of the tapes in the study one day and said 'Mum, who's Rosemary the beautician?' 'What?' I screamed. 'I've been searching for that tape for two years!'

When he handed it to me I could see it was not 'Robot Electrician' but the precious tape I thought I had lost, 'Rosemary the Beautician'.

Rosemary has had a worse deal than many. She was not diagnosed dyslexic until she was sixteen, she had tried to commit suicide and was put into a mental institution. But now she has a most successful career.

* * *

13

I have two sisters. I am in the middle which made it quite bad because they are quite bright. They both read at very early ages. I suppose I knew that there was something different about me at the age of three. I just decided I did things differently or things seemed different to me.

PARENTAL SUPPORT

Looking back, I suppose my parents were very good because they tried everything. They took me everywhere from the first signs of me having problems learning and reading. I went to eye specialists, ear specialists, people to teach me how to read, I went everywhere. They really did try everything they could.

I was only diagnosed as dyslexic when I was sixteen by which time I already had lots of problems with my schooling and generally with my life.

I knew I wasn't basically stupid but all the teachers who I came into contact with thought I was and I suppose because I am quite a strong personality I used to be very disruptive. I was a rebel with a cause and my cause was proving that I wasn't basically stupid.

NERVOUS BREAKDOWN

After I had been diagnosed as being dyslexic I couldn't be helped to overcome my dyslexia, because by that time I had got myself into such a state that I had a nervous break-down.

I suppose the only people the diagnosis actually gave relief to were my parents – now they could say there was a reason I was like this and why this happened to me. It was nice for them to label it.

SUICIDE ATTEMPT

I tried to commit suicide by slitting my wrists. From about the age of nine I felt sheer frustration at not being understood and not being able to get across to people how I was feeling and what I felt needed to be done with me. My family were so geared towards getting a good education and going into a good career and succeeding. At age nine I still couldn't read and had great difficulty writing, and I felt there was an immense pressure on me. I did not know what was wrong and I didn't know who or what I was. I think I am a perfectionist. I always strive towards doing things to my best ability, and when I couldn't do things, then I would get so frustrated within myself that I created my own problems.

Perhaps *if*, when I was nine, somebody had said to me I was dyslexic, and we could have worked towards doing something about it, I could have avoided all this agony and I probably would never have gone through what I went through.

I went to see Professor Miles at Bangor University and he gave me all the tests. I think my father went to the Dyslexia Association during my nervous breakdown and they recommended him.

PROBLEMS AT SCHOOL

At sixteen I left school without any qualifications. I had a sort of bust up with school because they took me to all the school psychiatrists, psychologists, special remedial learning techniques and all this sort of thing, and, because I was so rebellious, I was probably very rude and not very helpful. I tried to make my own statement. I literally wanted to be left alone.

CATATONIC

I went catatonic and I was totally agoraphobic. I had a terrible time. I wouldn't go on public transport at all and I literally sat at home next to a radiator rocking back and forwards, for months and months. The only thing that got me out was drama which I was very interested in. I joined a drama group and met a boyfriend there and decided that he was strong enough for me to collapse on. I felt I couldn't do this with my family. They in a way were trying so hard to help me that they were pushing me away.

MENTAL INSTITUTION

When I tried to kill myself they put a care order on me and put me away in a special unit which was set up in Macclesfield for the care of children with emotional disorders. Putting me there meant that it didn't actually go on a medical record because I was still sixteen.

My parents were very against me going into any place where it would be stated that I had had a mental illness. I was given all sorts of drugs, drugs to make me sleep, drugs to make me perk up, mogadon and valium, which just make you worse really.

It took me about six months to purify my system having been in the unit for four or five months. I really shouldn't have been there because most of the children there were in a much worse state than I was. They were menaces to themselves and to society. Quite a few of them managed to kill themselves while I was there.

Not a nice experience, but it did give me the determination to get out and to decide that there was only one person who could do something about the way that I was feeling and that was *me*.

GETTING A JOB

So I got out and I decided I had to get a job. That's when I went into the beauty world. I saw an advertisement in the local newspaper – and I wrote to them.

They phoned me up two days later and said yes they were very interested and would I go and see them. I had an interview with them and they literally offered me the job there and then. Wonderful for my morale.

I must admit I have had experience of beauty before that. My parents had shops, my grandparents had shops, so it was something that I suppose is in the blood. I had worked in a shop since being five years old and I had always liked the experience and it always fascinated me. So it seemed an easy thing to do in a way.

PROMOTION

Within two years of the shop opening I was manageress, at nineteen, which was very good. Then as the company evolved – they work on a franchise system – and as franchises were opened I would go and help set up the franchises and work with them and train the staff.

I believe selling is an art. To do it well gives so much satisfaction. It's such a challenge and I don't think half the people realize what's involved in it. Everybody needs a little bit of advice when buying. Everyday somebody is buying something somewhere – salesmanship could be so much better.

HEADACHES AND PROBLEMS WITH WORK

I might be frightened when I first go into a new job or a new situation, or feel that I have to prove myself, but it means that I do do it extremely well because I am thinking more about things than most people. Because I am dyslexic I am concentrating harder.

I suppose when I first started work I used to get terrible headaches and terribly uptight because I was trying so hard to do things right.

When I started work I still couldn't really read properly. I couldn't spell at all. I still carry a dictionary around with me everywhere, but now that I am more confident within myself I can pass it off as a joke. If somebody asks me how to spell something I say 'I haven't a clue, hold on a minute, I'll just get my dictionary out.' The thing is that with working with lots and lots of people, you find out that they are exactly the same as you. They still can't spell things properly. They still don't know how to write or how to do arithmetic extremely well in their heads. They all have calculators.

I used to think that I was so imperfect and I used to worry so much about it. I went through a whole period in my life not reading, not putting anything down on paper, except perhaps for my own private use because it really did look like double Dutch when somebody else tried to read it.

I think, and I hope now, that my parents are very proud of me. I still feel I've got a long way to go and there's a lot that I'd like to accomplish but I think perhaps I have done more than they thought I would ever do.

Because of learning disabilities, in particular dyslexia, my memories of school are not some of my favourite things. It was different in those days. There was less understanding about conditions like dyslexia. Those of us who had the condition learned to cope and survive the best we could.

Not many years ago there was a disease called polio. No one hears about it any more because of the good efforts of Dr Jonas Salk and many research scientists. The same is happening for learning disabilities. I guess the most important step in research is just knowing that a condition exists. Once people are aware, then understanding can happen: and before you know it, a solution to the problem becomes available.

Whoopi Goldberg
Actress

Theatre Designer

SALLY

In 1986 I was invited to a lunch with the judges of the Central Criminal Court, not really the place where one would expect to talk about dyslexia. Yet while there I met an Old Bailey circuit judge who told me her daughter Sally was severely dyslexic. Sally is a theatre designer.

In fact Sally's and my paths had crossed in the past, when Sally was probably too young to remember. After rehearsals of The Sleeping Prince I would go back to the director's, George Baker's, house to work on the lines with his wife. On many occasions I saw an extremely shy and very sweet little girl having tea and playing 'nanny' to the director's daughter. This was Sally.

*   *   *

For a long time no one knew what was wrong with me. I found it very easy to communicate with people of my parents' age group but with my peers I was a clown, I was ridiculed, I was an outsider. I had to play the clown, a sort of silly little girl.

I am the eldest child and I have a brother. My parents are divorced. My father was a late developer and was almost self-educated. I mean he didn't actually start learning until he

20

was fourteen. My father is a lawyer and Member of Parliament and my mother is a circuit judge at the Old Bailey.

I went to a school where I stayed behind a year in the class and nobody else had done that. I couldn't spell and I couldn't write my name. I genuinely, very obviously was behind everybody else. I never told anyone about how I felt as I thought it was something definitely wrong with me, and that I wasn't coping – if I was dealing with it in a different way it wouldn't be happening to me.

BULLYING

I went to a really horrid school. I was teased very, very badly and I got very badly bullied in the playground when they played with skipping ropes. Children are very horrible when they gang up. They used to get me and put the rope round and round me and I used to end up with terrible rope burns. I had no ability to know how to stop this.

MENTALLY RETARDED

I was told that I was not able to be educated and then they thought I was mentally retarded and the only people who believed in me were the private tutors. All of them said that I was highly intelligent.

I had one wonderful teacher called Kirsty who was a great lady and she used to say 'Darling, you are completely unteachable,' and take me off to St Paul's and do wonderful things and then say to me 'You can find your own way home can't you, girl?' and I used to say 'Yes'. She was wonderful.

PARENTS' ATTITUDE

I think my parents were very in the dark. There was no one like you around, talking about dyslexia. Nobody knew about dyslexia at all. My mother believed that I wasn't mentally retarded and my father, to his credit, did as well, but they had me psychoanalysed. They took me to a psychiatrist, and he told them that the most they could ever hope for was that I would marry well or work in a flower shop. That was about all he thought my ability would allow. I was eleven when they said this and I still couldn't read or write.

Jackie Stewart was on the radio recently and he was talking about conditions at birth. I had a very bad forceps delivery. My mother nearly died. I heard him say he was immensely dyslexic. He said he thought this was to do with the trauma of the birth. Maybe I was the same. I was a very serene baby – I never cried. That's the thing people always say about me when I was little. I never ever cried, I slept through the night, I was like a model baby, like the baby you write about in little books. I have heard of one other person who is dyslexic and who was a model baby. I wonder if that means anything, very quiet, never cried.

When I was eleven I changed my name from Sarah to Sally because I could spell Sally and I couldn't spell Sarah because I still to this day have a block about where the H goes in Sarah. I had no idea and so I changed it to Sally. I thought that was pretty easy, but my surname, Gardener, forget it, I couldn't spell it. And I had a lot of problems. I mastered tricks, I wrote my name on the inside of my hand. I was not dumb at thinking up ideas of how to disguise how bad the situation was. Then finally when I was eleven I met this very crackpot woman who said this incredible word that I had never heard, which was 'dyslexia'. I couldn't say it, and I thought how extraordinary to give a word to something that is unpronounceable and I thought how sad.

GETTING HELP

Suddenly everyone was terribly relieved there was this tag which actually fitted this little person. But I couldn't say it. People would say 'Well, what is it?' and I would just sit there thinking I'm sorry. Then I heard the words 'word blindness', that was a great relief because I could say 'word blind'.

She was horrendous, this crackpot lady who supposedly cured me. She cured me in a series of awful lessons and she would say 'I've got a patient with me.' I had a little red book and I was terrified of her beyond all description of fear. I went and saw her for, I think it was a year – the most agonizing year of my life. She would do all the words like cat, mat, sat, that business, and she had thousands of clocks that all ticked. They all chimed on the hour. I used to look forward to that because you couldn't speak while the event happened.

EXPELLED

I went away from there and I went to a very smart girls' school. I was there for precisely six weeks. I couldn't spell anything and I couldn't write any of the subject names on the books. Eventually I was told that I had beaten up a girl in the playground. I was expelled.

Finally the school confessed that they just couldn't cope with me. They had never met anything like this and they couldn't teach me anything.

CHILDREN'S HOME FOR MALADJUSTED CHILDREN

So then I went to a school for maladjusted children. I had no confidence. I wouldn't have said boo to a goose if it had jumped out at me. I think looking back I was very depressed. My parents both remarried, I knew I was loved but I felt totally locked in a world where there was no way out, there was no route out of this complexity.

I went to this school for maladjusted children. I had never been a boarder before and at eleven I was chubby and unhappy. A girl said to me, 'Well, do you think anyone will pick you up at half-term?' and I said 'What do you mean?' and she said 'There are lots of children here who never get picked up again.' I discovered it was a school for children with very great difficulties, one step before reform school. Then obviously on for a happy prison career.

I just looked and realized I was so lucky, that I was really loved, I was really wanted.

MENTOR

Dr Pullen who ran the school was incredible. She didn't believe in dyslexia but believed that there was a me. She said I could do anything I wanted to as long as I wanted to do it. I think it gave me a lot of courage, seeing her and this amazing way she had with children. I mean she was very rough and immensely cruel in a way, but she was totally on our side. She was fighting for us against great odds. There were about two hundred children. There was no bullying. Nobody bullied anyone. There were all sorts, there was a spastic child there and mentally retarded children. There was such a feeling of brotherhood and camaraderie and helping each other.

We were all in this same boat together and sticking with one another and we really loved each other.

DISCOVERING THE JOY OF READING IN MY TEENS

I had always wanted to read *Wuthering Heights*. I loved it. My mother read it to me. I had tried to read it but it was all a jumble. I thought it was all set inside a toy box, in an attic box. I just couldn't understand it. I found a collective works of the Brontës and I picked this up and I was reading it, and suddenly it was like falling into this wonderful pool. Instead of these words becoming agony, I was getting through it and wasn't using my finger to follow the words. It just happened and I was thirteen when it happened, and I never to this day know why I did it, or how it happened. I suppose no one had ever worried about my reading when I went to this school, they stopped educating me, bullying me, they just let me be.

NO ENCOURAGEMENT

I went to a terrible school after the one for maladjusted children. I went to a school for girls, an awful boarding school in Hastings where you were made to wear walking shoes with slippery soles and brown horsehair uniform and I hated it beyond all belief. My mother said to me if you get five O-levels, you can go to art school. I have to say, all through my education there was one woman who said I was very talented at art, but nobody at any of the schools ever recognized it. I think mainly because they did not want to see any ability in me.

It's easier to say there is no ability in a child than to say 'Well, she actually does have one thing that she can do really well.' Especially in an academic private system, *it is not the thing to say she is artistic*. It is much better to say she is brilliant at her maths. So encouragement had been denied to me.

EXAM SUCCESS

Then I passed my O-levels. I worked out the art myself because I have a brilliant memory. I memorized pages of this stuff, pages upon pages that I thought would get me through this exam. I sat in loos and I memorized it. I have no idea of the order of words until I focus in on them. Even now I still make mistakes. But I did block memory it.

I was so determined, as I thought freedom lies in getting this. I was told not to make a fuss when I went to do my O-levels, to sit quietly and to write my name and to sit still because other children were going to do really well. At the end of the English Literature, because I never got English Language, I was asked 'Why have you scribbled so much on the paper?' I never forgot that. I had been writing, but to them it was as if I couldn't, so what had I been writing on my paper? They didn't think I could ever pass any of these exams.

I passed the exams and in fact I did better than some of the more intelligently spoken members of the school. They wrote to me and asked if I would like to go into the Sixth Form, and it was a great moment of my life, and one of delight, to tell them where they could put their Sixth Form!

BEING TAKEN SERIOUSLY
FOR THE FIRST TIME

Because I was very young, too young to go to a proper art school, I went to one which sadly no longer exists. It was like the doors of heaven opening. My first drawing you could put a thumb over it, but nobody laughed.

We were having a discussion afterwards like you do, about painting and drawing, and I remember going hot in the face saying my point and almost waiting for everyone to laugh. But absolutely nobody did and they were saying 'That's a very interesting point, now I think what Sally has said . . . .'

I thought 'This is the first time in my life that contemporaries have ever said this or taken me seriously.' No one was laughing and they came back and asked what else I thought. I have never forgotten that. It has stayed as one of the big red letter days of my life, that this was the day that I was actually with my own age group and no one had seen me as the clown. It just got

26

better and better.

I did art school for one year, then one year at Hammersmith College, and then three years at Central where I got a First Class Honours degree. My mother said I should tell you this because it's a lovely story: I got this First Class Honours degree and I phoned up my mother and I said 'I've got a First Class Honours degree, Mum!' and there was a terrible silence and she said 'Oh, darling, go back and read it again, you may have read it ⸱⸱rong,' and I said 'Mum, you can't read 1 round any other way!'

CAREER

I immediately got a job. I was asked by the wonderful theatre designer John Napier if I wanted to become his assistant which I only sort of wanted to do. But I thought it was pretty good to be asked, so I was his assistant for a while, at the Royal Shakespeare Company in Stratford.

HIDING BEING DYSLEXIC

Then I was very determined to get an Arts Council bursary. They have a bursary to pay for you to be in a theatre as a resident designer. I went to Newcastle University Theatre which was lovely and I was very lucky and I worked on and designed some fabulous shows and I met a director who believed in me straight off without a question. The first show I had designed on my own within twelve months of graduating was *Woyzek* which was wonderful. Then I did *Good Person of Sechuan* and then I came down to London. Newcastle was an amazing experience but it's funny that I never told anyone I was dyslexic and this was a big mistake.

I remember when we were doing *Good Person of Sechuan*, the production manager called me into his office and said 'Sal,

I hear you are looking for someone to do this Chinese writing,'
and I said 'Yes, I am really desperate,' and he said 'Well, it's
amazing but there has been somebody in this building about
a year now who can do the best Chinese writing I have ever
seen,' and I said 'Who?' and he said 'You!'

He got out all my notes and he said 'Would you kindly
explain to me what all these mean?' and I said to him, sitting
there feeling very embarrassed, thinking I had got away with
it for so long, 'I am dyslexic,' and he said 'You have really got
to tell people because this is quite chronic.' He had been back
pedalling for me all the time and I thought I was being quite
clever.

Then I went to the RSC and did Barry Kyle's play. I did
a lot of opera and then I got ill in 1980, I slipped a disc and I
ended up in hospital. I was about to go on a scholarship to China
which I had applied for. Then I slipped a disc and nearly died,
which was really rather dramatic and all quite unnecessary.

And I have to say in all honesty I think that experience really
did change me, I stopped being so worried about my career, I
stopped being so anxious about work and being dyslexic. I had
known my husband for years, so we then got together. He is
an industrial/product designer and a couple of years after we
were married we had twins.

THE EFFECT OF BEING DYSLEXIC

It's a funny thing to say this, but I would be very frightened
if I wasn't dyslexic now, and it's taken, I suppose, quite a lot
of time for me to say that. It's so much me now that I sort of
think half of me would fade away.

THE ADVANTAGES OF BEING DYSLEXIC

I see totally visually. I don't see in words, and words still stay

28

visual with me. The most wonderful thing in my childhood was the Coca-Cola sign in Piccadilly, to me it was the greatest work of art I had ever seen. The lights at Piccadilly Circus were just poetry. And the minute I could read, all that went, which was very sad.

Schizophrenia is the most beautiful word in the English language, visually it is absolutely beautiful. I would hate to lose all that ability to look at words that are completely incomprehensible to me and see such beauty in them.

DISADVANTAGE OF DYSLEXIA

Frustration, with writing, is the greatest disadvantage of being dyslexic. I used to have to write 'It's a fine day' or 'It's a sunny day' when my heart was bursting with, nearly every other word in the English language apart from those pathetic squirts, but I knew I could spell them.

MESSAGE

I would say to other dyslexics not to give up, and to be determined about what you are going to do, and be single-minded and get out and do it.

Q: How does an octopus go into battle?
A: Well-armed!
David Bradley (11), Foremarke Hall,
Repton Prep School

When I was sixteen or seventeen I went for a job at the New Cross Bus Garage and they gave me a form to fill in. I couldn't do it so I walked away. Being dyslexic can be lucky. If I could write I could have filled it in and have been driving a No. 47 bus for the rest of my life!

Ron Shaw
Successful business man

Business Man

RON

Ron is a very successful entrepreneur. His enterprises range from building retirement homes to airports. One of his horses has won the Grand Military Gold Cup, a highlight of the racing calendar. He has met most of the members of the Royal Family, and hunted with Prince Charles and he and his wife have raised thousands of pounds for charities including dyslexic causes. But to this day he has never written a letter. He left school before he could read and while he was there he suffered terribly. He was made to stand in a wastepaper basket as the master thought he was so stupid.

When I spoke to Ron I identified very strongly with one aspect of Ron's character: Feeling the need to keep giving and buying friendship, because you imagine no one would really want to be real friends with 'a fool'. Giving, you feel, makes you worthwhile, or worth liking (although it's hard for dyslexics to think of themselves as worthwhile).

We had our talk over lunch in his club. Everyone seemed to know him and I thought as I left, 'I expect everyone's had their lunch paid for by him too!'

*   *   *

How I didn't become an out and out crook, I shall never

31

know. It's probably largely thanks to a man by the name of Arthur Protheroe, a solicitor. I used to go round cleaning cars, and I used to clean his car. When I was about ten or eleven he said to me, 'Don't ever let me catch you in that court because if I do, I'll put you away. I will definitely put you away.'

He's even my friend now. He is ninety. I still say to him, 'You used to terrify me.'

SCHOOL

At the age of seven I attended a school in Deptford and one of the teachers was a Welshman. He obviously thought I was an absolute 'dum-dum', because I couldn't understand any of the reading or writing he was trying to teach me. So my punishment was to be rapped over the knuckles daily and then given a prod, or the worst thing he could do was to take me to the front of the class and stand me in the wastepaper basket. After this happens on a number of occasions, you feel something is wrong with you.

You've not worked it out, and no one's told you what's wrong. But if you're made to stand in the wastepaper basket and everyone else is not, you definitely think something is funny about you.

BULLYING

Then the children think you're a bit funny, so when you go in the playground they ridicule you and you're laughed at and joked about.

The worst thing that happened to me was once when I was in the toilet – one of those stand up jobs – I found five or six children urinating on my bare legs. The thing I remember was the warmth. The terrible feeling of warm pee.

I think when you're young, you become foxy, you become

crafty, because what you're doing is hiding from everybody that you're a berk. You are not whole. If you had one leg off, they could see it and say 'Oh, the poor chap, he's got one leg off,' but if you're dyslexic you are not whole because you can't do what the average person in the street can do.

My parents didn't worry about how I was doing at school. They were living to survive, you were just keeping the wolf from the door the whole time. The last thing you worried about is how your son was doing at school. Reading and writing didn't matter to them.

I have never kissed my mother in my life. I was the middle one of seven children. We had an indifferent relationship to each other, and my problems at school weren't important to them. But I have always made friends very, very easily and kept friends for a long, long time, for ever.

At school I was always naughty. I was just a naughty person, probably because of the frustrations.

I left school at the age of thirteen and a half. We were allowed to leave school early in the war, because of the bombing. I never did any exams. I was about twenty-odd when I learned to read. I still can't spell. I have *never* sat down to write a letter *ever*. When I left school I got a job as a sweeper-upper in the local drapery store. You did any job you could find.

ARMY CAREER

Then I went into the Royal Army Ordnance Corps which is not the nicest thing you can go into, but not the lowest thing. But you were always made to feel a secondary citizen as it were, because you were dyslexic, but because of your personality you got on all right. You could act the goat and you were funny so you got on with the chaps.

I became very clever at getting other people to do things for me. If you went on leave you had to make out a form as to when and where you were going, I would get someone to do it for me for money, that meant I had to make money.

MAKING MONEY

When I came out of the army I thought 'What can I do for which you don't have to read and write and that you can get good money for?' I decided that the answer was to get into some kind of artistic job with no reading or writing. I got a job in a shop and then worked much harder than anybody else so they let me do the interior displays. Then the guy who owned the place came along and said, 'Who did that?' It was a very simple thing, I went to the park and got a load of autumn leaves and then got a fan, and before you know where you are, there is a window-dressing!

I became Display Manager of Scotch House in Knightsbridge and I worked on the *first* Regent Street Lights Display.

When I was twenty-two I started doing freelance display stuff, because I found creating things was easy, just lighting and colour. I then got a job as Display Director with Gussy Group where you get everything in a room, have it photographed and then branches all over the country copy it. I was making a lot of money.

Then I thought, now what can I get into and I decided (I was about twenty-seven or twenty-eight) that the boom thing was going to be those motor scooters. So I got going with a lorry driver who knew about mechanics and we opened a scooter shop in Bermondsey and another in Deptford.

From the very first minute we started making money. I got involved in different businesses because I wasn't really into scooters or motor cycles or cars.

Then I decided that the place to make money was in banks so I took out a money lender's licence and started lending out money. Basically it went from there, it just sort of snowballed until I had all sorts of different types of

34

business. If I like a thing and I think it's got potential, then I'll do it. But I've been in the business of building hospitals and old people's homes since about 1970 so that's eighteen years.

HOBBIES

Horses are strictly for pleasure . . . it's never returnable, it's always money outgoing. But then like all these things, you try to make it a business. I took out my own licence and trained my own horses and tried to keep my other business going as well which was very difficult.

But horses lead me to lots of people that I never would have known (the Queen, the Queen Mother, Prince Charles), because you've got to have lots of money to own a racehorse in the first place.

There is a cup called the Grand Military Gold Cup. When I was in the army I was the lowest of the low, a private. There were officers there that were very unpleasant to you. You were scum. There was this race at Sandown Park which is the Grand Military and I remember going to Sandown Park and looking at the Race Calendar to see who'd won it. It'd be Lieutenant-Colonel this and Brigadier that, and General this, and I thought 'One of these days I'll bloody well win that race.' I used to tell people I was going to win it. Anyway the first time I put in a horse we came third, the next time we came fourth.

I just kept trying and eventually we won. We beat the Queen Mother's horse which was 11-8 on favourite.

The name of my horse was Columbus, and he won at 50-1. It was fantastic and afterwards we were invited back to Windsor Castle.

DISCOVERING MY DYSLEXIA

I think basically dyslexic people tend to blame themselves for their shortcomings. It was only when my wife was called to my daughter's school, when she was fourteen and I was forty-plus, that we ever knew that I was dyslexic. My wife took my daughter to see Dr MacDonald Critchley and he said it was hereditary. Then he wanted to see me. So I went up and spent hours with him, literally hours, in London going through all the things that happened to me in my life. And he said how well I hid my dyslexia and how well I managed to put a shell over it so that nobody knew, and so you see you definitely have to tell a fib or two!

COPING WITH MEETINGS AND LOSING OUT

I go to a board meeting sometimes. When they are all talking about the project, I'm thinking 'Now I wonder what they're going to ask me to write in a minute, because I know there is some writing to come up, I can feel it.' I have lost out so many times on big deals that way. For instance the property round the corner. I bought it for about half a million and sold it for six hundred thousand pounds. It was then sold to Christie's for *five and a half million* and nobody had even stepped in it. But you see they are the type of things you lose out on, because you're dyslexic. You can lose four and a half million pounds!

But 'Man is rich by the fewness of his needs'. In other words you don't have to have all the money in the world, providing you don't want a lot.

Now at the moment I'm flying a jet, but when I come to analyse the real me, first of all I don't need a jet, secondly I don't need a big house, thirdly I don't need any horses because I get just as much joy out of watching somebody else's horses. I don't need to have dinner parties, I don't need to go to functions or charities and the rest of it. I would be quite happy without it all but because of the mantle, you become trapped in that which you have created.

For instance, everybody expects me to look after them. I look after masses of people. I do it because I want people to like me, because nobody can like a berk, a dyslexic.

SELF-ESTEEM

I have always thought of myself as insecure – I have never felt secure. I don't feel that I have achieved anything. I have achieved money but that's nothing. It's much nicer to have other things.

I think basically that if you're dyslexic you have a problem with managing yourself. What I mean is – for example I liken it to a racehorse – if you bought a racehorse and took it out every morning for a gallop, to make it go faster, and faster, and then all of a sudden after three years you take that racehorse and say 'Now I want you to be a dressage horse.' Forget it, you can't do it. It's impossible because he's been racing all his life.

So what is happening to me is that all I have been doing is rushing and rushing, to make more money, to make more money, and by doing that I have never learned to manage myself. I haven't said, hang on, let's stop and make sure that the money I have just earned is well invested, and that I am getting the right rate for it, and so on. You can't manage yourself because when *it comes to something where you have to read and write* it's a problem.

But what amazes me is when I go to an important meeting, I know that people are scared of me. How can they be scared, but you see they build up a picture of a big executive who is flying in in his jet to come and see them.

BUYING FRIENDSHIP

You feel you have to buy friendship. Back at school, when they thought you were daft and stupid, they didn't like you. Let's face it, nobody likes people who are idiots. So you're the one who *buys* the football and brings it to the guys. Dyslexics do it more than most people – until very recently we'd entertain lots of people. Our house in Antigua would be full of people from beginning to end of the holiday. Why do I do it? When you really work it out it's because you want them to like you. You are giving all the time. But you don't stop and say 'I'm not going to do that any more'.

I think the biggest disadvantage of being dyslexic means you are not whole. There is something missing. Therefore you are always wondering what it would be like to be whole.

Angharad Rees

ACTRESS

Angharad Rees is an actress whom I have always greatly admired. Television viewers all over the world fell in love with Angharad in *Poldark* and marvelled at her performance in *Forgotten Story* and *The Way We Live Now*. She has captivated audiences when on stage in both Shakespeare and Shaw. In 1983 she was nominated for a Best Actress award for her performance in *Moments*.

But it was only when I went to interview her about her son that I discovered that she was also dyslexic. She had always kept it 'very quiet'. So I was doubly happy that she agreed to talk about herself for this book. We sat among the builders' tools drinking Perrier water and trying to concentrate while the builders were working on the finishing touches to Angharad's new home which she shares with her husband Christopher Cazenove and their children.

* * *

Funnily enough, I didn't face up to my dyslexia until I discovered that my son is dyslexic. Then I looked back on my life and all the things joined up, like being a very anxious child, wetting the bed when I was small, or being terribly ashamed of myself sitting in the dunces' row aged eight. I loathed having to stand

39

up in class, even at the age of fifteen, to read. Then discovering at school that the one thing I could seem to do and enjoy was acting.

When I was thirteen, I discovered I actually did have quite a lot of academic ability. But I was totally self-taught. The other thing I found very difficult was *absorbing* what was said in class. I don't know whether that's anything to do with dyslexia, but it was much better for me to go home, slowly read everything and teach myself. I found it very hard to remember things. My younger brother could read before me and do everything before me. He was quite a tease about it. Not at all in a hurtful way, I'm sure, but I hated it.

I was very blessed with my parents. My father being an eminent psychiatrist was able to explain to me at a very early age that my problem was dyslexia and although in those days there was no remedial help, my father said that I would grow out of it. My parents never put any pressure on me and obviously did not suffer the confusion that so many parents suffer with dyslexic children. My father became Professor of Psychiatry at St. Bartholomews and housed Beve Hornsby's Clinic in his department. He gave pioneering support to this problem and I always love to think it's because of his dyslexic daughter.

TEACHERS

I had a wonderful English teacher, Miss Clarke, who was totally inspiring. She seemed to 'light up' talking about Wordsworth on Westminster Bridge, and I was just totally wrapped up in her. She was terribly strict and quite scary but she was a wonderfully inspiring teacher, and another person was my drama teacher, Miss Budd, who was brilliant. Both of these people greatly inspired me from the age of thirteen onwards.

As a child I was only bullied in the sense that I was never allowed to be any different from anybody else. I had to stand up and read in class and go through the shame of not being able to. I was a very anxious child, but a terrific ringleader. I was always the leader of the pack, a bit of a bossy boots. But everybody was very happy to follow me around and let me organize them. My friends never teased me.

If a teacher was explaining something in class, I found it very difficult to absorb and remember. I had many learning difficulties, I think, in the end. I think probably some of them were psychological, but I got a lot of GCEs, did one year in the sixth form and left, because I got into drama school with a scholarship.

EXAMS

Until my GCEs I think I failed most of my exams. I didn't ever pass any. It worried me and I was quite confused, because I knew I wasn't stupid, but then I would think, 'Oh, I must be!' I was so hopeless at everything. I wasn't at ease with it but when I did start working for my GCEs, I did very well and everyone was so surprised that I got so many O-levels.

I went to Rose Bruford Drama School. It was the only one that my parents would let me go to because you did a teaching diploma there as well, so I did that.

After I went to drama school, I went off the idea of acting. Drama schools can do that to you. I knew this wonderful family in Spain, so I just wrote to them and asked if I could work in their psychiatric clinic. I taught English to the patients as they were getting better. Most of my work was oral, but it was therapeutic for the patients and fascinating for me.

I got one of my first jobs quite by accident in the Play of the Month with Maggie Smith and Robert Stephens. I was so lucky, one thing led to another. When I started it was the vogue for directors not to ask you to read the script you were auditioning for. They just talked to you. Nobody asked you to read and I was jolly lucky that I was never asked to read.

STUDYING PARTS

When it came to work, I learnt my lines very quickly because I can't, I still can't, work off the written page. So it's only if I have learnt something that I can even slightly bring it to life. I can't 'half' bring things to life like some people can. So for that reason I have always questioned my ability as an actress, because I don't have this quick ability to do things.

I didn't do plays on radio for years, but once I discovered that my son was dyslexic I took myself in hand and started to do things like radio. Actually within two years of doing radio, I was nominated the best radio actress which I thought was jolly good.

When I am doing a radio play, I spend hours working in the evenings. I tend not to go out when I'm working on radio.

I hardly mark the page of the script at all, and I often don't even underline my own lines. I actually put a tiny little pencil mark against my part but none of this underlining people do. Because, you see, I have learnt the work without a script and what's the point of writing things on it? With a bit of luck I will have learnt it by the first day and won't need it anyway.

Working in television and theatre I used to panic so much on the first day of rehearsal, when the cast sat in a circle and read the play from beginning to end, that I used to ring up and say I was ill, because I couldn't face it.

But I remember once playing Juliet. I did go to the read-through and in the end I just had to say to the director, 'I'm sorry, can you read my part?' I was in such a panic and with the anxiety and the embarrassment I just couldn't go on any longer.

ADVANTAGES AND DISADVANTAGES

The kind of mind that dyslexic people have seems to have extra dimensions to it. So very often when you get over your dyslexia you seem to be extra equipped, very often intellectually, and can excel in certain areas. For example my son who is dyslexic is wonderful at English, he is intensely interested in writing and he writes the most wonderful things. It's something he really is not only good at but takes off in.

I think the disadvantage has been that it made me compensate terribly for the rest of my life, because I felt inadequate. It made me a perfectionist and I have made life difficult for myself later because of it. I now understand it better, but I think one grows up feeling very insecure about oneself.

I think the great problem for people with dyslexia is self-confidence and the lack of self-esteem because people are constantly making you feel bad about yourself. I think it's criminal the hurt that teachers inflict on children by just silly words like 'slowcoach', 'stupid', 'concentrate' and how in our schools the care of dyslexic children has been so bad.

MESSAGE

Although I don't think it's an advantage for anybody to have disabilities, I do think it is wonderful if in the right atmosphere as a child you can learn self-discipline, the ability to overcome something and to understand from an early age that working on something makes you good at it. So many people never learn that the discipline of putting effort into something reaps rewards. If you discover your dyslexia young enough before psychological blocks happen, you learn these lessons very early like my son.

Q: Shall I tell you a secret about butter?
A: No, you'll only spread it!

James Johnstone, Wilmslow

Farmer

HARRY

**Several years ago I visited a stately home in Warwickshire
and as we were shown round I started talking to the owner.
The conversation veered away from architecture to dyslexia
and I discovered his son, Harry, was dyslexic. So I decided to
write to him. Harry agreed to see me and I spent a fascinating
afternoon listening to his story.**

**As a child he was cut off from the world due to deafness.
He struggled through school and was kept in every Saturday
for doing poor work. He eventually got into farming.**

**Despite his difficulties he went to agricultural college at
Cirencester and he says, 'For the first time in my life people
were actually trying to teach me something that I wanted to
know. In farming no one cares if you're dyslexic.'**

* * *

I was probably eight or nine when my dyslexia began to
be apparent. My writing more than my reading was most
affected. The thing about a mental problem is that to oneself
it seems quite normal. You are only aware that you have made
a mistake when someone else actually points out that it's wrong.

At preparatory school, where I was from age eight till

44

twelve, they refused to recognize dyslexia. I was diagnosed by a doctor a year before I left my preparatory school. My mother wrote to the headmaster and his reply was, *'Dyslexia is a modern fad and we are not going to tolerate it here, it is simply an excuse for laziness.'* Through the four to five years that I was there I very rarely got a Saturday off. Every Saturday was spent writing lines. I got incredibly good at it.

I think I suffered through being punished and being kept in in the evenings and on Saturdays. That definitely altered my entire character although I had been quiet before then.

But I did suffer from another problem which is the main reason for my liking solitude. The first five years of my life I was deaf, and it wasn't diagnosed for a long time. I was my mother's first born. She used to cover up to guests. At three or four years old I wandered around paying absolutely no attention to anyone and when they said 'Hello, Harry,' she'd say, 'Ignore him, he lives entirely in a world of his own,' and how right she was.

I didn't speak. I had some hearing. The left ear had failed. It hadn't worked from birth, and the right ear was overloaded to such an extent that it very quickly packed up.

HANDWRITING

I failed simple tests through poor spelling and handwriting. Work would come back 'Spelling not good enough.' Any kind of exam, it didn't really matter what the subject was, it didn't have to be English, would be returned 'Failed, spelling not good enough, handwriting too untidy to be decently legible.'

The best present I have had was when I was about sixteen or seventeen, my father gave me a typewriter and after that, if anybody gave me something that they required me to write on, and which wouldn't fit in the typewriter, I'd throw it away. It was a new lease of life. I didn't have to write any more, although more spelling mistakes came through because I was, for the first time in my life, writing almost as quickly as I thought.

I was given some remedial help at Harrow where I managed to survive for three years. I arrived at thirteen and left at sixteen. When I found that I could leave, I did!

I took my O-levels. I took six or seven and I failed all but about one, I think, English Language. I have always had a liking for language, this language and the other European languages. Russian is, I think, the most interesting because it is made up.

LONER

I never had any really good friends at school. I have always been a bit of a loner. I was not a generally popular boy because I wanted to be alone. I became very introverted and closed myself off with a sort of steel door.

The masters tried very hard. But dyslexia was a problem that they weren't too sure how to tackle. It very quickly built up into a sort of direct confrontation. I wasn't happy at Harrow but I was at Summerfields.

REACTION TO THE PROBLEM

When you find that you are unable to do something as easily as other people, whatever it is, whether it is writing or whatever, you tend to build up a certain amount of resentment, and after a while, that's got to spill out in some form or another. Rather than being aggressive, I went the other way, I just became totally introverted.

When I left Harrow aged sixteen, a rebel and a bit of a hermit, nobody could understand what was wrong, especially me, and that didn't help. People were saying that I was anti-social. My sisters and my parents tried to nag me in a loving way, trying to encourage me to go out and do things, but I just wanted to get away, and so as with many sixteen year olds, I was faced with the problems of my father saying, 'Well, if you don't want to go to school, what do you want to do?'

I thought about it. I had considered joining the army, but they said no. Their last letter said I *had* to do quite well in my exams. I always knew that there was no hope of doing that. I was surprised how many A-levels you need to be able to kill somebody! Having not been able to follow that one through, I said I'd like to be a farmer, which is nothing to do with my family's background.

FIRST JOB

I didn't imagine myself going and sitting in the farm manager's chair taking command. I wanted to get my hands dirty. I got a job in Buckinghamshire, and for the first time in my life I was given a responsibility that didn't involve writing things out and therefore there was no chance of being punished or being held up to ridicule for not being able to do something so simple as to write. It was just a case of 'There's the tractor, there's the plough and the field is two miles down there, and don't come back until you've ploughed it.'

SHEPHERDING

I have never found it of supreme importance to be able to get on with people or to have contact with people. I worked as a shepherd in various parts of the country. I loved that, that was definitely the best job that I have ever had.

The first year that I became a shepherd I was working as an office boy in an estate office on an estate in Northamptonshire. One morning the shepherd was carted away in an ambulance. He had contracted a disease from the sheep, something quite terrible, his arms swelled out and went red, and he couldn't move, and breathing was very difficult, so he was taken away in an ambulance.

That left five hundred hungry sheep and it was February and very cold. There was snow on the ground, and the manager said to the office staff, 'Do any of you want to become our shepherd?' so I said 'Yes', simply to get out. The manager said 'Have you had any experience with sheep?' I said 'No, none. I can't tell one end from the other, I'm not sure if I like them.' He said, 'Well, there are five hundred sheep out there, you have got a tractor and trailer, and they are going to start lambing in about six weeks' time.' So after that he pushed me out of the door, and there I was standing in a field, freezing cold, with all these hungry sheep, saying 'Our boss has gone and where's the dinner?' I just got down to it and did things really by instinct.

LAMBING

The first lambing six weeks later was possibly the most tiring and most exciting time of my life. I don't think I will ever get over a thrill as big as that. I got virtually no sleep for about eight weeks as I didn't know what was happening. No one told me.

I rang up my mother and she said 'Be there', and so I was – two o'clock in the morning, freezing cold, snowing, and there I was stripped to my waist with a ewe who was obviously in difficulties, and I didn't make any mistakes. I didn't lose any.

There was an old shepherd who lived across the road and he used to come and lean on the fence. He gave me some very good pieces of advice, but he used to annoy me. He just used to lean on the gate while I was drowning in problems.

He gave me one very sound piece of advice – when you see a ewe in trouble, go away, go and have tea, have a drink, just leave it, because most problems are made a great deal worse by humans rushing in without fully understanding the problem and saying 'Well, I'm here, I'm God, I'll do it.'

BOOKS

It was the second day that the lambing was going in full swing, and going quite well, I went out and bought a book on the subject. I don't know what the bookseller must have thought, I came in in my boots, my hair just a matted mess, mostly sheep's dung, and blood the whole way down my front and up my arms. I went in and said, 'Have you got a book telling me how I can lamb a ewe?' Luckily he said 'Yes'. So I went back and I read it, and it gave me a bit of help, but books aren't really that good. It's like cookery books – first dice a chicken, and I've got the dice and I've got the chicken, so what do I do next, throw the dice? If I hit a seven it's cooked!

I studied at Cirencester and I found for the first time in my life people were actually trying to teach me something that I wanted to know.

Now I have been running the farm for just over a year. I have to do all the administration side and I find that writing can be a problem. I find when taking notes during a telephone conversation my writing tends to go all round the page, it doesn't go in straight lines. It doesn't even go in a gentle curve.

I like the camaraderie of farm workers. They are quite happy to spend twenty hours without meeting anybody else. When you do get together it tends to be great fun. Rather like cowboys in America, they're exactly the same.

I went to America a few years ago, I worked as a cowboy in Texas, North Kansas, and that was marvellous. In farming nobody cares if you're dyslexic.

I can appreciate now that if I wasn't dyslexic, I don't think I would have had a natural liking for language, especially, one of the great loves in my life, poetry.

MESSAGE

There certainly are a lot of disadvantages in being dyslexic, but that word 'If', what if? The thing is to make the best of what you've got and hopefully one day you'll be able to understand the reason you haven't been able to do something. Afflictions of the brain, however temporary they may be, are very much the same as being physically disabled. If someone is physically disabled, it's obvious to everybody and to yourself that you can't walk. The positive aspect of being dyslexic is in a word – individualism.

Make-up Artist

SUZY

As I slumped into the make-up chair one April morning almost before the birds were awake and all I could think of was how lovely it would be to have a cup of China tea, Suzy, the make-up artist, leant over and said, 'Your book has been such a help.' I immediately perked up. I thought she was referring to the gardening book that I had come to promote on television that morning. But it turned out that it was another book, *Susan's Story*, and Suzy was dyslexic.

Suzy, who lived in care until she was fifteen, was taught to read by her brother. She now relies on her husband to help her with any paperwork. She is a much in demand make-up artist who trained at the BBC.

* * *

I was brought up in care since I was seven to fifteen. At fifteen, I went back to my mother.

The early part of my life was the most difficult because I was always feeling stupid. I was late learning to read, maybe twelve or thirteen. I couldn't have managed to learn to read without the help of my brother. But spelling was my main problem.

TEACHERS

I had great difficulty with maths. One day in class, when I was eleven, the teacher said, 'Sit at the back and read a comic.' He thought I was too hopeless to teach.

I used to be physically sick – I actually had to go to the cloakroom and was sick whenever I was asked to read aloud in front of the class, I would panic, I couldn't even focus on the words. I remember my brother saying, 'You'll never go to the Grammar School.' I said, 'I don't want to go to Grammar School, I want to go to Glamour School!' – which is what I eventually ended up doing.

CAREER

I was always interested in theatre and got a job as a trainee hairdresser in a shop and then, through a client, got a job as a trainee make-up artist at the BBC.

When I initially went for a job and had to fill in forms, I would have to take the form away and do it at home as I couldn't do it there.

As part of the BBC job, I had to read scripts and mark them up for continuity and for a while I found that difficult. Then I got my own system of using photographs of the artists in make-up, and putting them in a folder rather than writing lengthy descriptions of wigs and make-up details. And I would use make-up charts which I found much easier.

I suppose in a way dyslexia held me back in my career. I could have become a supervisor if I had been more confident about not making mistakes with scripts, official forms and filing reports and so on.

Now I have to get my husband to oversee any paperwork. But I still get letters back to front.

DRIVING TEST

It took me ages to pass my driving test, as I couldn't work out the left from the right. I took it four times.

As I get older I find my memory and the problems with left and right and so on are getting worse, but it might be the hours at TV AM. I'm up at 3 a.m. every morning when I'm working, so it could be that.

TIPS

I find it easier to type things than write. Also coloured perspex has been very useful for me.

A man came on the programme talking about dyslexia and he said that one of the tricks was to use coloured perspex which you put over the written page of the book. It stops the words 'jumping' about so much and it slightly magnifies, which makes it easier.

MESSAGE

Don't be embarrassed by your dyslexia. Tell the truth about it. Get people to understand that it's not that dyslexics can't read or spell, it's just that it's very much more difficult for them. This needs to be got through to people. Also that dyslexia makes you more understanding.

University Lecturer in Computer Science

JIM

I knew David Austin, an exceptionally brilliant rose grower, through my love of gardening and roses. Over the years David mentioned that he had the same difficulties as I have with reading and spelling when he was young. Yet this did not stop him writing the enormous and remarkable book *The Rose*, and running his own extremely successful rose growing business. David's son Jim is also dyslexic. It was thought that he was possibly brain damaged when he was a boy. He was bullied at school and became very withdrawn. He now lectures in Computer Science at York University and does research into robots.

* * *

I was the worst at school. When I was seven years old the teacher said to my mother 'Something is dreadfully wrong with your son. He can't read or write.' And that was it as far as the school was concerned. I had meningitis at nine months and my parents thought the reason for my difficulties was brain damage.

54

A psychiatrist friend said to my parents 'This is nonsense. This is not the case,' and to prove it he arranged for me to see three very eminent people in the 'brain field' in London. A paediatrician, a child psychologist, and a brain surgeon, for a brain scan. The result showed that I was *very*, *very* dyslexic, but no one knew what it meant in those days.

My mother wrote to Child Guidance and they interviewed me. Afterwards I was accepted into a *reading clinic*.

SCHOOL LIFE

I was dreadfully bullied at school and there were awful behaviour problems. I didn't want to go to school. I screamed and cried and was ill. I became very withdrawn but luckily was interested in clocks, drains (where water went), and loved making things.

I didn't have many friends, at my big school the teacher said, 'Not trying', and I always came home in tears saying, 'I did try, I did try', but I was made to run round and round a field as a punishment for 'not trying'.

My mother was accused of being over-protective and defensive, and apparently the staff thought 'What a stupid woman, her son is stupid.'

Eventually a psychologist said 'Remove him from school and find an alternative.' David Jones at Shropshire, chief psychologist, said to my parents, 'He's an exceptionally bright child,' and proceeded to build into my system the thoughts 'don't worry', and 'ignore that reading and writing are difficult', and '*concentrate* on the things you *CAN* do'.

Now I'm lecturing at York – as my mother always says – 'Not bad for someone who was thought to have brain damage!'

Television Producer

'ANNETTE'

I knew of 'Annette' when she was just a little wisp of a thing, but I didn't actually get to talk to her properly until, quite by accident, years and years later we were both waiting for an internal shuttle flight to Boston. I was struggling with the names of different places on my itinerary on a whistle stop promotion tour for a television series and it was Annette of all people who helped me read them.

'Thanks. Sorry I can't read, are you English?' I asked.

'And dyslexic,' she smiled. 'I'm Annette. You know my mother.' Annette! Need I say more. Of course, Annette is in the book!

Annette was labelled 'A dear sweet child' at school, 'but not academic.' She was even put into the National Hospital for Nervous Diseases after it was discovered she was dyslexic. Yet she went to Cambridge, read English and is now a successful television producer.

* * *

At about the age of seven I couldn't read or write a word and I think my mother got rather concerned, as any mother would, and I think from then onwards she gradually realized that there

56

was a problem. My local church primary school told her that I was a 'dear sweet child but not academic', which luckily she didn't accept. She took me off to a couple of educational psychologists, because dyslexia at this point was a very new thing and they said they thought I was dyslexic.

HOSPITAL

So I was sent for a week to the National Hospital for Nervous Diseases under a chap called Dr MacDonald Critchley as an in-patient, for tests in what can only be described as a semi-mental ward!

I was about seven at that point and all the other women in the ward were about thirty-five, and they were all in for some sort of nervous breakdown and things. Luckily I didn't notice it at the time, being only seven.

As an in-patient I did all these tests, like co-ordination tests and throwing balls and catching balls, and writing with both hands going in opposite directions, which of course was a complete disaster, I couldn't do them at all. MacDonald Critchley decided that I was the most brass bound dyslexic he'd ever seen in his life. The genuine article, the original dyslexic.

At the end of the week my *pièce de résistance* was that he used me as an example for a lecture for all medical students. He asked me to throw things and catch things and make paper darts and this sort of stuff, which I loved. Apparently I caused a complete sensation because I couldn't do it . . . Having an audience of about forty people didn't faze me at all – I thought it was wonderful. So that got mummy all the relevant bits of paper to be able to tell the school that she was taking me out of school for one afternoon a week whether they liked it or not.

REMEDIAL HELP

I was sent off to Mrs Gray for extra tuition with a couple of other kids for remedial reading and writing.

I used to hate reading and writing. There are the famous Dr Seuss books which I had and couldn't read at all, but my mother was never quite sure for about six months whether I was dyslexic or not because every time she said to me, 'What's that word?', in the Dr Seuss book, I'd tell her the word. The reason I could do it was because I'd memorized where the page turned. So I knew where the word came on the page although I couldn't read it. I knew what each word was, like a memory test, and she couldn't catch me out.

It was only when I went to school and I couldn't read anything that I had behaviour problems. I was doing all the things that one does to avoid having to read and write, like disrupting the class, making sure you were always at the back of the queue to get your prep checked, all this sort of stuff, so that it would never be seen that I couldn't actually do it.

It was only when my mother sat me down and tested me that she discovered that I couldn't actually read or write at all.

Then at the age of nine I was taken out of the State system and put into the private system. I went to a boarding school in Dorset, Hanford House, which was much smaller and could give much more concentrated attention to the fact that I was dyslexic. That's where they really got the reading and writing going.

Hanford House was not specifically designed for dyslexics because there were not many of them about . . . I mean basically the class that I was in was for disturbed and difficult children.

There were only seven in the class. They taught us things like the basics of grammar, most of which I've forgotten now, but it broke me from the habit of remembering reading by rote without actually understanding the mechanism of it. I had to go back two or three paces so I could actually learn how to read properly. I still had, I think, until I was thirteen, extra lessons in spelling and grammar, and in writing and reading, just to help me.

TYPING

Later, the only concessions I had were for exams which meant basically that I could type them, because when I was ten Mummy took me to a secretarial college to teach me to type, with another boy who was dyslexic as well. She decided, which was actually quite wise on reflection, that the problem was not what I was writing at that point, but the fact that nobody could read it! Of course with O-levels coming up this would have been a bit of a problem.

So I learnt to touch type, and when I did my O-levels and A-levels and Oxbridge, I had a concession that I could type the exams, and they would disregard the spelling in the paper, which was just as well. But I didn't get extra time which I think was quite right. I got ten O-levels and then three A-levels plus Use of English. I had an A and a B and a D. I did English, physics and design. At the time I was thinking about doing architecture. If you sit for Oxbridge you don't need A-levels anyway.

Technically you don't need any exams at all to sit for Oxbridge, certainly when I sat it, except Use of English. But the college that I went for, New Hall, had its own exam papers as well as the general paper.

GETTING INTO CAMBRIDGE

We had this really extraordinarily good English master John Batstone, at Bedales school, who had a word with my mother and said it was probably worth a go at getting into Oxford or Cambridge.

In Oxford at St Anne's, there was only a compulsory Old English paper. We asked if they were prepared to make a concession but they wrote back a very snotty letter saying quite frankly if I was going to need concessions, was there much point in my applying for Oxford anyway.

59

So I got into New Hall, Cambridge, on two interviews and they asked me quite a bit about dyslexia there, but didn't seem particularly fazed by it because they'd seen my papers, and I'd had a good recommendation from the school.

TOUCH TYPING IN A DIFFERENT ROOM

I find it very difficult to work in longhand now because I haven't done it since I was eleven.

All they did for the exams was just lock me up in a room in the sick bay. Somebody started me and finished me at the right time. I actually quite enjoyed it because you're sitting by yourself typing, you can think, and you're not worried about the pressure of people scribbling around you, which is awful.

COPING WITH WORK AT CAMBRIDGE

I read English which was great really. I got a 2.2, principally because I didn't do an awful lot of work. I did an awful lot of other things. I did lots of sport and I did the university newspaper. I edited and wrote for that for three years which was a real scream. I think the reason was because I'd written a couple of things for *Harpers & Queen* just before going up to Cambridge.

It was a very good student newspaper and it won a few awards which inspired me. Also I felt that I was actually achieving something which might help me get a job after university, and having a good time at the same time.

I also edited a thing called the *Varsity Handbook* which is a guide book, published by the same company as the newspaper. I came down in July, having typed my finals and typed my prelims at university, and I typed all my essays.

TRYING TO GET A JOB

When I left Cambridge I tried for the BBC because I'd enjoyed journalism. But I didn't get into the BBC straight away, I got in third time round. I failed to get into the BBC while I was up at Cambridge. I did odd jobs and really bits and pieces, and I worked briefly for a publishing company and other places until the following February when I was offered a place on a post-graduate journalism course in Cardiff.

They gave me a spelling test at the first interview and I think I must have got the lowest ever, and every now and again they used to give spelling tests halfway through the course, and I used to get the lowest by miles on the test . . . I'd get twenty-eight out of eighty and everybody else would be getting fifty or so. The fact that I couldn't spell, they thought, was because I was a southerner. If I'd been to a proper northern school it wouldn't have happened.

I did this course to improve my job prospects of getting into the BBC because everybody who went on the course quite honestly got a job. Anyway, I chose the radio option on the course. I thought, if you're doing radio, nobody looks at your scripts except you, so it doesn't matter if the spelling is wrong.

I also thought that radio was going to be better for getting a job. I completed the course in radio and I did the BBC interviews again, and in August that year they offered me a job to start the following Easter, which I accepted. At this point there had been no mention of dyslexia or anything like that and everything had gone absolutely swimmingly.

A NEW PROBLEM

I had done written tests for them and oral tests, and then they started to take up my references at this point and there was a slight hitch. Because unfortunately my tutor at Cambridge was away on holiday when the letter arrived, her secretary sent an old reference for me. It said something like, 'Annette is fantastic, particularly considering she is dyslexic.' The BBC had a seizure . . . 'Dyslexic! Nobody ever told us about this.'

'What's all this about dyslexia?' they said. So I said, 'Well, what about it? What's the problem?' And they said, 'Why didn't you tell us?' So I said, 'Would you actually have given me an interview if I'd told you?' And they said (bearing in mind that there are 4,000 people applying for these jobs and there were twelve jobs), 'I don't suppose we would have, no.' Then I thought, well, case rests, m'lord.

They wanted me to see the BBC doctor, but my mother first took me off to an educational psychologist to have a new assessment done on my ability, because the last one we had was when I was about twelve.

He came up with an assessment saying that I was *not* a fruit cake and that I was perfectly competent and I could read and write like a normal human being.

So I told the BBC doctor I wasn't a fruit cake and I was perfectly normal and I walk, I talk, I read, I write and I don't mix up my left and right. So he said 'Off you go then, that's the end of that.'

There was then a deathly silence for about six weeks, nothing happening, and then finally the contract just arrived out of the blue and that was it.

It's immensely satisfying. I enjoy it immensely. Now, after several years there, I am a senior producer.

Duncan Goodhew MBE

OLYMPIC GOLD MEDALLIST – SWIMMER

Today Duncan Goodhew is a conference speaker for leading commercial companies and his enthusiasm and wit when sharing his battle with dyslexia and other personal difficulties, have inspired many executives. Duncan also delights children with his pantomime performances, and spends a great deal of time helping with fund-raising for charities including those concerned with dyslexia.

Over the years Duncan Goodhew and I have met at various dyslexic fund-raising events. In fact Duncan, who is a tremendously witty and clever public speaker, was responsible for my deciding that I should abandon public speaking on behalf of my fellow dyslexics, as by comparison I was so BAD! Among his many business interests, he is a director of the Barbican Health and Fitness Centre in London, an extremely well equipped health club, where I went to interview him.

Duncan says he considered himself 'a stupid oddity' at school, but he has certainly achieved remarkable success in his teenage and adult years. He was one of Britain's leading breaststrokers by the age of eighteen and five years later captained the British swimming team at the 1980 Olympic Games in Moscow. At the

Games he won the Gold Medal for the 100 metres Breast Stroke, came 6th in the 200 metres Breast Stroke, and third in the 4 x 100 medley relay.

* * *

I was called Duncan the dunce. I was quite often made to stand in a corner in the class, up front by the teacher. I was always poor academically. I didn't like reading or writing at all. In fact in my junior school, I was such a fidget that on one occasion I was tied to the chair and put in a corner. I always felt so acutely uncomfortable in school.

It was at the age of eight that it came to a bit of a head when I actually got up in a class and I couldn't read, hardly at all. I could just read a couple of words. Ever since that time I was absolutely terrified of getting up and reading to people. It was a most uncomfortable experience. Even now, having been to university etc, I still find reading out loud the most horrific experience. The teachers and the headmaster did make an effort, but they just didn't understand at the time. They weren't cruel, it was the other boys that were cruel, and it was myself being cruel to myself. The school was trying to do everything it could. Some of the teachers were not as understanding as others, but generally all the staff were pretty good.

But at my first school, which I won't name, it was just diabolical. It was one of those very old fashioned schools and they just didn't understand. You read by numbers.

FAMILY

I have got one brother who is probably more severely dyslexic than I am. Mine I suppose mainly manifests itself in reading and I suspect is largely visual. In my brother it manifests itself as writing and spelling especially, even now spelling is a great problem. I think my mother might be slightly dyslexic. My father might have been but he died when I was sixteen.

64

I found school life just hugely frustrating. The school I was at formed a class of 'rejects' and I was put in there and we had a few dyslexics and a few people with other problems.

I think my father probably understood. He was quite good at mathematics and never very good at English. I mean he would have been very proud if he had been alive to see me going to a university. But I think he probably didn't expect very much academically, which was good in a way because it took some of the pressure off.

To be dyslexic and to write yourself off, then have all your school chums write you off, then if you go to a bad school all the school teachers write you off, and to have parents write you off as well is just beyond everything and you can't accept that.

PRIZE

Dyslexia was never mentioned to me. We were just classed as stupid. However, when I was about ten or eleven in my junior prep school I was awarded a prize for effort, The Bishops Prize, and that was a particularly good moment for me because I think at that point they had realized that I was trying very hard but not really getting anywhere.

I was at boarding school from the age of seven. Even though I didn't enjoy it, I appreciated what all of them were trying to do for me and I will give you an undyslexic related story.

MY HAIR .

My hair fell out when I was ten. I fell eighteen feet from a tree and damaged a nerve, and about eight months later all my hair fell out and it came out very quickly. I was wrestling on a mat, and it wore the top of the hair off. So I had a huge bald patch on the top of my head.

I went down next morning, and it was all a bit of a joke

as it was coming out by the handful. It was quite funny at the time. I went down to assembly at school the next morning and I can always remember the headmaster, who was a most superb chap, looked at me and did the classic double take as I walked through the door. I walked down the corridor. At the end of the long corridor I looked back and at the other end there were these big wooden doors up the stairs and there was just one little window. Framed in the window was the headmaster's face still staring down at me. It was then that I really appreciated his reaction, and how serious this was going to be.

The accident was at school and when I lost my hair it was also at school. The headmaster talked my parents out of letting me out that weekend. I went absolutely barmy. Obviously he had realized that if I had gone home to my parents I would never come back to the school, or come to terms with it. So that was an example of how somebody away from the family can make a hard decision. If I had gone home I am sure I would have had a lot more trouble coming to terms with losing my hair.

DISCOVERING DYSLEXIA

Then I went on to Millfield. What happened was I think at Windlesham House School, the prep school, they recognized that there was something wrong, and I think they appreciated it wasn't stupidity. It was just something they didn't quite understand and they couldn't explain it to me. I went to a meeting at Millfield with Jack Meyer, the headmaster ('Boss' they called him), and he asked me to count across a bookshelf and he gave me one or two little tests and things like that. Suddenly he said I would like to tell you that I suspect you are dyslexic. My parents asked what it was, then he explained and we went down to the swimming pool and then he accepted me into Millfield.

COMING TO TERMS WITH BEING DYSLEXIC

I think that adversity makes or breaks you and that's the problem with dyslexia. Either you end up *not* coming to terms with it and life in general, or you come to terms with it. Because reading and writing is almost essential in life and making a living. You have to come to terms with it or else the consequences are pretty horrific.

After my father died my mother came up to me and said 'Duncan, I can't really afford to keep you at Millfield any longer, what are you going to do with yourself?' – and this was when I was seventeen. I said I wanted to swim. But there was no sponsorship and I realized I was going to have to give up.

I only had a handful of O-levels and the coach said to me 'Why don't you go to an American university?' which I thought was the most hilarious thing I had ever heard. But I got a lot of help with sending off all the applications.

UNIVERSITY

I then had to take the standard aptitude test, very similar to an IQ test. You have a bit of English and maths and they test you on logic etc and of course I'm fine on that – it was multiple guess! I got a high enough score. My reports were broken down into two sections, effort and my actual performance. I had always got As and Bs for effort, and that translated well for university because they look at how you perform as a person. Hence I got a full sports scholarship to North Carolina State University and studied business and economics. But, I had to maintain a pass grade or above, in most cases it's above a pass grade, otherwise the scholarship is taken away from you.

There is one thing that happened to me at university. English was prerequisite for the course. The English teacher was a very southern American lady. In the past they had had problems with English from some of their undergraduates who had been accused of being illiterate. The university took this personally, so they put this very hard English programme together.

I remember sitting down in class when the paper came back. It was covered with red, I mean all over. To give you an idea, if you make two spelling mistakes you fail. But it was just unbelievable at the bottom of my work, this southern American lady had written 'Somehow in this paper you have managed to ruin the King's English.'

Now as an English person who had just gone to America I found that the most insulting thing I ever read. I was an eighteen year old, fairly highly strung, very stubborn lad, so I went up to her and said 'Madam, when I put pen to paper I may ruin the King's English but that's mild to what you do to the Queen's English when you open your bloody great mouth!' I failed the course, but I didn't half enjoy saying that to her.

RELATIONSHIPS

Dyslexia still affects my relationships. It's water under the bridge. But what happens forms your character and what happened to me I wouldn't wish on anybody else. I am not asking people to feel sorry for me, but it has made me like an armadillo. If someone gets nasty with me, then I can just pull out the iron shields and nothing they say will upset me. So it has affected relationships and it continues to affect relationships.

I am just glad now that I experienced the privilege of my position in this country, because people are so nice to me all the time. It is a constant reminder to me that a lot of what has happened to me at school was done out of ignorance rather than out of malice or vindictiveness which has been a great healer for me. But *you can never completely heal the scars that were caused in childhood and that's why it is so important that every dyslexic child, as you well know, is diagnosed in class.*

I have described it like a knife being thrust into the heart of your self-confidence and then moved around. Children are so badly damaged. I remember just the other day somebody was talking about physical education to me and said 'Well, if children are hurt when they are young physically they repair themselves so quickly.' I thought that was a pretty extraordinary thing to say because if someone is hurt, there is a scar whether it is physical or mental and quite often the mental scars are the ones that affect people the longest. They actually are part of what forms their character.

Life is not easy, it's very tough and nobody should give anybody else favours. But I think with dyslexia you have got a situation where you have potentially very, very bright people and they can actually contribute a huge amount to our society. Because they quite often see things in a different light, Churchill and all the rest of them.

MESSAGE

This is a message for parents – concentrate on what the child is good at and encourage them in a positive way. Try and avoid 'You are bad at . . .' or 'No, that's not the way to do it.' Try and encourage them to do it a different way but in a positive way – 'Hey, maybe you'd find it's better to do it this way', or whatever.

If you are in the kitchen pouring out some milk into new glasses and you've got the glasses full and feel a bit wobbly you say 'Jack, why don't you go and take the milk for me.' And Jack picks up the glasses and as he goes towards the door you say 'Whatever you do don't drop them.' Well, that's what's called negative reinforcement.

The worst people of all are children and teachers, parents do it, friends do it. What you should say is 'Jack, you're really good at carrying glasses. I'm useless, can you take this round?'

Unfortunately I have had so much negative reinforcement

from childhood that I still have trouble coping with reading out loud in front of people because there are so many negative experiences in my mind. That's what parents should be especially concerned about – always putting through a positive reinforcement.

It is unbelievable, when you actually know a child is dyslexic, that that child can be treated as a fool by teachers and you treated as a neurotic parent. I don't know how many years it will take, but eventually dyslexia will have to be accepted and understood everywhere for the children's sake. It's something I feel very strongly. Every barrier of this hidden handicap should be lifted.

Felicity Kendal
Actress

Poetess and Painter

ANNE

The first time I met Anne was when she won the poetry prize. She had been invited to London for Dyslexia Week to talk to the press on the top of the Dyslexia Week Bus in Covent Garden. Her story was so moving that she had most of the press in tears. They identified with the tragedy of not being able to read what you have written.

Afterwards I asked if she would be prepared to talk to me for the book. Eight months later she came to London and we met back stage after the matinée of *Married Love*, the play I was in at the time.

Anne, who is in her forties, has only just learned to read her own poems. She is a perfect example of triumph over adversity. She recently had a very successful exhibition of her painting and has been asked to paint some murals in the entrance to the geriatric ward of her local hospital, and a book of her poems is currently in the pipeline.

After not being able to read or write when she left school, she moved from job to job without much success. She trained as a nurse but found it so difficult to cope she had a nervous breakdown and was forced to leave. Still no one recognized the cause of her problems.

She finally decided to pursue a career in art and poetry.

After an interview for art college she was diagnosed as dyslexic and had special lessons with the Dyslexia Institute for two and a half years. Anne is one of the most successful adult dyslexics at the Institute. She won their National Poetry Competition and came third in an essay writing competition with her first essay, written at the age of thirty-nine.

* * *

The first thing that was mentioned when I was at school was how inattentive I was. I couldn't be held to any one subject for any length of time.

I was born in 1947 and classes being large they sort of preferred to forget my existence almost. If I was lucky I would be given a large colouring book or some paper to doodle on in case anyone came in. By the time I got up to secondary school, not only had they abandoned me but I had abandoned them.

FRIENDSHIPS

I was considered to be thick to the point of being stupid and the other children tried to bully me. I never did make many friends because I was nearly always spending playtime and lunch breaks fighting off children who just wanted to be nasty.

I very soon learned how to disappear within the school, all the hidey holes and how to just sit quietly at the back so no one took any notice of me. The only lessons that I really enjoyed were the art lessons and the bits where the teachers actually read to us. We had a very highly creative English teacher who used to read poetry and I think that's what sparked my interest.

I got through from the age of eleven to fifteen very nicely. I left school, couldn't read or write at all and found a job in a shop. My parents had realized by then that there

73

was a problem. There was a problem, but not a problem that they could cope with. I wasn't ill in any way. I wasn't unintelligent, but yet there was something, they didn't know what. The shop job lasted about six months and such was my lack of maths that I am wondering now why it didn't end before then. It was all guesswork. There were many people who walked out of the shop with some item free and the manager was always at me because the till was wrong. I mean I could be ringing up £200 or £2 or whatever and I wouldn't know.

FINDING A JOB

After that I thought well obviously I can't work in a shop. What am I going to do? And then I thought 'Ah, kitchen work, in a hospital or a large canteen or whatever.' I walked into our nearest hospital and asked if they had any jobs for kitchen staff. I was interviewed for the job of very lowly nurse helper which is a post given at that time to young girls prior to them becoming student nurses. They didn't know I couldn't read and write. My mother came with me to the interview, but she would probably be too proud to admit that her daughter had this problem. I was not particularly bothered by it.

NERVOUS BREAKDOWN

The problem started when I was made up to student nurse for the year and we started doing theory. But they still allowed me to muddle along because I was picking up the practical side of it so well. That is until I became a second year nurse and then whether it was the pressure or whether it was just the nature of the work with psychiatric patients I don't know, but I had a fairly severe nervous breakdown and had to leave.

I started sleep walking. I had sudden losses of temper that

74

were inexplicable and finally I went to the doctor with a cold which was most unusual for me. It just wouldn't clear up. I developed a nasty cough and he said 'This has just nothing to do with having a cold. This has got everything to do with you having a breakdown.'

INDUSTRY

So then I got into the steel works. It was heavy work, dirty, not without danger and I got on quite well. We were working three shifts, that is mornings, afternoons and nights. Unfortunately, I was nineteen going on twenty then, it proved too heavy. We were lifting anything from between 12 lbs to 1 cwt of steel quite frequently and this was just too much. So I had to get another job.

In all the jobs that I had in industry, which were quite a number and of quite a variety, I went through the lot without being able to read or write which means that I had only one chance at picking up the instructions that were given to me and getting on with the job.

Unfortunately a back problem that I had had from the steel works suddenly began to make itself felt and I gradually began to be more and more in pain and had to stop work altogether.

I began to go to the classes at the Mappin Art Gallery on a semi- and full-time basis, got my folder together and then my problems really began.

DISCOVERING DYSLEXIA

An appointment was made for me with the Poly doctor in Sheffield and I explained it all to him, how I had never been able to learn to read or write, how the words were just a chaotic jumble, and he said 'Oh yes, well, I don't know if there is anything we can do for you but I'll put you in touch with the

Dyslexia Institute.' He made the phone call, put me in touch and off I went for a preliminary interview. I began to go for lessons, all the while thinking 'Well, if this is like school, I'm not standing it.'

It wasn't until about my third lesson that I realized that they weren't going to belittle me or just leave me to my own devices. Gradually some of the words were beginning to make sense. After two years and a good deal of coaxing I entered the National Poetry Competition and also the essay competition which at the age of thirty-nine was the first essay I had ever written. I won the poetry competition and came third in the essay writing competition.

I had arrived at the Dyslexia Institute in Sheffield without being able to read or write. They thought having coped for so long that they were going to have difficulty teaching me. But they didn't. It was partly determination on my part that gave me the incentive, I wanted to do well at college. I wanted finally to overcome what had always been a problem.

ANNE'S WINNING POEM

WINTER

Wild roaring seasons gale
Lashing swirling snow across
Bowed forest, bleak moor, huddling town
Ever colder as each noisy storm
Arranges drifted snow's new patterns.

Quiet frozen nights eerie stillness
Broken when hunting owls sob
Hauntingly, alert to clutch small prey.
Forest heart slows, sleep becomes coma
Only fierce Robins utter defiant challenge.

Tall evergreens shake shaggy green sides
Denying foothold for enfolding snow
Oaks grown snow laden, grass sleeps
Snow piling on snow, hoar forest,
Chilling breezes stir stiff rimed rushes.

High towering clouds loom skyward
More snow falls, astringent winds
Sough cold, bitter lullabies, frost
Assails small pond, mighty river alike
Pale ice grips with deadly force, cold on cold
Winter a years slow stumbling old age.

Soldier

IAN

I heard about Ian when I visited the Dyslexia Institute in Lincoln where he was taught. Although I never actually met Ian I found his story a very interesting one and one which I felt I wanted to include in this book. I'm sure he will be an inspiration to youngsters with similar aspirations.

* * *

Ian Davies is another of the Institute's success stories. When Ian reluctantly accompanied his mother to the Institute dressed in a studded black leather jacket, he hated school. He was of average intelligence, yet his reading age was that of a seven year old, and his spelling age that of a six year old. The teachers hadn't bothered with Ian, and he had been left at the back of the class where he dreamt of a career in the army he thought he would never have. Or, when he became bored, he would draw attention to himself by playing the fool and disrupting the class. This, of course, got him into trouble. Understandably, Ian arrived at the point where he wanted to have nothing to do with the school or the teachers, as he felt they weren't able to help him.

78

Mechanical Technician/Engineer

DAVID

Adult remedial classes can improve the quality of life and the job prospects of many people who otherwise would have been dismissed as stupid.

'Mature students' are increasing in number now that dyslexia is more talked about and adults are less shy of admitting their difficulties.

I met David through the Dyslexia Institute and after much correspondence and changing of dates, David, who is a mature student, and I got together one weekend.

David was behind at school in every subject but maths. However, he didn't know there was anything wrong until he was sixteen. It was his first day as an apprentice mechanical technician and he couldn't fill in the personnel form. Being told he was dyslexic shattered his confidence completely. He became very depressed and moody, even violent at times. So his boss arranged for him to have special lessons. His work is going well, he was made Apprentice of the Year in 1985. David's hobby is making model aeroplanes.

* * *

I knew I was dyslexic when I was sixteen. I had an interview at Newcastle College in late September 1983 with the training

81

instructors and they offered me a job there and then. I didn't do any tests, unlike all the other apprentices, who had to go through about three or four tests and about three interviews.

They discovered that I was dyslexic the very first day I started, as a personnel form had to be filled in and I did it very badly, even worse than normal. I was in front of the boss within about five minutes of filling it in, and he said 'Are you dyslexic?'

THE EFFECT OF DISCOVERING I WAS DYSLEXIC

Finding out that I was dyslexic knocked my confidence for six and my ability at work was really shattered. One particular job which was just making a set of clamps, which normally takes an average apprentice around forty hours, took me about seventy-nine.

I felt terrible, I couldn't see the point of anything. I had the tests, I knew I was dyslexic and I was beginning to ask myself what I was going to do. I wasn't going to pass.

At home those first six months, I moped around thinking to myself, ignoring everybody, shouting at them. I smashed a model aircraft and went really over the top.

I have models all over the place. It's my general interest. It's mine and nobody else's. They may be bad, but I've made them. Something I can enjoy on my own and the associated thing of going out and watching air shows without worrying about being dyslexic. Everybody should have a hobby. My mother was dusting and one of them dropped, then the shelf followed and landed on top of it. I went mad.

Then I had a confidential conversation with my training officer. He said that the training manager was thinking of dropping me from a technicians' course which I was on, to a craft course. The craft course is the toolmakers and fitters ... they actually build and assemble the tools, whereas the technician designs and organizes other things around – products. He thought that I wouldn't survive the job and I sort of agreed with him.

Then over Christmas I thought I might as well have one go. So I had a go and passed reasonably well. My boss arranged for me to have lessons. I started going to the Dyslexia Institute in Stowe which was a great boost, knowing there were others like me.

SUCCESS

I survived the technicians' course for the next six months, passed the first lot of tests with reasonable marks and started the next stage. They take on an average of between eight and ten apprentices a year. I'm surviving. They didn't expect me to get this far.

I was Apprentice of the Year in 1985. 'Apprentice Achievement' was the title. One of the training instructors died and they created a memorial for him and I was the first to receive it.

I finally completed and received my Higher National Certificate in engineering last year. Since then I have started a part-time degree course in physics. It's hard going but I have just completed the first year exams. It's a four year course, and I don't know whether I can complete it, but I believe it's worth a try.

British Telecom Engineer

DAVID

Another mature student, David Brown, has a younger brother and sister, both are dyslexic. He was considered a trouble-maker at primary school. The headmistress thought he should go to a special school but his parents objected. He struggled through school, leaving at sixteen without any qualifications. After a series of unsuccessful jobs, David eventually sought help two years ago. He was found to be dyslexic and has been going to special lessons ever since. He now works for British Telecom and plays bridge as a hobby.

* * *

I'd just started school in Croydon and I'd been there about six months before we moved down to Bracknell. Within those six months I learnt to write my own name and count up to ten. Then we moved to Bracknell and I went to the primary school there but they didn't seem to do the same things.

So I became a little trouble-maker. I was always getting into fights, with other kids. Then the headmistress decided that I wasn't clever enough and that I should go to a special school. But my parents wanted me to go to a normal school. I was about five or six. So they had a psychiatrist come down

84

and have a look at me. He said I should go to a normal school.

MASTERS' HELP

In my junior school I was struggling all the way through. In the third year the headmaster took an interest, and at that time he had his own special class where he had his group of all the really intelligent kids in the school. He had me transferred to his class, so that he could teach me whenever he was there. All the other kids would help me as well. The headmaster and his wife spent hours after school trying to help me. But they just didn't understand and didn't know which way to go around teaching me to read. As far as I knew there was nothing known about dyslexia at the time.

I left there at about eleven and then went to a secondary modern school. At my secondary modern school the teachers tended to be more unkind than the kids, and put me into an idiots' course. But that's not their fault. I don't think they really understood. *It wasn't until one teacher started finding out about dyslexia that her attitude changed and she knew it wasn't because the kid was being lazy, it was more that you'd got to find some way of teaching them.* I think this is why sometimes the old-fashioned way of teaching probably would have been the better way for me.

Another teacher tried his hardest and gave me confidence to say that at least I'd tried. Most of my school reports that I had, especially from him, were that in the class situation I'd done well and probably got average marks, but when it came to sitting down and doing exams, problems built up and I couldn't make it. If I'd had someone to sit there and read the paper out to me I'd probably understand the questions and be able to do them, but trying to sit there and read it in half an hour and then write down the answers as well was just too much for me.

I left school at sixteen. I actually found a job making contact lenses, so I didn't bother taking any exams because I knew I'd

85

have trouble passing them. I'd been making contact lenses for six years and then got made redundant, I then went and drove a big steam roller that flattens the ground for a company, and that lasted for six months. I then started cleaning cars in a garage, but got made redundant from there. Then I decided I wasn't going to just jump into any old job for the sake of money.

REMEDIAL HELP

I'd heard about people being dyslexic and I'd always wondered about it while I was working. I was quite happy working and it didn't really bother me. But being out of work, then you start looking for ways of improving yourself to help you get a job.

So that's when I went to my doctor to find out whether I was dyslexic and the best way to go about it. She gave me Barbara Foster's phone number at the Dyslexia Institute and I called her and made an arrangement to meet and ever since then I've been going to the Institute once a week. It must be two years that I've been going to Barbara. Any spare bit of time I have now I practise the spelling cards. Before I'd become quite lazy in certain respects. I would always try to find the easiest way to get round things. Through the hardships of not being able to read and write clearly, I had to find other ways.

I think if my parents had been more academic with that sort of skill they would have had the intelligence to say, 'All right, he's struggling, let's sit down and help him.'

COPING WITH WORK

I've worked for British Telecom for two years now. There was a cleaning job going so I applied for that and they also asked me if I would like to apply for the job I'm doing now called jumper running. It means that you provide the lines or re-numbering lines to different addresses within the exchange. It takes some engineering skills but you've got to have a good memory basically. I don't think the bosses really know I'm dyslexic.

I've a good visual memory if things are explained well. I can work on it. The biggest drawback is if someone said to me to go and fix a telephone and gave me a diagram, I'd be there a month of Sundays. But if they showed me – undo this screw, put that wire there, I could probably do it. That's the worst thing about being dyslexic – being frustrated.

I have just to *dot* the *t*'s and *cross* the *i*'s

Doctor

SAMMY

Some dyslexics feel a strong sense of injustice. They know in their hearts that they will eventually be able to live up to their parents' expectations, but not at the exact moment the education system demands. This sense of injustice manifests itself in a variety of ways. In Sammy's case he admits that he finally resorted to cheating, which quite a number of dyslexics said they did in order to survive in school. Sammy is not proud of the fact but he is honest about it.

Sammy had a really hard time at school, he was half English, half Pakistani and his tanned skin and funny accent gave rise to endless teasing. Sammy's dyslexia just added to the problem and the teachers thought he was lazy. However, he went to university, qualified as a dentist then continued to study and qualified as a doctor despite rather unusual circumstances.

* * *

I was sent to school in Boston. I had tremendous difficulties in actually learning to write. Dyslexia was unknown then but they knew that I wasn't lazy, I wasn't stupid and yet I was having a considerable amount of trouble just formulating words and moving my pen across the page from left to right.

My spelling was atrocious. I had no idea how words or letters linked together, so it was a feat of memory. I could only remember words in short term memory, the next day I wouldn't know them. It took me a long time to learn to write my name.

My reading ability was nil. I was always having my knuckles rapped for 'dreaming'. So I was told to sit at the front of the class each semester and was ridiculed by the teachers. I was told I was useless and that my mother was over protective. All my reports said, 'Inattentive, lazy and disruptive. I see no future for the boy. His grades are a disgrace'.

Then I moved to another school and I started to get some extra teaching at the end of the day, and I was eventually diagnosed as dyslexic. I was very unhappy at school because I got such bad grades.

I was teased cruelly, I wetted my bed all the time. I went on wetting, then I learnt a trick in summer camp. I never slept in my bed, but on the rug on the floor. I saved myself the humiliation of the 'wet patch' when each morning we had to strip the beds back to air them.

RESOLVING TO CHEAT

I realized I was going to get nowhere fast so when my parents moved and I was sent to school in England I decided to change my own life by being a cheat. I realized I wasn't stupid, I was just a little behind and would catch up later.

There was a landmark. There were the exams at sixteen and I realized I had got the ability of a fourteen year old and I didn't see why I should be taking this test at the age of sixteen when I knew I would be ready for it at seventeen. If only the clock would stop for a year it would make a whole difference to my life.

EXAMS

I did geography and sciences. Coming up to the last six months before the exams I realized I would have to devise some plan to cheat and I knew I was to be given special privileges because I was dyslexic. A room on my own to do my exam with additional time.

In geography I had anticipated some questions and had the appropriate answers with me, hidden away, which I just put down on paper.

In chemistry I knew I could get all the answers to the multiple choice from a scholar who had done the exam before. Because I was in a different room I was able to get the answers off him without him knowing it. I got distinction in chemistry which as I said wasn't entirely all my own work! I failed the first part of the exam because I had done it on my own. So I worked out the second part of the paper because some chap had had to do the exam the day before and I had managed to crawl in through the window, see the questions, crawl out and write all the answers out on the examination paper which I had kept before, because I knew it would take me too long otherwise. I must have got a distinction on that paper and that gave me a pass on the compiled score.

So that was enough to get me off to university. The point was that I wanted to leave the place with some honour and I knew I wasn't useless. I knew I could have done those exams when I was nineteen but I had to do them at seventeen and a half. And I had worked and worked and I wasn't going to throw everything away.

UNIVERSITY

Then I promised on the Koran that I wasn't going to cheat at university, but in the end I had to. I did my first year at dental school in New York and failed. I was devastated and thought this is it. The crunch had come. I did the exam again and had to cheat to qualify.

BECOMING A DOCTOR

Then I decided to do medicine, so it's been a long haul but I have enjoyed it. I had to go back to university and I got distinction in everything and became a doctor *with no cheating*. I got honours, prizes, all sorts of things which just goes to show that I was two years behind my learning age and these obstacles were just a little bit too close for me at the time. Had they been slightly further apart I could have done it, and done it well.

MESSAGE

I think the most important thing is to believe in yourself and have a lot of determination to succeed and to carry on in spite of the handicap you may have. By working hard you can achieve and become very successful in life. Don't be held back too much by your own handicap and the pity you might receive from others.

It is a problem that you can have all your life but I think you can get around much of it. Some people may find it very difficult, if it is severe, to actually get started, and may have missed all their opportunities. That's the difficult thing, the way education works. You have got to achieve certain goals at a certain age and if you don't, you then get relegated, and that is the biggest handicap of all.

So when in your youth you want to be climbing trees, I think you have to realize fairly early on that you have to work hard in order to get somewhere, and climb the trees later!

Jackie Stewart OBE

RACING DRIVER AND BUSINESS MAN

Jackie Stewart is one of the world's most successful racing drivers in the history of motor sport. He began Formula One racing in 1965 and retired in 1973. During those nine years he was World Champion three times and won twenty-seven Grand Prix victories out of ninety-nine races. He was honoured with the OBE in 1972 for his achievements. Jackie has also written several books and is currently working on a new one. He is in great demand as a speaker at functions and frequently appears on television. Jackie now has several business interests and has set up the Jackie Stewart Shooting School in Scotland. When he finds the time his hobbies are shooting, golf, tennis, music and, perhaps surprisingly, reading.

His two sons – the elder is a racing driver like his father, the younger one works in television production – are both dyslexic.

When we met it was 9 a.m., but it was already Jackie Stewart's second meeting of the day. There were doubtless a few more to come before he flew to America that afternoon. I arrived at the hotel early but may as well have been late, as I had left the tape at home and had to borrow one from a painter redecorating one of the rooms. Then I couldn't work

the tape recorder. In the end Jackie had to get me a new tape, and work the tape recorder for me as well!

Not the best way to start an interview with a busy man. Nonetheless it was a riveting three quarters of an hour.

* * *

I was born in Scotland on 11 June 1939 in the house where my father and mother were living, literally in the house. It was a small bungalow next to the garage that my father ran – a small family business.

I was the second son. My elder brother, Jimmy Stewart, who is eight years older than me, still lives in Scotland. He also turned out to be a racing driver but retired after a couple of serious accidents in the mid-fifties.

I had what I would call a normal happy childhood in the sense that my parents were very kind to me. We were brought up very comfortably.

I am the only one in the family who is dyslexic. I have no knowledge of my father or mother's problems in learning, and certainly I don't think my brother was. He was considerably better at school than I was. But because of the large difference in age I did not have the communication that I might have had with another brother or sister of a more uniform age.

UNHAPPY AT SCHOOL

My youth was based in the unhappiness of my inabilities at school, and unquestionably they were the unhappiest days of my life.

I went to the village school at the age of five or six. I don't recall having problems there. Then I went to Dumbarton Academy which was fee paying at first, then it became a grammar school. Very over classed. I mean forty-five pupils per class in each subject. I went there I suppose from the age of eight or nine. I was held back a year to try and pass my eleven-plus

93

because then I was a disaster, in almost everything outside of sport.

Although now I have largely overcome it, I think I had a real problem of reading aloud, and I had problems spelling and I always had trouble with comprehension. That's to say, comprehending everything – the spoken word and the written word.

The blackboard was the same. Nothing could I absorb. I mean I was like the eternal plastic sponge.

ABSENTEEISM FROM SCHOOL

At home there was frustration. The constant disastrous report cards. I had very poor attendance figures at school. I was always ill. There was some reason for me being ill, I think. I don't ever remember playing truant. I always had maladies of some kind or another that I would have to go to the doctor for. I had everything, I think.

My parents thought I was just generally weak as an individual in the sense of my health. They thought I had anaemia and I went for blood tests and I had. I was much slighter than I am now in build. I had a lot of time out of school and that was looked upon as an excuse for the poor report cards.

ELEVEN-PLUS EXAM

As I prepared for the eleven-plus, I was sent to a friend of the family who was the head English teacher in the secondary school, D. J. Thomas. I went there two or three nights a week for private tuition to try and cram for the eleven-plus.

That was equally frustrating and I found my capacity for consumption of information very poor. My concentration span was very short, probably up to twenty minutes, and then I was lost. I would find excuses to captivate Mr D. J. Thomas in conversation about other things that would take the heat away from my problem of not being able to listen to him and comprehend. That was a frustration that has lasted all of my life.

In the eleven-plus I got a C which meant that I couldn't stay at the Dumbarton Academy and had to go to Hartfield School which was very much looked upon as the poor school. My friends of course were all much cleverer. They teased me. I was ridiculed because of my (a) stupidity, (b) thick, stupid and dumb attitudes. I had to somehow overcome that in other ways, in my case by sport. I was good at soccer. I played outside right for the school team, and for the county in the end, and that was through just sheer determination. But I had very little self-esteem as far as school was concerned.

DREAMS OF SUCCESS

When I think back I don't think there was anything wrong with me at all. I think it was all part of this dyslexia problem and it was always frustrating.

I was always wanting to be an achiever. I always dreamt of success. I always dreamt of fame and fortune and all those other things I think all young people dream of. I had always had enormous ambition, but I mean it just seemed so futile when clearly the only identifiable standard you had to meet was that of others in a system. There was no alternative, it seemed, so therefore if you were daft and stupid and dumb, my goodness! You had to expect it.

PARENTS

My parents were certainly not unsupportive. Certainly not. I mean I wasn't being ridiculed. I wasn't being abused for my inadequacies or ridiculed because of any stupidity or any lack of intelligence. Somehow or other it was 'My God, you know Jackie's ill again' or 'My God, Jackie's report card'. I'm sure they thought I was not working hard enough or was not concentrating. It was just a depression that I knew was there and not from them, but from me, from inside me more than anywhere else.

I left school at fifteen at the earliest possible minute without any qualifications and worked in my father's garage. I felt the unhappiness, frustration and the pain of being identified as not being able to do anything in those days. I covered it well, with a personality that made people think I rushed around and did this and did that. My energy level was always high.

FRIENDS

I never had any great friendships at school. I have always been very much a loner in almost everything. But one of my friends in that school is still one of my best friends today.

A TASTE OF SUCCESS

At fourteen I started to shoot clay pigeons and at fourteen and a half I won my first competition on New Year's Day, which brought with it a very large trophy. I then saw the opportunity to be good at something for the first time in my life and I suddenly started to beat people. There were no other young shooters, so I was beating grown men. Then I thought 'My God, I can be good at something!' For the first time in my life I was being credited as achieving something. Not only did I win that event, I won something wherever I went to shoot. So from fifteen years of age I was being picked up on Saturdays or at weekends to go shooting with friends of the family.

I went on to shoot very successfully. Winning local events and winning slightly bigger events and then shooting for Scotland, winning the Scottish Championship and other national championship. Then shooting for Britain, winning the British Championship, the English, the Welsh, the Irish as well as the Scottish, the European and Mediterranean. Travelling to do the World Championship, the European Championship, nearly going to the Olympics in 1960 when I was twenty-one. It was a two man team and on my final day qualifying I lost my position in the British team by one point and therefore was reserve for Rome.

All this was going on besides my job at the garage and night school. My failings now were not nearly so important as they had been when I had no other focus point. Now I was having pride in myself because here I was shooting for my country with my Scottish lion rampant or my St Andrew's cross and then my Union Jack – and that was big time for me. I was travelling to places and I was being *given* my ammunition because people thought I was good enough. When I started to shoot I suddenly saw a light at the end of the tunnel that simply wasn't there before, and it saved my life as a person of self-respect. I mean I just thought I was a disaster until then.

JOB

I worked on the farm next door after school every day. That was great because I would go and I would lift more turnips than anybody else, and I would lift more potatoes than anybody else, and I would move more hay bales than anybody else.

It was important for me to lift more potatoes and turnips and bales than anybody else. Because it was my only way of showing myself to be any better than anybody in anything. The only standard that I had was at school.

At school I played football and because my position was outside right I ran more than anybody else. But when I left school to work in the garage I was able to actually do something physical that I was given credit for. I was earning £3.16 a week and I made double that in tips, because everybody was so pleased that I would do this and that. Obviously looking back it must have been with a great amount of spirit and enthusiasm.

At first I served petrol then I repaired punctures. A year later I got into the lubrication bay. It was brand new and I tell you I kept it the cleanest and the best in all the county – you could eat your breakfast from it. I would do the 1,000 mile service faster than anybody else. I had great pride in the lub-bay, it was mine, my responsibility. Dyslexia only then started to cause a problem, because as a mechanic in those days you had to serve a six year apprenticeship to become a genuine mechanic, and for that you had to go to day school or night school.

NIGHT SCHOOL

I chose night school because day school suggested longer hours, so I went to night school three nights a week at a place called Stowe College. An engineering college in Glasgow. We went to night school to get a City and Guilds certificate. I was frustrated again. I passed but I don't know how. I mean I certainly didn't get it by passing exams. It was the practical application.

Still nobody had identified my problem. I was still having learning difficulties.

When I found out how to do something, then I was magic. Then I would do it faster, better, tidier than everybody else. I have always been fussy about the appearance of things. That's always been so in my racing and my shooting and professional life now. So I have always been very pernickety about detail.

THE THOUGHT OF LOSING MY JOB

My father wanted to sell the business at one point and none of us wanted him to sell it. I more than anyone else didn't want him to sell it, because if he sold the business, it would mean

I would never get a job anywhere else! Who would give me a job? Because I certainly wasn't good enough under normal circumstances to get a job.

RACING

Then I started to prepare cars for other people to race. My brother had been a racing driver when I was at a very impressionable age at only ten years old. Whilst still at school I went to see him participating in this very exciting sport. For a young person enormously stimulating.

As a family we did not have a lot of money and my father had given my brother quite a lot of money to go racing. Therefore there was no opportunity for me to go racing. But in any case I was shooting and it didn't mean anything to me really. But when I started to prepare cars for other people to drive, again it was that meticulous preparation of eating your breakfast from any part of the car that made the difference.

By the time I was twenty-two or twenty-three, this person who I was preparing a car for gave me the chance to drive the car as a reward for my hard work. That's how I started racing which then fired me up. At the same time I had married in 1962 and I couldn't afford to shoot any more because of the expense. I was earning a small wage, and although I had a car from the garage I couldn't afford to shoot and be married. So I gave up shooting and retired in 1962. And then I took up racing because it wasn't costing me anything.

REMEMBERING NAMES

My dyslexia never affected my shooting or racing. Other than in remembering people's names. My mechanics' names took me years. Then I would never forget them because they were part of my life. Roger Hill, or Alan Challis, or Roy Topp, all these names come back to me instantly because they were part of my life.

But when I was racing it took me a couple of years to learn the names of my mechanics whose life they had in their hands – my life.

DESIRE TO LEARN

I have always mixed with people more successful than myself, because it's the only way you learn. I love meeting successful people because they have done something, not because they are famous but because they have got a skill level which is usually enormously high.

Perhaps if I had been a traditional business man dyslexia would have been a disadvantage. But you see I entered the business world through my name as a racing driver. I mean my calling card did everything for me in a way because I was famous. When I called somebody up they were impressed that they had got a phone call from me if you like.

Now then, if I had let them down or more importantly let myself down by bad presentation, by not knowing what to say or not being able to project, then I would have got nowhere. But I think dyslexics and people who have had learning difficulties of this kind have a unique opportunity.

I find dyslexics have an ability to communicate better than most others, if they really set their mind to it. Because we are so concerned that they the listener may have the same problem of comprehension as we have when someone is trying to tell us something. So I tend to be more specific, more colourful and more demanding of myself to be sure that they understand what I am trying to say.

I speak too much but I am always frightened that I haven't got the message over. So I go further with my pictorial work of painting the picture of what I want to pass on.

BUSINESS

So if I have something to sell, I will generally sell it through my enthusiasm and my energy and my words. Now I have learned that I can never do business by only selling concepts. I have got to close deals. I think anybody can open a deal but very few people can close them. So I have learned at the age of fifty how to do that.

AMBITION

It was ambition because of my dyslexia that did it. The desire to be good and it wasn't a desire to beat other people. *It was a desire to beat myself that was important.* I stopped being competitive as a racing driver long before I retired from racing. People think that you have got to beat other people. It's nothing to do with beating other people, it's controlling your own emotions and beating yourself because other people make mistakes. I'm not allowed to make mistakes because I am my judge.

THE RELIEF OF DISCOVERING I AM DYSLEXIC

My son was having difficulties and we took him to have him assessed and that is how I discovered I was dyslexic. We sat down and I said, 'Well, you know, I don't see how Mark's really much different than I am. Because I had terrible troubles at school etc.' I did a few simple tests and they identified it there and then.

Now that was at forty-two and I tell you even at that age it was a relief to have somebody turn round and say, 'Do you know all that trouble you have had all those years ago – well,

101

you know, there's been a reason for it.' Even at that mature age, after all the success I had ever had in my shooting and my racing and financially, I thought, 'Oh, my God, I'm not stupid after all.' Until that time, I felt inadequate, because I wasn't able to read as well as I should.

When Mark was identified as being dyslexic it was a fantastic relief for him too, because until then he would have a little girl friend saying 'I'm not going out with you any more because all my friends tell me that I shouldn't go out with you because you are stupid.'

I write things phonetically now and I don't care because I don't have to justify my ignorance any more. That's more important than anything else. Suddenly now if I ask anybody how to spell a word, someone alongside me in an aeroplane or anywhere, I don't care any more. I know they'll go home and say, 'You'll never guess, I sat next to Jackie Stewart and he asked me how to spell so and so for God's sake.' But you see they don't think I'm dumb any more. I have achieved. I've come out of the wood.

PERSONAL APPEARANCE

I was doing an appearance in America introducing the Scorpio car and I spoke to a young lad. The boy had trouble with eye contact and obviously had an inferiority complex, he even had trouble shaking hands. But after my talk when I spoke about my problem of learning disability at school and so forth, the boy came up to me because he wanted to share the fact that he had a problem and tell somebody who would understand. But I told him 'For God's sake don't even worry about it. I mean I've done it – look I was up there and everybody stood up and applauded,' and he suddenly saw somebody who had all the same troubles as he has, and I think suddenly the boy had hope, just a little bit, and if that's all he's got then that's fantastic. Because he now sees something that maybe is a role model, or whatever, *but he at least has hope, not everybody can be the World Champion or an Olympic Gold Medallist or an actress on a silvery screen. That doesn't matter as long as he can attain his full potential and be a great deal of use in this world.*

USING YOUR ABILITY

God gave me a gift which in my case was to drive a car. If I was able to channel that God-given talent in the most positive way, without interrupting it by distractions of any kind, then I was going to be better off. There are twenty-six God-given talents in the field that make up a Grand Prix start.

All twenty-six probably have a fairly equal distribution of natural talent. It is only the ones who are more able to mentally adapt their skills to the fullest extent of their ability who will hit the big time. Somehow or other when you get the chance you have to be able to use it most positively.

THE POSITIVE EFFECT OF DYSLEXIA

Ultimately dyslexia has affected my life in a very positive way. I am sure without it I wouldn't have achieved what I have. Because if I had only been a great shooter, I mean to shoot for my country and to carry my flag in my blazer and to have won all the events I won, I could have satisfied my future life even at that young age. To have won the World Championship three times as a driver and won all my Grand Prix victories would in itself have been very satisfying.

Perhaps for some other people that would have been my life's achievement. I know that it's not my life's achievement. I know that I have something else to do and to give that hasn't yet arrived. I know it. All the material benefits that I have got have manifested a comfortable way of life and a privileged life,

103

but I know that I haven't yet succeeded. I have more to do.

THE MESSAGE

Everybody has the ability to improve their own personal performance. I don't care if I run out of money today. If I had to go to work I could be a window cleaner. But I bet you I would be successful because I would clean the windows better than anybody else. Now who has to be Einstein to clean windows? But windows all have to be cleaned and if you do them better than anybody else you're going to be asked back to clean the windows next week or next month.

As the father of dyslexic daughters and the grandfather of five dyslexic grandchildren, I think the more open dyslexia is, the better it is for everyone. There is no point in shutting someone up in a closet and pretending it doesn't exist. The most important thing is to discover it early and then be able to do something about it scientifically.

His Majesty King Olav of Norway

Dentist

SUE

In New York there is a school of dentistry where a large percentage of students are dyslexic. I was told by one of the administrators that dyslexics make wonderful dentists. This is obviously the case because when I made enquiries requesting a dyslexic dentist, a dozen dyslexic dentists in America and England were put forward within a few days. I chose Sue as she was the only woman.

It was a Friday night, I had been working all day with my editor Mary and my mind was swimming with dyslexia stories. I knew I had another five people to see over the weekend in London, Leicester, Oxford, Reading and Sussex and the thought of driving out in the rain through the Friday night traffic on the M25, getting lost, misreading the road signs and ending up on the A369 instead of the A396 made my heart sink.

To make my life easier Sue had said 'Let's meet at the Post House just off the motorway.' Very wise, as I had warned her that I was often as much as an hour and a half late after struggling with road directions.

Well, the rain stopped, the traffic wasn't too bad, we met, found a quiet corner where I could plug in the tape recorder and we sat and ate toasted sandwiches, and Sue's remarkable story unfolded. When she was little she used to say, 'In so many hours' time, and in so many minutes' time, in so many seconds' time, the English lesson will be over! If there was a day without English that would be a good day.'

Sue didn't pass her eleven-plus at school. She was teased and the teachers were cruel. She never imagined she would qualify as a dentist. But she did and is now running a practice of her own with two other dentists.

* * *

When I was a child, they realized that being strict wasn't the way to deal with me. *It had to be love.* I think it has been very much the thing with me, that I have needed more love.

I think I felt that I wasn't particularly wanted because I was so stupid and I wasn't the sort of little girl that I felt my mother could dress up and take out and be proud of. I was the only one in the family who was dyslexic. I think I was awkward and difficult. I have had to come to terms with a lot of my early life. Even going back to the little girl in the classroom and saying, 'I forgive you being like that, for being awful and stupid, not able to read or do silly little things like not being able to follow a knitting pattern and having the knitting thrown at you at school.'

You were never one of the special little girls that the teacher always chooses.

When I was very small we lived in the country and so before I went to school I didn't really meet anybody else. There was just me and my mum, my brother and my father, and relatives that lived away, so I really didn't have any contacts till school came, which was a bit of a shock!

SCHOOL

I had troubles in school. I didn't notice anything until I was about seven. Before then I just had one or two problems when I thought the teachers were being a bit nasty. I remember once the teacher was very cross with me and sent me back down to working on a slate because I had done something wrong. You worked on a slate with chalk and then you progressed to a book with a pencil. I had progressed to the book with a pencil and then got pushed back to the slate!

In the last infants' class, suddenly everybody else seemed to know their alphabet. I could never understand it because I thought I worked fairly well at school but everybody else seemed to know things that I didn't know.

The worst thing was when I was in the first class in the junior school – they added up the exam results wrongly and so I came about 9th in the class and then they realized their mistake and I was *last* but one.

My brother had gone through the same school. It was just an ordinary primary school, and it had a very good headmistress, my mum used to go and see her and plead with her to keep me in the A stream because she felt if I ever went down to the B stream, that would be it. As long as I kept in the A stream I would be all right. I was very lucky really and stayed in the A stream.

TEASING

I was teased a lot, I was plump as well which didn't help and so it was a mixture of the two. I always thought I was stupid and that my friends were much better than me – that I wasn't capable of doing things because of it.

108

BEHAVIOUR PROBLEMS

I think I was quite naughty. I didn't want to relate to life. I was quite happy in the little world that I was in. I didn't really want to face school and growing up and all that sort of thing.

I was teased more by the teachers than by the children. The children really didn't notice except that we always used to sit where we came in the class. But then as I got older because I was very intelligent, the gap started to narrow and the teachers would say, 'Well, you can actually do maths!'

PARENTS

I think I was more unaware of my problems than my mother was. She was more aware of the difference in me. My parents were fantastic really. If it wasn't for them I think I would still be blissfully unaware.

When I was about seven, Mum realized I had a problem because I wasn't reading, and I didn't intend reading. So I went to elocution lessons – that was the only thing that the headmistress could suggest. They got on to the problem fairly quickly which was great.

But I didn't realize it was dyslexia until only about ten to fifteen years ago – in fact it was a programme that you were on, on television. I watched it and I said to my husband, 'Oh, I think that's what is wrong with me!'

EXAMS

The first barrier was the eleven-plus because in those days if you didn't get your eleven-plus you couldn't go to a decent school. It was obvious I was going to fail my eleven-plus so my mother got me some extra English lessons which were hilarious because the lady was very strict and I was just a pain and couldn't do what she wanted.

109

FATHER'S HELP

I remember my mother talking to my father who wasn't very well at the time – but he came downstairs out of bed and said to me, 'Well, will you work with me?' So we sat down and we worked every night for about an hour after supper – it was pretty consistent. You could get those papers of English, intelligence tests and things, so we just worked through those.

My mother wanted me to go to the local convent because it wasn't as big as the girls' grammar school, so there were small classes and she thought I would be happier there. You had to get an entrance exam for that. It was a direct grant school so I still got in but I got into the bottom class. Their English exam was really awful. I just didn't know what it was all about.

Then when I got there, I began to realize that subjects that I liked I could do really well in, so there was really no barrier then. In English I used to do appallingly, but in maths and science and geography – things I was interested in – there was no problem.

I actually got an English O-level which was an absolute fluke. I didn't expect to get it but I was quite interested in what it was about, so I did actually get that.

I got two A-levels. I changed subjects because I wanted to be a dentist. One thing I found was bad was that because I had started off in the lower stream they didn't realize that there was a reason for this and they wouldn't change me. I wanted to do science and they said, 'No, because you are in this stream you are not capable of doing sciences.'

So, when I got into the sixth form, I had to start sciences from scratch which was quite late to start.

CRUELTY OF THE TEACHER

I didn't pass the chemistry A-level, because of the teacher, I think, as much as anything. I had one awful incident at school.

I remember in one exam I got about seventy per cent on content and the mistress took the whole lesson tearing me to shreds saying *'This paper is terrible, the spelling is disgusting. I am going to take ten marks off your paper – you have now got sixty per cent.' This went on the whole lesson until I got thirty-two per cent at the end. It was absolutely demoralizing. Especially as it was never mentioned to me at all that I had a spelling difficulty.*

UNIVERSITY

I applied for various universities and when I got my A-level results I applied to Edinburgh and got a place to do dentistry. I had decided when I was about fifteen that was what I wanted to do.

I went to Edinburgh because I failed my chemistry and they do an extra year there. In Scotland they take Highers instead of A-levels. Then I got distinction in chemistry in the first year so I felt justified.

BEST STUDENT OF THE YEAR

I was worried about anatomy because of all those Latin names so I used to sit up every night and repeat them until I got them absolutely right. We used to have to do a little bit and then have a spot test at the end of every fortnight. So I really got into it and spent lots of time learning the words and I won the prize for the best student in the year. It was just literally sitting down hour after hour studying. I qualified as a dentist.

My English is still terrible. I remember we were in groups, and I was in a really good group, I think I was the only girl in this bunch of six boys and they were super boys. In one particular exam, biochemistry or something, I got way above the rest of them – they thought I was a swot but they just accepted that I

111

was a swot. I was. I had to be a swot to actually get through, but they accepted it. I got eighty per cent, they'd all got about forty per cent, so the tutor said 'Sue's got eighty per cent, and what does it say on your paper, Sue?' The last thing I wanted him to do was put me in an awkward spot with these lads, but written at the bottom of my paper was, 'Your English is terrible' – so it cleared the air.

PRACTISING DENTISTRY

I have to be very careful about left and right when I'm working. I also have to be careful about what I write down. I find it very easy to think one thing and write another thing which would be very dangerous if you were to refer somebody to have teeth out. You have got to make sure you put the right teeth down!

I double check and sometimes I think I am not terribly quick in deciding what I want to do. I like to have time to think the situation out with my patients, but I think they appreciate it when I say, 'Look, we are not going to make any snap decisions, we'll see how it goes.'

ADVANTAGES AND DISADVANTAGES

I would prefer not to be dyslexic but having said that, I don't think it has done me any harm. My brother is very intelligent, with all As at O-level, and a First at Oxford, but I think he probably finds life more difficult than I do.

The worst thing about being dyslexic is people thinking you are stupid. The most inconvenient bit is not being able to remember things.

FAMILY

I have got three boys. Two of them are dyslexic. The little one is probably not quite as quick as he could be but I don't

112

think it's dyslexia, just the first two boys. One is really quite bad. I was upset when I discovered – it's a struggle.

My eldest son wasn't picked up until he was about ten, as nobody really wanted to know. I knew that he was dyslexic and I think because of that we worked with him, homework and things, to try and keep him going.

Then I was ill and hadn't been able to work with him, and his teacher at school picked it up which was probably quite a good thing. She got him assessed and again he is incredibly intelligent and they suggested that perhaps we went out of the system and put him in a private school.

We looked around one or two and now he goes to Leighton Park which is the Quaker School. They are just super with him. It's still hard for him because they call him 'slow man'. I suppose as you get older you tend to regulate yourself. I write lists for everything but he doesn't know how to do that. He is terrible at organizing himself.

I try to give my boys a lot of love. You do need more love because you do feel rejected and you feel stupid – 'Why can't I do this simple thing when other people can do it?'

TEACHER'S ATTITUDE

I know that the teacher of one of my sons said to me one day 'How did you manage to get where you've got?' And I thought if she doesn't believe in the kids that she is teaching, how can they get there? I think too often dyslexic children are kept at the basics, but they should be allowed to forget the basics and learn to spell when they are older – just get on and do what you want to do. To hell with the basics and get on with the rest!

TIPS

Lists – that's my secret. Getting organized beforehand. I find when I get with other people I tend to go to pieces so I try and get myself organized beforehand so I know what I am doing. *Be very well prepared.*

I have tended to use my dyslexia as a bit of a joke and almost make out that I am more stupid than I am. Perhaps that's one way that I deal with being a woman in a man's world.

SELF-ESTEEM

I think that I did suffer very much from having a low self-esteem. I know Mum said to me that she realized that when I was little I needed a lot of love. She wanted me to do ballet and I wasn't very keen – I think I was taking Grade 1 – and she rolled back the carpets and made me practise and apparently I just went completely to pieces and she shouted at me and I wouldn't do it.

MESSAGE

Believe in yourself, that you can do it. There is nothing that you can't do if you really put your mind to it. Aim as high as you can and don't be afraid to fail. I have failed lots of times, I don't think I am frightened of failing. I am quite used to picking myself up and getting on with things.

Taxi Driver

RAY

I had the good fortune to get into Ray's cab one Friday afternoon when the traffic was the usual end of week West End madness. The rain was pelting down and everyone was rushing in circles screaming 'TAXI!!!'

Ray's cab's light was off (he was on his way home), but he pulled up to the kerb where I was waiting and yelled, 'Jump in! Can't resist a lady who can't read!'

That was my first introduction to Ray who is also dyslexic.

'I know,' he began again, 'you're the one who has trouble with her spelling and doesn't read books.' Before I could answer he continued, 'Got the same trouble myself,' and so I asked Ray about his dyslexia. I never seem to get into a taxi these days without a cabby mentioning my dyslexia. Word gets round. The fact that I have been acting for thirty years is irrelevant.

* * *

I was in the fish market at Billingsgate before I was a taxi driver. A good East End boy, and my daughter who's dyslexic has also got good street sense! School was horrible, I thought I was thick and left school thinking I'd never learn anything.

When I was studying for the 'Knowledge' I discovered that anyone can do anything if they exercise the brain, dyslexic or

115

not. A lawyer said to me, 'You, learning the "Knowledge" is like getting a degree.' I was really chuffed. He said, 'You've learnt all those street names and where they are and you're dyslexic. It's as hard as qualifying for a law degree.'

Since I've stopped studying it's become more difficult. Now if I read a new street name or a street I haven't seen for a long time, I have to ring on the radio and say if I spell it to you, you tell me what it is.

To learn the Knowledge, I had all the streets put on a tape and I had earphones on, so when I went round on my moped I could hear them as well as read them.

MESSAGE

If you're down on one thing, you're up on another, like common sense, street sense and will-power. So having this trouble is OK as you become a survivor.

I was thinking the other evening about Winston Churchill whom I'm told was supposed to have been dyslexic. I'm not the least bit surprised that he became such a good wordsmith, because if you've got one arm tied behind your back, you'll learn to use the remaining arm twice as well.

'Tim'

Historian

'TIM'

As I have said earlier, in some cases being dyslexic can be an advantage in that it gives you an extra special quota of determination. This is something that 'Tim' believes too, although when Tim was growing up dyslexia was not really talked about. At school when he was made to stand up and read aloud, he failed so miserably, that the master, who knew nothing of his difficulties, made him stand on a chair and thumped the desk with his cane so fiercely that Tim immediately burst into tears. Although he disappointed his father by not going to Oxford, and following his footsteps in the City, Tim nevertheless has enjoyed a very fulfilling career holding many prestigious jobs and he has found his dyslexia has been an asset in the respect that he sees things differently.

* * *

I was lucky because at eleven and a half or thereabouts my headmaster, a chap called Sir Richard Basil Smith, identified that he had got two or three children with this problem. I remember before that at about the age of six I had a terrible time at pre-prep school. The headmaster used to make me stand on my chair and then thumped the desk with a cane at the poor quality of my reading.

118

But at my new school Sir Basil had heard of Helen Arkell, so he sent his mother off to Norway or Denmark and had his mother trained as a teacher for dyslexics. So three or four of us dropped Latin and started doing remedial lessons. We did things like read the *Daily Telegraph*, we had a Helen Arkell box of letters and we were also taught to use typewriters. I also had some tuition from Helen Arkell herself and I did a short course at Bainton House. And I had quite a lot of extra tuition at home.

When I was thirteen and a half I managed to shoot myself in the left eye with a starting pistol so consequently I was blind for a bit. It was a silly accident but as a result of this I had about six weeks of both eyes covered. It was an amazing experience and one that I wouldn't have missed. To actually experience being blind was fascinating. One's other senses become so much more alive. One's sense of touch for example, one's sense of smell, one's sense of the feel of one's skin, one was aware of whether the sun was shining or not by the heat on one's skin.

So I think similarly with dyslexia. One is bound to develop other skills to substitute for the difficulties. For example, I think that in my experience, and I have known quite a lot of dyslexics, they tend to be highly creative, fairly exuberant and outward going, usually rather good at communicating verbally. Interestingly enough, the vast majority I know have been highly intelligent.

FINDING A JOB

When I left school with not one damn exam to my name I went out to Canada and through a letter of introduction got a job as a sales clerk with the Hudson Bay Company in their Vancouver store. Subsequently I was offered the opportunity of joining their management intake course.

When I came back to England I tried very hard to go into television because of my verbal skills. I thought that commentating or particularly interviewing would be something I would take to like a duck to water. But I discovered that the majority of television interviewers and newscasters were doing nothing but reading off boards and teleprompters, and of course my voice drops two tones when I start reading out loud. The colour disappears and it becomes monosyllabic. So that was hit on the head.

PARENTS

My parents were very supportive really. But, I think having a fairly successful father is no great help if you are dyslexic. My father was chairman of one of the oldest banks. I'm not sure whether or not he was expecting something special of me but presumably he was. Certainly I think had I not been dyslexic, then my career path would have been very different. It would almost certainly have led through Oxbridge and probably into the Diplomatic Corps. It would have been a much smoother path.

If you're dyslexic you can't really be one of the crowd so instead of going into the City when I left school I decided I was going to do my own thing. I worked damned hard, but at least at the end of the day one can say one did cut one's own swathe.

JOB

I've always been interested in history. I think it stems from a love of heraldry. Because heraldry was visual, it was something I could relate to, it told you things. It was a code. You could see who married who and it was really rather interesting.

Also my father was very interested in archaeology, so I was quite interested in that. I also enjoyed history and the three things merged together.

Having got up to being a Director of a firm I was then made redundant in 1981. I became a professional glass engraver for a year and during that year I wrote to a large number of people for work. The long and the short of it was that Allied Breweries and Allied Lyons were looking for a historian. They read my C.V., looked at it laterally, studied various component parts and knitted it together and said 'Right, this chap is an information intelligence expert. He's interested in heraldry and history and clearly he's a people's person. We want an historian. This chap could do it!' and I got the job.

WORKING RELATIONSHIPS

I think being dyslexic means one tends to be more outward going and perhaps a little more human because one is aware of one's own shortcomings. I am sure that my dyslexia helps because I could forge relationships quite well.

I was thinking the other evening about Winston Churchill whom I'm told was supposed to have been dyslexic. I'm not the least bit surprised that man got where he did. And I'm not in the least bit surprised that he became such a good wordsmith, because if you've got one arm tied behind your back, you'll learn to use the remaining arm twice as well. So providing somebody is prepared to be open minded enough to give a dyslexic a chance and be understanding initially and particularly to help with the confidence, then they will succeed.

MESSAGE

Buy a book you want to read. I bought a Dennis Wheatley, which was very easy to read and a thumping good story. It wasn't great prose or anything. But I think that from a dyslexic point of view if sentences are relatively short and simply constructed, one can read them that little bit faster so you can actually enjoy the story. Then you are tempted to buy another book and read that, and that can really start you actually enjoying reading.

I may be dyslexic but I still like a good read.

Knitwear Designer

WENDY

I can't think of anything more difficult than reading a knitting pattern, other than deciphering Japanese roadsigns. So in my eyes Wendy is nothing short of a genius to cope with instructions that would daunt many a non-dyslexic.

She now runs her own knitwear business. She mostly designs her own jumpers, as she says, 'Often I find there are mistakes in knitting patterns, and if I made it the way they said, it wouldn't be the jumper that they have in the picture! So I like to design my own.'

* * *

I did have problems at school. I had extra remedial classes in my last year at junior school. I think only because people thought I was a bit slow.

As soon as I went up to middle school, I had problems because in a lot of the classes the lessons were dictation. I always had half the notes missing.

I certainly didn't have any help from the teachers. They weren't nasty. But I think I was one of those children that went through without really registering.

123

ABSENTEEISM FROM SCHOOL

I missed practically the whole of the last year because I *just hated school so much they couldn't get me in there*. I stayed at home and I had a private teacher but when it came to the exams some of the things I had done didn't really correspond with the things they had done at school.

I passed Grade 1 CSE English literature. Then I went to college and did a course in professional design. We needed three O-levels and I had O-level art, needlework and English literature. At that point the college were aware that I had problems and had missed school and they were a great help.

WORK

Now I have my own business designing mohair knitwear but I trained as a pattern cutter. Basically all the jumpers are done on a machine and I sell most of them to boutiques.

My fiancé Chris types the letters for me and the accountant does the books. So, I just design the knitwear and then make it on a machine. I parcel it up and send it off. On average I work from 8 a.m. till 6 p.m. except at Christmas time when everything goes mad and I have to work longer hours.

I get a lot of pleasure from running my business and making it work although I find the paperwork very tiring and difficult and I try to avoid doing it. If I did it more regularly it would be easier.

SELF-ESTEEM

I think being dyslexic affects your confidence. Partly because I haven't read very much. I have learnt to cope with it and if other people can't cope with it, that's their problem. At school I used the fact that I had to wear glasses as an excuse for not reading out loud in an English lesson. Now I very rarely actually read out loud because people just collapsed in heaps of giggles.

I think the worst thing about being dyslexic is that all the way through school you have one major problem – your reading and writing. When you leave school you are unprepared. You are not sure if you can read the books for university which is something that should have been conquered back in junior school not when you are leaving secondary school. So your biggest problem still is the reading and writing, when you should be thinking, 'My biggest problem is learning this new course.'

MESSAGE

If you are dyslexic don't let other people spoil your life. People are quite harsh. Particularly at school which is when you are developing, and that's when it damages the most.

Bruce Jenner

OLYMPIC GOLD MEDALLIST – DECATHLETE

My husband, Eddie, watched Bruce Jenner win his gold medal at the Montreal Olympics, so it was only natural that Eddie, knowing that Bruce was dyslexic should encourage me to write and ask him to be in this book. I did, and he very kindly replied by return.

Bruce Jenner won an Olympic Decathlete Gold Medal in 1976 and has been called *the World's Greatest Athlete*. He is now a film star, successful business man and creator of a fitness video. He has been very outspoken about furthering the understanding of learning disabilities, always mentioning his own battle with dyslexia.

* * *

I grew up in a middle-class family in New York and Connecticut. In school I experienced problems, but it wasn't because of my learning abilities, it was due to my dyslexia, which affected my ability to read properly. I thought of myself as a 'slow kid' until the disorder was diagnosed in high school.

I've always had to work harder than anyone else. Mentally I had it tougher than anyone. I was not a good student, and not knowing I was dyslexic until high school, I had a poor

126

image of myself. In fact I failed the second grade, but then sports changed all that for me.

I think the biggest problem with dyslexic kids, or any learning-disabled person, is the image they have of themselves. When I was a young kid I wasn't very smart. I thought I was pretty dumb and that's unfortunate because I wasn't dumb. The biggest fear I had in my life was getting up in front of the class to read, because I knew I wouldn't do a very good job. The process didn't work. Every day in school I'd sit there and sweat, thinking that they were going to ask me to read in front of the class and I'd look a real fool. I didn't want anyone to know I couldn't read very well.

ATHLETICS

There were kids in class getting an A on every test, while I was getting Cs or Ds but I could go out on the athletic field and hold my own against them and that gave me confidence. The reason I think I grasped on to athletics and took off, is because it's important for any kid to get a pat on the back. I was not a very good student and, not knowing I was dyslexic, my image of myself while growing up was really of this 'slow kid' in school. Sports changed all that. I could hold my own.

Through high school, I involved myself in a variety of sports, I was good at all of them, but not great at any one thing. As a football player at Tarrytown (N.Y.) High, I had my picture in the *New York Times* when Tarrytown beat arch-rival Ossining in a battle of unbeaten teams.

CONFIDENCE

You can't correct dyslexia by taking a pill and making it all better. It's just something you learn to deal with and learn to adapt to. You learn to work with it.

The tough time for me was growing up, learning to read and being slower than the rest of the class. Once I got past that point, and found out that I was somewhat an intelligent human being and I could deal with life, then it doesn't become quite as much of a problem. But it's mainly in growing that it's tough.

MESSAGE

What I try to do now is tell young kids in school, 'Hey, I have this problem and I didn't turn out to be the guy in the gutter, I turned out OK. So, keep your head up high, keep working on it.'

Paediatrician

MARY

**Mary has difficulty with road directions and I would certainly
put myself into that category. In fact I drove past her road
three times before I realized that I had not read the signpost
correctly.**

**It's not only the inconvenience of arriving late, it is the
state in which one arrives and the state one gets into when one
gets lost that is so taxing (or exasperating). Anyway I found the
house and it was well worth the trip.**

**Mary is the youngest in a family of dyslexics. Thanks to the
support of her parents she gained high enough exam results to
go to medical school. After five years of consistent hard work
she qualified as a doctor. She is now a paediatrician working
with children suffering from cancer – a highly responsible job
which she finds very rewarding. She has two sons, one is probably dyslexic.**

* * *

We are nearly all dyslexic in our family and I struggled
through school by hook or by crook I think really.

I loathed reading and I can remember my first boarding school. I was the youngest in the class and probably
the youngest in the school. I always misbehaved in reading

129

class, so I was always sent out. It's a classic thing. As soon as there were only two or three to read before me, I would misbehave by talking or whatever, and get sent out of the room.

PARENT'S HELP

I didn't read until I was nine. I still hate reading. I can remember my mother spending hours trying to teach me to spell. She used to sit me in the bedroom with my eyes closed and make me draw out all the words. It was probably the best treatment.

Then when my parents decided to send me to another school where I needed to pass the Common Entrance, they all said, 'Oh, she won't get it' and I am not quite sure how I did get it really.

But I was never pressurized in any way at home. I was allowed to do just what was within my potential. There were never any aspirations that I was ever going to do very well, although I was always congratulated when I did. When I had bad reports I can't remember ever getting into trouble. It was a very relaxed atmosphere. We were quite lucky really. I am sure it was because my father had the same problem. Therefore he didn't get cross. It's a very bright family, although many of us are dyslexic, but our little section is not as bright as the rest.

TECHNICAL COLLEGE

I did my O-levels at school and then I left and did my A-levels at technical college. I think I got seven O-levels, my lowest grades were in English. Technical college was a real eye opener and I really struggled there and then my cousin who is

130

a scientist gave me extra coaching. I did three A-levels. Then I went to medical school.

I learned the tricks of the trade and I had a very good memory. So I used to learn everything off by heart, like the back of the French dictionary. And I picked up a lot of oral clues. I almost had a photographic memory. I was able to train it, I don't have it any more, I seem to have lost it, but I think that's laziness rather than anything else. I certainly could train my mind. My writing was always appalling and my spelling is awful. I still can't spell. I could always write but my writing was appalling.

TRICKS

Anatomy was horrific. I couldn't spell the names. I spent more time learning to spell the names than I did learning the positions. But I had a very good friend who was very, very bright. She didn't realize why but I used to say 'Oh, I'll test you.' I did a lot of learning like that. I used to test her and she used to give me the answers and I used to learn that way. So I didn't have to do that much reading.

I worked very hard. I'm a night worker so nobody knew how hard I was working, but I always had to be on top of my work otherwise I couldn't cope. I always had to feel that I knew a lot more than I needed to know to pass exams.

I never admitted I was dyslexic. I never showed anybody my notes either, they were so appalling. No one can read my writing anyway so it was all right.

I qualified as a doctor first time surprisingly. I'm glad to say they don't have grades.

FAILED EXAM FIVE TIMES

As soon as I qualified as a doctor I did my house job for the first year. Then I went to Africa. When I came back I wanted to become a paediatrician but my membership exam was a disaster. I failed that a lot of times. There are two parts. Part one is multiple choice and I failed that five times, I think. I had to get a special dispensation to take it again. My boss at that time was a very wise paediatrician. He was a marvellous man. He was the only person who recognized that I was dyslexic and he in fact wrote to ask if I could have another go which was wonderful. So I did and luckily I got it.

I did oncology, that's care of children with cancer, quite early on in my paediatric career. I have enjoyed the intensity and the fact that you can actually offer children something. Fifty per cent of children don't just live, but are cured of cancer. So it's much more rewarding.

You get to know the families very well and you feel you are doing good. These kids come in terribly sick and you feel at the end of the day you are actually going to make them better, even if you're not going to cure them. At worst you can give them a couple of years maybe.

PROBLEMS AT WORK

Once I started work the only problem I found was my left and right. So when I had to mark whether they were operating on the left leg or the right leg, I always asked a nurse to double check. They must have all thought I was mad, but I always asked somebody to double check and I was always very careful.

I would let somebody else answer the phone and they would write the results down, in case I wrote it down incorrectly. I think you get into a routine of things you do automatically and with pleasure, and things which you hold yourself back from and don't volunteer to do. I find at work there are certain things that I certainly don't volunteer to do.

I don't think many people know I'm dyslexic. The secretary at the hospital only recently realized. She couldn't understand why every time I asked for a number to telephone somebody in another department I never managed to get it right. She never ever said anything, but eventually I said 'Well, you know the reason why I'm so bad at it.' And now she is very good because she does it very, very slowly and then repeats it again. And while I'm dialling it she says it again, so she's actually cottoned on. I suppose it's the first time I've ever admitted it in my working life, and I think probably that's because it's becoming more difficult and perhaps because I feel a bit more confident that I can admit it. I certainly would never go into an interview and say look I'm dyslexic.

FAMILY DYSLEXIA

My father was a doctor. He qualified as a doctor but failed his exams, *he got nought per cent once because he got so many spelling mistakes*, and the next time he got ninety per cent so he obviously knew the stuff and it was just that the first time they failed him on spelling mistakes.

I do find it difficult keeping up though. My self-esteem is sometimes terribly bad. My sister and I have talked about it a lot. She has always had tremendous problems and self-esteem has been her big problem. It really affected her, in marriage and everything. The person she may have wanted to marry, she felt she couldn't keep up with academically. I admire people who are very bright. I never ever see myself on that kind of level.

DYSLEXIA GETS WORSE

I feel that the older one gets the worse the dyslexia gets. From

133

around my A-level time for about eight years, it wasn't a great problem, although I found I had to work all the time. Now if I stop working for any time the dyslexia regresses again. It's much worse now than it was ten years ago and I'm dreadful on the telephone taking numbers and things.

I do have complete blanks and when I am writing notes my use of English is appalling. It's because I can think of a word but there's no way I can remember how to spell it. I can't even get the first letter right sometimes. If I can't get the first two or three letters right, I can't do it. I find that when I am stressed I am much worse. I have to take myself away from everybody and have a bit of peace and quiet or go for a walk.

DIRECTIONS

I find directions impossible. Absolutely impossible. My mother, who is the only member of the family who isn't dyslexic, always had a most amazing memory for finding places and we always thought she was just marvellous because none of us could find a place anywhere. Travelling on my own is a nightmare. I take a long time finding my way. My eldest boy is very good and he takes me wherever I am going.

I loathe reading too. It's not a pleasure for me to read a book and everybody else finds it is a pleasure and that does upset me.

MESSAGE

I think you should talk to other dyslexics and realize that it's a common problem and that at certain periods in your life you are going to hit it again. It's never going to go away.

Advertising Photographer

PETER

Many dyslexics have a wonderful visual sense and photography is a profession in which this gift can be put to good use.

When one thinks of the enormous influence advertising has on our lives it is curious to think that it might be Peter's, a dyslexic, photograph that is persuading us to change products!

Peter left school at fifteen without any qualifications and hardly able to read and write. He didn't know what his problem was until his late twenties when he heard me talking on the radio! He now runs an extremely successful photographic advertising business. But, as he says, a man who has worked his way up to running his own business can employ a staff that will 'pick up' his mistakes.

* * *

The thing that used to horrify me at school was dictation, because it was really difficult for me to keep up as well as trying to spell. It was just like a disaster.

My younger brother went through the top stream in the comprehensive school. My parents were aware that I was trying hard, and that was the way that I was going to progress.

They didn't think I was going to be a particularly bright child so there was no pressure.

FUTURE

At fifteen heaven knows what you really want to do in life. Holland Park Comprehensive was a wonderful school, it had two and a half thousand children and it also had the most amazing facilities of which part of that was a photographic section. So I actually took photographic lessons during the course of the week and it did build up. I left school at fifteen.

JOB

I wanted to get into photography and I applied for a job in the Easter holidays after I had done badly in the mock exams. I got exactly what I wanted – a job as an assistant photographer. I had no idea of what a wonderful life it actually is. But it was what I wanted to do and it was the first interview I ever went for and I got the job.

The only problem was that I thought I just couldn't spell. But it was really a lack of understanding. Early on I used to read advertising hoardings, posters or copy lines and I couldn't make sense of them. It's as if your mind focuses on a word and reads something totally different. That was when I started to understand that maybe something was wrong.

OWN BUSINESS

Now I am in advertising. I run my own business. I have my own studio. I think that maybe I have a fair amount of confidence now and it doesn't worry me that I can't spell even the simplest of words. I wouldn't hesitate to ask.

STAFF'S HELP

My staff for Christmas bought me one of those tiny computers. You put in how you think the word is spelt, then it gives you a list of words that you could be trying to spell.

A lot of paperwork that I do at the studio is repetitious, so the same words occur and my secretary recognizes the mistakes because she is expecting them.

I have a problem with figures as well. Things like writing phone numbers down. It's almost like my hand pumps in numbers into a phone in the wrong order. Or I can write figures on a cheque and write them the wrong way round. I can't stop doing it although I can see it happen. My staff picked up on that! I employ staff who can spell very well and they are also good at reading my handwriting.

COMMITTEES

I think my writing is my biggest drawback. If anyone was to look over my shoulder at something I had written down they wouldn't be able to make head nor tail of it. It really would be such a mess. It's just like a shorthand in words that look the same sort of shape so that I can read again what I had written.

MISTAKES

I have made some terribly expensive mistakes. I print my own Christmas cards each year, which go out as an example of my work to past and present clients. One particular year I read the copy for the card and didn't pick up the fact that the card was written 'Hapiness' – instead of 'Happiness' and they were all printed, so that was a very expensive error.

I still have great difficulty in spelling the simplest of words and have great difficulty in getting companies' initials right. I get the initials the wrong way round.

There are lots of words I have problems with. I quite often write 'Birthday' with the 'i' in the wrong place. 'Etc' I put 'ect'. Trivial Pursuits I find quite embarrassing. When I have to read a question by the time I get to the end I know I have read it incorrectly.

I actually thought when I was younger that dyslexia was something dumb kids use to explain why they were dumb. I really didn't think it was anything more serious, and now I have discovered more about it.

Social Worker

'JULIE'

It is interesting how many dyslexics go into professions such as nursing, or become psychologists, teachers, therapists, doctors or even probation officers and social workers. No doubt because of their handicap, their social conscience and compassionate nature come to the fore. One takes it for granted that dyslexics tend to go into the arts, but I found it was almost as easy to locate a dyslexic doctor or nurse as a dyslexic actor.

'Julie's' father, a clergyman, is dyslexic. Her mother, a teacher, taught Julie to read. At school, the teachers said her written work was so hopeless that at seven years old she was assessed as educationally subnormal. She proved everyone wrong by passing two A-levels and getting a degree. She is now taking a postgraduate course in social work and hopes to work with offenders with reading and writing difficulties.

* * *

It was in the first year in the local primary school that it became clear that I was not responding. I could always read, because I had been taught to read by my mother before I went to school but in everything else it was getting much more difficult.

139

BEING TOLD I WAS EDUCATIONALLY SUBNORMAL

I think my parents were both probably very worried but they disguised it well. The only time I can remember feeling a bit peculiar was when I went for my assessment. I went to the Tavistock Clinic when I was about seven or eight, and they said I really was very ESN – Educationally Subnormal – and that there really wasn't an awful lot of hope for me.

I was also told that because my written work and everything else were so bad the teachers thought that I really was completely hopeless and that I ought to go to a special school.

NEW SCHOOL

My parents thought it was a whole bunch of kibosh, so they found me a tiny little school down in Duchess Hill which took fifteen children with learning difficulties. Although the school didn't specialize in dyslexia, they were interested in it.

It was a very safe environment and we were able to go at our own pace, so the pressure that I probably felt and which was obviously there at the infants' school went very quickly. Yet, when I was on a one to one, or one to two basis, I was damn well having to think and concentrate, and had to use my brain and not switch off. Because I didn't go to a school where I was seeing other people achieving so highly, the self-esteem bit was not too bad. But I suppose undoubtedly at the back of my mind was the thought I was at this school yet all my friends were at another school.

PARENTAL SUPPORT

All I know is that trying to do any work even at the special school I went to was a struggle. First of all what I would do is to actually speak an essay – a title had been given and I would then speak it out to my mother who would then write it down. My parents were both very supportive.

My father who is a clergyman is also dyslexic. For sermons he has got it to such a fine art that all he has is just a few headings. He goes from headings, so he doesn't have to read.

I found schooling difficult – trying to actually take in a message from a teacher talking, receiving and comprehending the message, and trying to get it down on paper, was incredibly difficult. Also because I had bad eyesight at that time too, to try to write from the blackboard was also very difficult, so that combination used to make me feel very constricted. I would miss what was being said because I was trying so hard to actually get down some of the stuff. Therefore I would miss the whole thread.

REPORTS

The struggle of doing homework when you didn't really understand what they were trying to get at was absolutely horrendous at times. I suppose even now when I'm sitting down and I'm writing a report, suddenly I just cannot spell a word and it just will not come. No doubt most people get something like that, but it's a total block about a word and you just have to either think of something else or put it down in a really bad way and go back to it.

I never thought of myself as clever. That is obviously something to do with how we do at academic work. Our education is so much geared to actually saying that GCEs, A-levels and further education are what we should achieve that *we don't actually get skills for life*. I suppose that I don't really think

I'm very bright at all. So doing this course I actually realized that I am slightly brighter than I probably gave myself credit for.

WORST PART OF BEING A DYSLEXIC

One of the worst things about being dyslexic is all those feelings you get from people not totally understanding you, or not listening to you, and thinking you are useless. I had a very good self-image, although at times it got knocked. I was able to think 'Well, stuff you'. But those feelings were there and they are being used now all the time on the course I am doing, and will be used in my probation work.

I think that there is an awful lot more behind offending, including what we do in the education system to kids. Reading and writing is such a middle-class kind of thing, and we assume that we are all going to be able to read and write. Somebody on my course, a friend who is in fact incredibly bright, and was at Oxford, said it made her really angry that on DHSS forms and things like that, there are no symbols. So people who perhaps aren't able to read quickly or easily, won't be able to fill them in. That's what I'm interested in and why I'm doing what I'm doing. I think that something has got to be done, to help people who have been poorly served at school.

THE POSITIVE SIDE OF BEING DYSLEXIC

I do believe that every dyslexic has got something that they can tap into, something that is a gift that they have. I came across someone whose brother went to a secondary modern school, the others had all gone to grammar school and they used to call him 'thick, thick, thick'. Around that time his mother died and that was what really broke him, but it also actually made him. He became so damned determined that he has just

142

finished a further degree, an MA at Cambridge University in mathematics. Although his English and his writing are still absolutely appalling, his brain functions in the mathematics and the logical sphere.

MESSAGE

I can't over-emphasize the struggle of actually doing homework and actually trying to get to grips with something you can't understand. You know you are trying to grasp at something and unless you have somebody sitting down there going back over something stage by stage, then you'd be lost. So get someone to help you.

Architectural Historian

CHARLES

I was first in touch with Charles, who is numerically dyslexic, nearly six years ago when he wrote to me after reading *Susan's Story*.

Although Charles is dyslexic and had a very difficult start to life, he nevertheless managed to turn his childhood passion into his profession. A profession which is not only of great interest to him but also historically important. Remarkable for a boy who couldn't speak at four, was doing brilliant drawings at six and in his teens contemplated suicide as he considered himself 'semi-mad'.

The Brooking Collection has been built up over the last twenty years and covers the development of the door, window, fire grate, staircase and rainwater head, from circa 1660 to 1960. Nearly all the architectural details in the collection have been preserved from demolition sites mainly in London.

The aim of the collection is to provide a permanent record of the development, materials and craftsmanship that went into buildings, particularly of the eighteenth and nineteenth centuries, and a valuable reference source for those involved in the restoration and study of historic buildings.

* * *

I run an architectural museum and this subject has been a passion which started when I was about three years old. I was always very aware of shapes and designs, and noticed buildings and details of the environment generally. But I did not talk until I was four, creating great concern in my family, who were going to send me to a special school to overcome the problem. I started talking by coming out with long words – like 'daffodil' – so I am told, and I was praised at my kindergarten for noticing a tiny ladybird in an animal picture which had never been noticed before in the sixty years the picture had hung in the hall.

In late 1957 when I was four, I was sent to a kindergarten school outside Ashtead, and I enjoyed modelling and painting, but the following year the teachers became concerned at my inability to form letters properly – and even more concerned at my total inability to understand sums.

FATHER'S INFLUENCE

My father was very annoyed at my artistic streak and wanted to stamp out my interest in old letter boxes and door handles which he thought was absolutely ridiculous. At this kindergarten, they couldn't understand why I could draw and rescue things from old buildings and yet I couldn't do sums.

My teacher said I was frustrated. I had psychological problems. 'The boy must be treated.' Of course my father told everyone that his son was a bit dim especially as my sister could tell the time when she was six. I couldn't tell the time until I was thirteen. I couldn't tie my shoelaces until I was eight and other things like that.

I was terrified of shops and getting on buses. We moved to Guildford in 1959 and I found it a great upheaval. I attended a local primary school and my problems started. Sums, reading and writing were incredibly difficult for me, and I was soon behind, especially with multiplication tables. Although

I learnt to read quite late, about the age of seven, without real difficulty, spelling and learning words parrot fashion were almost impossible for me.

My parents arranged for me to see a series of educational psychologists, who could not understand what my problem was, suggesting that I was of normal intelligence; they were all baffled by this blockage when it came to certain aspects of the learning process.

The first one, when I was four, recommended that I be allowed to throw sand and water around as a kind of free expression. It was at her consulting rooms that I first became consciously aware of older buildings: hers was a large Victorian house in Sutton.

BEHAVIOUR PROBLEMS

I suffered the usual fate so often suffered by dyslexics of being bullied at school and teased for my lack of ability in learning apparently simple things, especially the 'tables'! I ran amok at school, pushing desks over and generally misbehaving.

I was interested in old buildings and rescuing old windows and doors and fireplaces and things, but the other children at school weren't interested in my subject, and they would say, 'Gosh, Brookie's dim, you know he doesn't even know his two-times table yet.'

I became depressed and introverted and my social skills became fossilized. I became mute, walking around at break times on my own, suffering the jeers of the others who teased me about my continual 'laziness'. From 1960 to 1963 I struggled on, but excelled at art and history. My father was very upset at my lack of understanding of maths – his favourite subject. 'I don't understand,' he would say. 'It's easy.'

FEELING INFERIOR

At my prep school, which was a boarding school, the problems increased when I discovered a severe lack of co-ordination in games like football and rugby, further compounded by short sight. At times I became almost permanently depressed and considered myself semi-mad, as friends who were backward could at least learn these seemingly simple things. At some subjects I excelled, including history, English (apart from the spelling) and art. I never suffered from the usual symptoms of dyslexia, such as writing words backwards, although I mis-read some words, but figures and remembering, for example, the sequences of equations, were extremely difficult. The idea of dyslexia never occurred to anyone.

Homework became a nightmare and I worried myself sick as my father became more and more exasperated. In April 1963 I left Watlands School and was sent to Normansel, at Seaford.

SUICIDE

I remember a very low day at my prep school. I failed at maths and I skipped games. I didn't like games very much because it stopped me going out to look for things. A friend who was very fat and had been teased because of his size said, 'Shall we commit suicide?' We sort of planned it to the last detail and then the tea bell rang and we went down to tea! It was very depressing.

SPASTIC

I had a group of friends who had problems as well with maths. They were called spastic too. 'You're a spas, you can't even do this, you let the whole set down. You're dumb, aren't you?' Of course, if you weren't good at maths and sport you'd had it. The headmaster had a thing about this, maths and sports were very serious.

I began to believe that my brain had become damaged in a fall I had had the year before. Despite my introversion, I made some friends.

What seemed to rile my teachers and some of my classmates was that I was top of the class in some subjects and totally hopeless in others. The teachers put it down to 'Lacks the ability to concentrate'. In 1964, a special set was created for boys with big reading and spelling problems: there were five of them in the set and I was one of them. It was immediately dubbed '3B, the dunce set'.

I eventually left school with a few O-levels, Art A-level and a severe inferiority complex. I felt I could have done a lot better if I had had special difficulties time or something similar, as my handwriting was painfully slow and almost unreadable.

My mother was very kind and supportive but she didn't understand. She said, 'You're a late developer, you'll shoot ahead at sixteen or seventeen. Everyone says at thirteen, fourteen, sixteen you'll be fine. Don't worry.'

I was really so ashamed of myself. I hated myself for being so inadequate. How could I cope with the outside world? I went to a school outside Lewes when I was fourteen, which was for people who had problems. It was one of these typical sixties free places. No work was done. We weren't taught a thing and it was called a place for 'rich thicks'. Children with all kinds of problems. A lot of dyslexia, I blossomed in art and history.

MEETING PEOPLE

I never introduce myself to anyone at a party, I'll stand there until I'm introduced to someone. I always feel, 'What do they want with me? I'm awful and who wants to speak to me? How dare I push myself, it's a cheek.'

I find any form of public speaking and, indeed, speaking in front of a group of people – unless I get what I call a confidence boom – still almost impossible, stammering over simple words and clamming up completely, hating the sound of my own voice, turning crimson over the smallest mistakes. I would almost rather run out of a shop than dispute a small incident. However, I have given talks on the radio about my architectural museum: but I can understand just how you must feel going on air live. Hours before, I feel almost a nervous nausea coming on and my legs become like jelly!

FINDING A JOB

My parents were advised to get me trained as a furniture restorer, to set up in the antique trade. I went to work for a local man. The old man who employed me brought me a cup of tea one day and said, 'I want to talk to you a minute. You seem a bright young lad in many directions and you are obviously not unintelligent. But, some of the things you find difficult amaze me. What is the problem? Is it your home life, or what? You are not like the other lads.'

It was only my architectural museum project, which I had developed since 1966, that kept me going. I left the furniture restorer after six months.

FALSE ACCUSATIONS

For the next year, I worked on my architectural museum project. My confidence grew as interest in my project grew. I have worked in several areas. One in particular, at Sotheby's, Belgravia, involved my being asked to sort out various items using a rather complicated numbering system and red labels. My efforts caused complete confusion and havoc in the department. This gave rise to a suspicion from those I was working with, who believed I was deliberately messing up the job so that I could move to a more interesting one higher up, because people often did this to get over that particular stepping-stone quickly. I had no explanation for my stupidity in numbering etc, and doubted my abilities generally; I became still more depressed, introverted and inward-looking. However, I was a devil for punishment, and later joined British Railway's architect's department with the idea of becoming an architect, which was completely useless with my numeracy problem. Even sorting out plans with number systems became very embarrassing, as mistakes kept occurring. I became so embarrassed at my performance that holding a telephone conversation in an open-plan office became agony, and I began to pour with sweat if I had to speak out loud in front of anyone in my office. But on a one-to-one basis I have always got on very well with people.

Now, my museum project, which I have been working on basically all my life, has developed, and the numeracy problem has faded somewhat into the background; and, although I use calculators, there are everyday problems like change in shops at times.

DIAGNOSED DYSLEXIC

It was a tremendous relief to be diagnosed a dyslexic when I was thirty-one. One of the main reasons for taking action is my inability to master driving – and extreme problems when it comes to left and right, and managing roundabouts, gears and so on. I have never reached the Test stage, being too nervous to continue on manual gears, and have now decided to try driving an automatic.

I contacted an old school friend about a year ago: he is dyslexic, and I realized that some of his problems were not unlike mine, but in a slightly different area, and it was this that eventually led me to see an educational psychologist specializing in dyslexia, at the end of last year. He confirmed that I am dyslexic, and my problems, although according to him they are apparently not severe, are definitely undeniable and are slightly different from those of the usual 'everyday' dyslexic, who suffers from reading problems, which I do not. I am quite a fast reader, although I sometimes misread words. It was a great relief to know the cause of all this tribulation and depression. I had thought perhaps it was lead-poisoning or that I was going mad.

Learning disabilities can destroy lives. To get a really disturbing sense of this – we need only to look at the estimates of the learning disabled among juvenile delinquents. As high as forty per cent, and among prisoners, perhaps fifty per cent. No one knows for certain how many Americans are learning disabled. Like illiteracy, it is a largely hidden problem. The numbers, however, are huge: from thirty to fifty per cent of the students in adult basic education programmes. My heart goes out to these men and women, but I have hope for them as well. The knowledge is there to help them learn to read.

Mrs Barbara Bush
First Lady of the United States
Honorary Chairperson of National Advisory
Council of Literacy Volunteers in America

Judge

JEFFREY

Statistics mentioned in Mrs Bush's quote on the previous page show that illiteracy resulting in juvenile delinquency is alas an all too common tragedy. So, finding a judge who is not only dyslexic but also works on the family circuit in America, and is seeing the problem first hand, was fantastic good fortune.

* * *

Everyone at school said that I was lazy or stupid or both. After a while I began to believe them. Sometimes I just gave up. I couldn't write, spell, read or answer questions quickly. I didn't even know which hand to put over my heart when we recited the Pledge of Allegiance.

Once my parents were called to school and told that I had scored first in my class IQ test. That score, they were told, was evidence that I had cheated on the test. My father, a lawyer, argued that I must have been bright indeed, for I had copied only the correct answers. My parents never gave up on me although it must have been a great disappointment to those two scholarly people that their first born could barely graduate from high school.

They encouraged me to go to college and I did, graduating last in my class.

153

Brooklyn Law School took a chance on me. I responded with the best academic performance of my career – I graduated in the middle of my class! By the time I got to law school I had begun to learn how to compensate for my problems. Law school was easier than college because there was more emphasis on concepts and less on rote learning, my greatest weakness.

I was lucky. Loving parents, a college professor and a law school room-mate supported me, encouraged me and refused to let me fall victim to my frustrations and give up. They knew that I was neither stupid nor lazy, even though there were times when I was not so sure myself. By the time I was diagnosed as learning disabled at the age of thirty-five, I had already learned to deal with my learning disabilities. By the age of thirty-seven, I was a judge.

THE FAMILY CIRCUIT

Almost every week I see a learning disabled child who, un-diagnosed or untreated, is venting his or her frustrations in anti-social ways. I could have stood in that same spot. If not for loving, caring, involved parents, my frustrations at not being able to keep up in class, and to some extent in the play yard, could have burst forth in the same self-destructive way.

Hopefully, we will see a growth in programmes to halt the escalating conflict between the frustrated, angry, impatient dys-lexic youngster, and his or her overburdened, impotent feeling parents who are unable to socialize their children and integrate them into their peer groups. Too often in the past, the solution has been to place the child in foster care, an unsatisfactory and non-cost-effective solution which may very well do more damage than good.

It is the school which holds the key to avoiding the type of conflict we see in the family courts. An early diagnosis of the problem and an integrated treatment plan, including not only help for the child, but also counselling for the parents, *would save* many children now going astray. Unfortunately, too many schools have not focused their attention and resources on the problem and research proposals to find methods for early diagnosis of learning disabilities are going unfunded.

Judge Jeffrey H. Gallet
Circuit Judge, Juvenile, Family Courts

Reprinted from THEIR WORLD magazine with permission of the editor, Julia Gilligan. THEIR WORLD is the annual publication of the National Center for Learning Disabilities, 99 Park Avenue, New York, N.Y. 10016. Founder Carrie Rozelle.

Chef

IAN

I know from the hotel schools and from friends in the catering business that this is a profession in which there are a considerable number of dyslexics, including some of the renowned chefs of Europe, so I am really pleased to have a dyslexic chef for the book.

Ian, with his little daughter, kindly drove to London one Sunday morning to talk to me.

All Ian knew when he left school without many qualifications was that he wanted to do something with his hands and he wanted to be on his feet. Despite finding the written work hard, he is now a head chef.

* * *

I think my mother is dyslexic, but it probably wasn't heard of about fifty years ago.

When I was at school, people found my English and my spelling weren't very good. I was twisting letters round – putting them in the wrong order – that was my biggest problem. I think that's probably when it came to notice.

My parents helped me all they could. To start with I had extra English. My maths was so good that I could miss a few maths lessons a week and have extra English lessons.

156

APPRENTICESHIP

I just took my exams as normal, the same as any other schoolboy. But I didn't get to do what I wanted to do which was to go into management. So I decided I had better do something positive. I wanted to do something with my hands and I wanted to be on my feet. I managed to get two O-levels, but I didn't do A-levels. I left school at sixteen and did my apprenticeship in the Majestic Hotel in Harrogate. I did a four year apprenticeship there and worked my way up and left there five years ago.

FATHER'S HELP

I remember filling in college forms when I was first leaving school, it was quite hard. Letter writing was difficult. In the end I sat down with my father and we constructed a letter that we could use for every job application. I always used to write in longhand. And I'd have to write it about two or three times, after checking it and rechecking it.

WORK

The administrative side of my job is quite hard for me. I have to sit down and really think about it and things have to be written out two or three times before it's passable by my own standards. Menu writing and the occasional letter which has to be thought about and rethought are the worst. Then there is also writing out the orders but that's not so bad, because I have a system where I have got everything typed out already so all I have to do is go round and put a number in, but it always needs changing and updating. Within the catering industry things are always being updated, I find.

I left the Majestic as Junior Sous Chef and then worked

157

in Cheltenham for a short time and then moved to Teesside in my first position as Head Chef. I went to the Post House in Cambridge as Head Chef straight away.

EXAMS

I did City and Guilds 1761 and 7062 during my apprenticeship. It was just mostly practical but there was a certain amount of written work.

I am now doing another one. The written work is a bit harder than last time. I am doing an Institute of Public Health and Hygiene exam, advanced hygiene, which is all about controversial bacteria and it's quite intensive. I go to the local college in Cambridge once a week for four hours. There's a three hour written exam at the end of the course.

Because recipes are written using short statements, I don't find it difficult to read them.

Eventually I'd love a place of my own and to manage and run a hotel/restaurant on my own.

MESSAGE

I think if you want to do something you can do it in your own way. Disregard what anybody else says, within reason of course, but you can succeed. Certainly within the catering industry you can make it, because there are at least two or three people within our establishment who probably didn't realize that they are dyslexic until very recently.

Cher

OSCAR WINNING FILM STAR

Cher is an actress I have always greatly admired, most recently in *Moonstruck* and *Witches of Eastwick*. She has done a great deal for the dyslexic cause in America by her frankness when talking about her handicap.

The day a film producer insisted on Cher reading for a film part without allowing her to study the script first, reminds me of an experience I had in the less illustrious medium of television. In Cher's case the producer couldn't believe that she couldn't sight read as he had seen her in so many films. So how could she not read?! The sad irony is that when the producer did hear her read he was so aghast that he didn't give her the part. Unfortunately it is hard for some producers to understand that being a good actor or actress has nothing to do with being a good sight reader. In fact some actors are superb readers but not especially good actors.

Cher still can't spell or understand the words she sees on a billboard. She has trouble dialling a telephone number and finding the correct money for change. At the age of thirty her problem was diagnosed as dyslexia. 'Sometimes I feel so stupid,' she said.

Her dyslexia made her school years a nightmare – she dropped out in 11th grade – and her acting was a struggle. Yet

159

she has successfully managed to establish herself as an actress and is finally, at the age of forty, gaining the respect that has eluded her for so long.

* * *

I don't know what I'd do if I had a regular job. I'm insecure about everything. It doesn't take much to shake my confidence to the bone.

I never read in school. The first book I ever read was when I was eighteen or nineteen years old, and it was called *The Saracen Blade* by Frank Yerby. When I was in school, it was really difficult. Almost everything I learned, I had to learn by listening. I just couldn't keep up with everybody else. You can be really intelligent, but if you don't have a way of letting people know, you seem really stupid.

My report card always said that I wasn't living up to my potential. Teachers would see that I was a bright girl in class, and then I would hand in papers that you couldn't read. Also, I could never do the work quickly enough – most of the tests were timed.

My work was very sporadic. I got really bad grades – Ds, Fs and Cs – in some classes, and As and Bs in other classes. My mother would get exasperated with me sometimes: she just could not understand why I could do so well in one class one semester and fail the next semester. And I never could understand it either. Some things were so difficult.

LEAVING SCHOOL

Eventually I left school – on the second week of 11th grade. I just quit. I was sitting there one day and I just got up and left and said 'I'm not going back.'

For the most part, school is a very boring place for very bright minds. *I think what school does half the time is cut out your creativity and just make you fit into society.* I don't think

160

school is the place to really learn very much. It's evident if you see what's happening in the country – you know, there are so many people who can't pass a civil exam, or can't read. In Los Angeles, instead of using the word Walk (on street signs), they show a person walking because some people can't read a sign.

DISCOVERING DYSLEXIA

I was diagnosed when I was thirty. I found out about it when I took Chastity, my daughter, to be tested. She's very intelligent, but she just did so badly in school, and she was having such a hard time. Then I sent her to a special school, which was really a drag, because a lot of kids in the school had emotional problems and she doesn't. But she just felt that she was stupid because her oral scores were so much higher than her written scores.

One of the doctors who tested her recommended that I take her to a Dyslexia Center in Santa Monica. When I went there, I just said to the lady, 'I know Chastity is really smart – she's just like me.' The woman said 'What do you mean?' and we started talking about it, and that's when we found out we both had dyslexia.

DIFFICULTIES

There are things that I do that make me feel really stupid. Like the other day I couldn't figure out how much money to give the cab driver. In my mind what I did made sense, but he was just furious that I didn't give him a decent tip. Dialling long distance is difficult. If I really concentrate on it, I can do it. But if there's a number – for example, 472, I'll see 427. And the more numbers there are, the harder it is for me to retain them in sequence. And I see billboards that don't exist. Like, I'll see four words on a billboard, and I'll just put them

161

together in my own way. It'll make sense to me, but it won't have anything to do with what the billboard actually says.

I've pretty much got my own way of handling my dyslexia. Like the reading – I read very slowly. Now, if I read a script once, I know it; I almost never have to look back at it. I guess your brain compensates. If I had a regular job – one that uses skills that most people have to use, like eye-word, eye-number skills – I don't know what I'd do. But for what I do, the way I read is only an inconvenience.

EMBARRASSING SITUATION

I once went to an audition for a movie. I was supposed to meet the director and talk to him about a part, and he was going to see if I was right for it. Because he thought I was perfect, he wanted me to read. And I said 'I don't do this well.' But he gave me the script. Then Jack Nicholson (the star of the movie) walks in. We were sitting there, and I started to read, and I am trying to explain to them that I don't do this well at all. But they don't want to know about it. So we start to read, and when I was done, the director said 'It's a good thing I saw you in *Silkwood* yesterday because that is definitely the worst cold reading I ever heard.' And I said 'Well, you know, I told you that's not what I do well.' It was a tense moment. It was terrible. I didn't get the part!

I wouldn't do cold readings for a movie now. I would never cold read for anybody.

LOGIC

In *Mask* I tested, and I knew what I was doing. It's like, I saw a show once where they were looking for tap dancers. There was this little boy from Spain, and he was a flamenco dancer. He tried to tap dance, but he couldn't do it. But then, when

162

he did what he could do, he did it better than all the people that were trying out for the tap dancing job. So it just wouldn't make sense for me to try to cold read if what they wanted to do was see what I did well.

Now I read for pleasure constantly. I'm reading four books right now. I'm reading *The Mammoth Hunters*; I've read the first two Jean Auel books. I'm reading *The Vampire Lestat*, I'm reading *Goddess* and *Drama of the Gifted Child*, a psychology book.

I could not care less that the public knows that I am dyslexic.

(Extracts reproduced by kind permission of Redbook)

Many successful people in all spheres of activity have experienced great difficulties during their schooling and were termed 'failures' by educators. Yet they subsequently discovered that they were not 'failures' but rather dyslexics who had not received adequate help. I certainly 'failed' in school.

But once 'released' from the educational system, one discovers that new interests develop. I certainly experienced that and success comes in spite of the dire predictions of the educators.

A determination to succeed goes a long way to achieving that success, particularly for a dyslexic.

Alan Parker
Philanthropist and one of the world's most
successful business men

The Business Man

There are quite a large number of big business men in all parts of the world (Singapore, Hong Kong, Australia, Switzerland, Belgium, France, England and America), of different race and nationality, who are very sensitive about being dyslexic, and are reluctant to talk about it as they feel extremely inadequate, especially when they are face to face with an intellectual or bookish person. If only they knew, the bookish person may be only too happy to have some of the business man's natural aptitude for making money.

This feeling of inadequacy often drives the dyslexic to achieve more and more. Yet despite this, some still feel that people are envious of them for their money, not their skill in making it, which a non-dyslexic person may not always possess.

Kerry Packer, Australia's richest citizen, and cricket and polo promoter, is said to be dyslexic. But the disability certainly hasn't stood in his way.

In 1988 when the book *The Brothers* about the Saatchi brothers came out, its author, Ivan Fallon, suggested that Charles Saatchi, head of Saatchi and Saatchi Advertising Company, was dyslexic, as dyslexics, he says, often compensate with outstanding visual and creative ability. Charles Saatchi

165

was obviously a bright boy, but with his learning difficulties, he had a short attention span and overpowering impatience.

Another dyslexic who had a very difficult start to life even landed up in prison but he is now an extremely successful and respected business man in the north of England who runs a building firm.

In his youth, before it was known that he was dyslexic, he got into a lot of trouble at school. He was expelled at fourteen and then refused to go back to school. Within a short time, he was up in the juvenile courts and by the time he was nineteen, he was sent to prison for eighteen months for robbery.

Whilst in prison, he was reading an article about kids with learning problems. He identified so strongly with their problems that he sought help within the prison.

Once his difficulty was identified as dyslexia he vowed that he would overcome it somehow, as he didn't see why he should spend the rest of his life in and out of prison. He started literacy classes while in prison and when he came out, he was referred to ILEA for remedial classes where he ultimately did so well that he landed up doing an Open University degree.

Now, with his new found position in the establishment he is reluctant to disclose his identity, but he says, 'There's too many of us getting into trouble because we can't read, and we didn't get any help at school. It's before we get to the juvenile court we need the help.'

Another dyslexic business man, introduced to me by my husband, had a very successful sports equipment business. He told me that at school he was beaten constantly and made to stay in and write lines regularly, because of his poor spelling. Not a week went by when he wasn't called into the headmaster's office and reprimanded.

Even a lawyer for one of the great pharmaceutical companies confided that 'I have never read a book, everything is read to me. I can read each word on its own, but the sentences hardly make sense.'

David, another successful business man in the City, was severely dyslexic. He runs a business where people come to him with insurance business problems. 'Problems that they've been struggling with for maybe three years. I take one look at it and because I see everything in a different way I can solve the problem immediately. It makes me laugh, as they're so grateful and think I'm frightfully clever, I've always thought I was a fool. But I just have a gift for that sort of thing, seeing a problem and sorting it out, as I see things another way.'

Psychologist

DOROTHY

I carried Dr Dorothy Einon's telephone number around in my bag for about eleven months. Somehow I didn't connect that this was the doctor I was expected to contact for the book. I thought Dr Einon was an eye doctor with whom I was supposed to make an appointment and I just never had time to do it. So when I eventually rang to sort out my reading vision I was a little surprised that, firstly, Dr Einon was a woman, secondly, she was not an eye specialist and, thirdly, she is dyslexic.

Dorothy and I met at the Russell Hotel early one morning before she went off to give her first lecture of the day and I to record the commentary for a documentary. It was rather difficult to find a quiet corner and we landed up talking in the corridor!

Dorothy was put with the dunces at the back of the class because she couldn't read, and caned every Monday morning for her poor spelling. She failed the eleven-plus but her mother battled to get her a place at grammar school. Dorothy passed six O-levels without any concession. She got a job in computing at Reading University where she decided that she was just as bright as the lecturers. If they could do it, so could she. So after several years of hard studying, Dorothy achieved a Ph.D. in Psychology and is now a much respected lecturer at University College in

London. Dyslexia is scattered throughout her family and two of her three children have problems with spelling.

* * *

I didn't read until I was about nine or ten. When I was about eight my mother, realizing that I couldn't read and thinking it was a fault of the school, decided to move me to a very formal school. You sat in order of ability from the front to the back. I was a whizz at maths so they put me near the front of the class.

FOOLING THE TEACHER

We used to read once a week around the class. I was very cute and I knew how to cover up that I couldn't read. I used to wait until the teacher had caught the eye of somebody else and then I would put up my hand. It was too late, but the teacher was still impressed.

But one day it came round to me. I had this sentence and it started with 'the' which I knew and then there was this terrible word 'moon' and I couldn't read it. It wasn't a very nice school because, when they realized I couldn't read 'moon', without any ceremony I was taken and sat at the very back where all the real dunces sat, and that was it. That was where I was.

AMAZING TEACHER

But another teacher had fifty people in his class and during some of that year there was a teacher missing and he taught two classes of fifty. Nevertheless he found the time to teach me to read, for which I am eternally grateful. It was slow. He taught me, my mother helped me and my uncle helped. But I still couldn't spell or write properly. I remember there was an

169

exercise book without a name on it and it was passed round the class to see whose it was. It was mine but I didn't own up to it because I was ashamed of it. I mean what I used to do was write from the far side right to left.

'LAZY'

People used to imply I was lazy because I couldn't spell. The English teacher used to say to me things like 'Oh, you are one of the most able girls we've had in the school but you're also one of the most idle.' In a sense there was a truth in it, because there was something in me which said 'If you don't understand what I'm trying, I'm not going to try.'

The thing to do is to do as badly as possible so I used to get things like four and a half per cent. To get thirty per cent would have been terrible, to get four and a half per cent you see was a joke, and it was acceptable to me because I was noticed. On Monday mornings we got the cane for having spelling mistakes, so I had the cane every Monday morning. They used to come round for spelling mistakes and untidy books and of course I used to get it every week till I transferred to the grammar school at twelve or thirteen.

MY MOTHER'S FIGHT

Because I couldn't write well enough and I couldn't read well enough I failed the eleven-plus. At that stage my mother went into battle. We were in Staffordshire in Stoke-on-Trent at that time, she went down to Stafford nearly every day and fought to get me transferred into the grammar school. They said no.

So my mother then got all the teachers in the school behind me. She wrote letters, she rang up, she went down to see the local authorities. She went to the school. She went to the headmaster, she went to the headmaster's wife and talked to her. She got my form teacher and the headmaster of the school in firm agreement that there was no way that I should have been there. Eventually at the end of one term into the second year in the secondary school I was transferred to the grammar school. I was the first child ever to be transferred.

By then I was reading, and I am bright. I was clearly better than all the other people in my class at all subjects. I have a high IQ. If I hadn't, I wouldn't have been transferred. If it had been the case that I was less bright or I had not had a battling mother I'd have been stuck there.

JOBS

I got six O-levels without any concession. And I went on to do science A-level. After a term I dropped out of education for two or three years. I went from job to job, working in labs, reception work, that sort of thing.

Then I went to work at Reading University doing their maths and computing for them. I worked on the first computer that they had, and generally, filing was the job I went into.

I had never thought in terms of university, I had never thought I was bright enough. But, I suddenly looked round at the lecturers and I thought, 'God, if they can do it, you can do it.' That was three years after leaving school, I was about nineteen. I started helping with experiments. I started going to lectures. I started going down to the psychology department and listening to talks and everybody said to me, 'You should be at university.' I looked at the people who were doing Ph.D.s and I thought if you can do a Ph.D., so can I. I didn't think I was Cambridge material. I applied to do psychology but first of all of course I had to get A-levels.

I changed my job so I got a day release. I did A-level botany in the morning, A-level zoology in the afternoon, and A-level maths in the evening. I did this for one year and then I applied to university. I got accepted everywhere that I applied, by my references from the jobs. Also I was a mature student and universities like mature students. They all gave me a conditional place on two A-levels to read psychology.

I dropped the maths because I didn't need it and concentrated on the other two. I went to Durham and read psychology and zoology and passed well. I got a good degree, I got a 2.1 but I just missed a 1st. While I was there in my final year I did a research project and people said to me why don't you go on to Cambridge.

So I went to Cambridge to do a Ph.D. That was another three years. I had a grant through university and then I got a grant to Cambridge. So I did a Ph.D. and then at the end of that I got a research fellowship at Cambridge. I had a salary to do research. I had two research fellowships in Cambridge and after that I had an MRC personal award, Medical Research Council grant, for Psychology.

The grant was for studying animal play. Why they play, and what it means in terms of brain development, behavioural development, what happens if they don't play. Then I got a lectureship in University College where I am now. I had done some writing for *The Scientist*, and a book on children's play. I am ambitious and I think it comes from my dyslexia. I persevere, I keep at it.

MESSAGE

I think it is probably very important for children to know that they are special. I think that what helped me most is my mother and her absolute belief in what I could do. So it isn't just a practical support of helping children, there is this need to recognize that there are lots of doubts that you have as a dyslexic child in your abilities. The need to have that firm belief that you are special to somebody. Then you can always say 'Well, you don't know but my mum knows me better. She thinks I'm special.'

Builder of Custom-Built Motorcycles

NIGEL

I went to see Nigel, his wife and baby, one Sunday evening and as I drove away I was very conscious of the fact that, although Nigel had been diagnosed as dyslexic when quite young and has two dyslexic brothers, he is reluctant to accept it.

Nigel relies to a great extent on his wife who is a nurse, she fills in all the forms, pays the car tax, the bills and deals with the bank and building society paperwork. His mother says 'Nigel won't even open an envelope.'

Whether or not Nigel thinks of himself as dyslexic, his artistic gift prompted him to have amazing body art in fabulous colours (tapestry of tattoos) all over his arms and chest – not an inch of pink skin left. He also plays the drums brilliantly.

* * *

I left school as soon as I could at sixteen. I went straight to work. I took an art O-level, CSE grade 1, same with drama and music. I think the last two years that I spent at school were a waste of time anyway. If I had gone out to work at fourteen I'd probably have a proper business by now and I'd be a better mechanic.

At sixteen I went to work for a car mechanic, that's where I got my basic training. I worked for him for about four years. Now I work for a guy the same age as me in Chertsey.

AWARD

I've been interested in bikes since I was ten or eleven. Last year I won an award for one of my bikes. I was very pleased about that. It was awarded at a custom bike show that's held every year. Bikes come from Europe, Australia, and all round the world – it's a big event held in Kent. It was on TV, Derek Jameson did an interview on it. You take your bike down, there's a big paddock where all the bikes are displayed and mine was the best finish.

FIGURES

The only thing I have trouble with are figures which is a problem in my work as I have to get different measurements down to a 100,000th of an inch. My addition and subtraction are a bit weak.

Even though I can work the answers out, I always write it down and I always double check it because if you make a hole too big you may have ruined somebody's 200 c.c. or whatever. It can be costly if you make a mistake. You've got to get it right.

One of the things that puts me off running my own business is working out all the income tax and everything else, that doesn't appeal to me very much. But if I'm not sure about anything I will do it on a calculator until I am absolutely sure that it's right.

TATTOOS

I did a lot of the designs of my tattoos myself but somebody else actually did the work. I have had it done since I was sixteen all over my arms and chest. I like quality artwork. Some people are disgusted by it, but people who don't even like them are fascinated by the artwork. The tattooer is a very, very good artist. He's been doing it for a long time in England and travels all over the world.

DRUMS

I play the drums. I became interested in drumming when I was eleven. You need good co-ordination to be a drummer. There are a number of dyslexic drummers even though dyslexics often find co-ordination difficult. I have managed to master quite complicated drumming and play in a band.

You have to be able to do a separate thing with both hands and both feet. You would have four things happening at once. Your limbs are doing four different things at four different rhythms. When you get faster, everything will be doubled up and your feet will be playing twice as quickly. So depending if you're right or left handed, you would have the *left foot* hitting the base drum. The *right foot* hitting the high hat. (Like cymbals that go up and down.) Then the *right hand* hits the high hat with a stick, and the *left hand* plays the snare.

MESSAGE

I think anybody who has this difficulty should, as soon as they realize, find help one way or another, for whatever it is because I think the older you discover you're dyslexic the worse it gets.

175

I do know people much older than myself who are obviously quite distressed about it and find it very embarrassing and I think they should find help as soon as they can. Go to ILEA classes (for dyslexics) or go to remedial classes. Get specialist help.

It seems to me dyslexics tend to be quite bright people and they usually find or know what they want to do.

*"We were shattered to learn he was dyslexic.
We thought he was learning Bulgarian."*

Estate Agent

DICK

An information video was made by one of the dyslexia associations to help teachers, in which Dick was featured. A video is a good way of showing dyslexics' difficulties. Yet many of the teaching units are reluctant to show a child struggling to spell or getting the alphabet wrong on video as they feel to be shown making a mistake will embarrass the child or, worse still in their eyes, it will look as if the unit hasn't taught the child properly. So the result is that half the time the film leaves one wondering what exactly dyslexia is.

Anyway, Dick was the star of this video. With great style he revealed all his reading and spelling weaknesses which, of course, as he was already a successful estate agent, he didn't mind too much.

Dick was always the odd one out in his family, the only one who couldn't read properly. He was punished at school for not concentrating and punished at home for being lazy. He learnt to cheat at school and, in later life, developed a series of clever short cuts for writing letters and filling in forms. Dick ran a successful estate agency business for many years and is now retired. Many dyslexics get badly bullied at school. But there are also a large number who say that they became very aggressive to avoid being teased at school. Dick found being on

the attack was the best defence.

* * *

My school reports said 'Could do better, doesn't concentrate.'
I had to cheat. I had to crib from other people because I just
didn't know what to say. I remember on one occasion we had to
write about something and I hadn't got a clue how to go about it
so I thought right I'll copy his, so I copied his. He did something
wrong, spelt something wrong and I got it down, so I got caned.
This was how it was. I was punished quite a lot at school for not
concentrating. It wasn't because I didn't want to, I couldn't.

I didn't get bullied because I was quite noisy. I could
look after myself quite well. If anyone started on me I didn't
hesitate to go for them.

BEING LEFT BEHIND

The attitude of my parents is rather difficult. The family are
all quite intelligent. They have all got degrees, all my brothers
have got degrees. I was the odd man out, I was told to read
something and if I didn't get it right I had to read it to them
again, and if it was still wrong I didn't go out. They all went
out to lunch, visit friends or a pantomime and I had to stay at
home. I was lazy as far as they were concerned, I didn't try.

SORTING OUT WORK PROBLEMS

When I first started to work, I used to work for the Crown
Jewellers and then I thought I am just being used as a boy
running around doing odd jobs, I'll get out. So I then worked
at a nursery growing tomatoes and that was boring. Then my
next door neighbour who was an estate agent, a chartered sur-
veyor, said you can talk persuasively, would you like to come
and work for me and I said 'Yes' and I went to work for him.

Everything was written in longhand in his office. I thought this is terrible, so at lunch time I said, 'Could I have a word? Can I just be quite outspoken? Your firm is very go ahead, got a marvellous name, but you're very old-fashioned. Everyone should have a tape.' I knew that you have to look after yourself, no one else will. So he went for lunch, had a word with his wife, came back and said everyone is having a tape, so that's how I survived that.

I worked for him for about three years. I didn't like his old-fashioned ways. He wouldn't change, so then I got a very good secretary and got out and set up my own business. I've got a good eye, everything has to be in perfect order, photographs have to be good. I like that side of it.

The business did well and eventually years later when I sold out to retire I got a little profit, some 'sweetie money' at the end.

I never took any exams. It was absolutely impossible. I was made an honorary member of the Estate Agents Association.

TRICKS

I've developed a lot of tricks over the years. For instance in the estate agency world I used to get round by doing the *first* lot of forms, but when it got complicated, I would get them to sign it and I send it to the insurance company, or the building society, and they would telephone me back and say 'Hey, you've missed out half the words' and I would say 'Oh dear, I'm getting absent-minded.' And then they'd offer to fill it in for me and I'd say 'Oh that's marvellous, yes, well, that's all right.'

TIPS

All my life since leaving school, and that's about forty years, everything has gone onto a tape. I tape it all for my secretaries and then they do the whole lot. That makes life easier. It's only since I have retired and I haven't got a secretary that I got a Spell Master. It does save me sending out letters that people can't understand. I write my letter in longhand and then I go through it, and as I go through I put the words and spell them correctly and then I find I have missed words out and then I go through, and try and get it grammatically right, and this is sometimes very difficult.

It takes about three or four drafts of every letter I do. People say 'What terrible writing you have got.' And then you think for crying out loud, if you realized what I have been through to get this letter to you.

I think being dyslexic makes you realize you have got to fight for things. Nothing is handed to you on a plate.

MESSAGE

Don't imagine you can't quite make it. You're as good as anybody else.

There are an enormous number of dyslexic children going out into the world with their handicap still unrecognized. Hopefully one day there will be proper remedial teaching in all schools and this hidden handicap will no longer be the cause of damaged confidence and unnecessary unhappiness.

We have experience of dyslexia on both sides of our own family so we are even more anxious to see children and adults alike receiving the help they deserve.

His Majesty King Constantine of the Hellenes

Beryl Reid

ACTRESS AND AUTHORESS

I am a long time admirer of fellow dyslexic actress, Beryl Reid, whose wonderfully witty performances have given so much joy. When I interviewed her, and we were supposed to be talking about dyslexia, she made me laugh so much I found it extremely difficult to concentrate on the job in hand, and had to 'interview' her three more times in order to get any details at all.

Despite Beryl's dyslexia, she is the authoress of the bestselling books *So Much Love* and *The Cat's Whiskers*, and she has played many of the great classical roles in the theatre. On radio her famous 'Marlene and Monica' and her performance in the film *The Killing of Sister George* are but two of her triumphs.

In 1979 she won the coveted Olivier Theatre Award for her performance in *Born in the Garden* (which my husband produced), and in 1983 she won the BAFTA Television Award for *Smiley's People*.

* * *

I knew no fear as a child. I went to school at six, a wonderful school. There were only ten in the class. I lived in my imagination with 'Invigamis', my imaginary friend.

I never felt frightened. My first feelings of fear, I still

remember, were when I had to read aloud in class. I was ten. I counted the paragraphs of the people in front of me until it came to my turn. And while they were reading, all the time I was blocking my ears and trying to learn my bit. Suddenly I was asked to read and I didn't know where I was on the page.

I was always criticized by mistresses. 'I suppose you think that's clever' or 'You'd better leave the room.'

It was a self-discipline school which was terribly good for me but not very good for some of the others, they were defeated by it.

I could never criticize that kindergarten, though, because I learned so much common sense. It was boys and girls. But the boys couldn't take it, because they couldn't take that self-discipline.

I fell out of a window when I was about six, and I was sent to the headmistress who said 'I can't imagine how a *big* girl like you could fall out of a window.' We had this long talk and all I wanted her to say was 'Were you hanging out too far?' It was a very special school.

SPELLING

The trouble is that at this progressive school, I learned English, Latin and French, all when I was six, so I only learned to spell from phonetic sounds. 'H' to me is 'HEJ' and 'because' is 'becoz' – quite reasonable if that's the way you're taught, because Latin is from phonetic sounds.

I think learning so many languages at the same time made it difficult. I was in a muddle because I thought everything out to be just like Latin. I did a Latin play when I was six and it was marvellous, but it's not right.

I have a very good memory. I learned Latin and French by phonetic sounds but English, oh dear!

EXAMS

It was matriculation then. I passed on all the languages and art and biology and all those things, but I couldn't do maths. Latin was a substitute for maths which I could do standing on my head, because Latin had sensible spelling. It spells as it sounds so I could get that right.

FAMILY

My father had all the letters after his name you could imagine. He was an estate agent, lawyer and auctioneer. I am the only member of my family who is dyslexic.

My brother was a scientist, and my mother before she was married was a secretary to a lawyer. They were all quite academic except me. But I have written three books.

When I was small I loved being read to even by my brother. I learned to read like I do now by pointing to words. I taught myself.

I never read for pleasure. The only book I have sat down with pleasure and read is Roald Dahl's short stories, *kiss, kiss,* you know you can get to the end. I read all the *Winnie the Pooh* books now because I know them off by heart.

PLAYS

I can't go to the first reading of a play unless I have already three-quarters learned the part. You become a very good cheat. It looks as though I'm reading.

Learning the script beforehand is twenty times more work for me than for other people, as I learn one sentence at a time and mark the different words. I unscramble the syllables, syllable by syllable. And put a special mark on the 'words that got away' (those I don't know).

LEARNING LINES

I have always had some friends, actresses who are out of work, who are only too willing to be paid for helping me with line learning. I first of all have to go through every sentence pointing with my finger, like being six again, and put some symbols over the words that have to be stressed.

Then I start learning a sentence at a time. When I have three-quarters of the script learned I get somebody who is terribly good at reading to come and put it on tape for me so that I can have it in the car, in the kitchen or wherever I am, and learn it. Because I am now familiar with it.

When I was doing *Way of the World* and all period plays, I got an Oxford don to go through it with me first and tell me what all the Old English and difficult words meant. I couldn't have done the plays I've done without help.

Bill Bryden at the National Theatre knew I was dyslexic. I did *Spring Awakening* and *Romeo and Juliet* with him. If at the read-through we got to a bit I hadn't prepared, I'd say to him 'You said I could go to my appointment at 3.30 p.m.' and I'd stare at him, and he'd say 'Oh yes, Beryl, see you in the morning.' He knew I hadn't got that far.

Then before the next morning I'd catch up with them. As I say, I'm a good cheat.

WRITING BOOKS

I have written three books. But I dictate them on tape. First I do chapter headings with my editor. Then I dictate them a chapter at a time. I don't use notes. Afterwards I listen to it and add p.s.s like 'Going back to chapter 4, I want to add that cats only purr . . .' I've written all my books that way.

The Cat's Whiskers, it's still number seven in the charts and that's three years later. It's all about the history of cats – theatre cats, cats in Egypt, and then all sorts of cat facts like how they put them in those leather bags known as ferkins and they were used for archery practice – that's where 'letting the cat out of the bag' came from.

I have loved cats all my life, since I was a little girl. My mother always had a cat, but of course then I wasn't responsible for them. But since I got into the RSPCA as an active member, any little thing that's going spare I have to take in because I can't see them go wanting.

FATHER'S REACTION TO STAGE

My father was the estate agent and auctioneer for Kendal Milnes in Manchester and he said he'd rather see me dead than go on the stage. He thought it would be a dreadful life and so he said 'You must go to Kendals because there is a pension.' I was so determined to do badly, I had such awful determination that I was only there for six weeks! I was put into six different departments because nobody would have me.

TRYING TO GET THE SACK

I posted all the fur coats to the wrong addresses. I had to get on my hands and knees and polish the glass cabinet that the furs were kept in. When I was in the toy department I had to demonstrate Bakelite bricks, the one thing I could do, and that was like doing a performance. At the end of it I used to look round and see if the buyer was in earshot and I used to tell the people not to buy them as they were awful and would all fall to pieces.

186

GETTING INTO THE THEATRE

I had to have lunch at 11.30 in the morning as I was a junior and I went to Leslie's Pavilion which was a famous concert party theatre where the Cabaret Kittens appeared – quite a highly thought of theatre then.

They were holding auditions for a concert party in Bridlington so I went at 11.30 and I got the job and I got £2 a week. I went home singing on the tram saying 'I'm going on the stage,' and there was a terrible silence, not from my mother because she knew that's what I had to do, but from my father. He never asked where I was for a year. But he was a swank pot when I did quite well.

I wish that mother could have seen other things that I have done but she died too soon. She was seventy-two when she died, she could have been thirty-five because she was so bright.

THE BONUS OF DYSLEXIA

Dyslexia has been a very good part of my life because I never forget anything. Once I have learnt something, I can't forget it.

I remember when I was terribly ill with pneumonia after they operated on my arm, I fell and hit my temple on the windowseat in the loo, so I had a brain scan. The consultant said 'I have never seen anyone with so many brains in their head,' and I said 'Are there any I haven't used?'

MESSAGE

For the children who are dyslexic, it is terrible and it makes you afraid and terrified, but if you just work at it diligently you come out the other side.

187

Oxford Academics

Anxious to discover how dyslexics were achieving at university, I made enquiries when I started the book, at one particular university, Oxford. Within no time I had 'traced' six dyslexics. I waited to hear of their progress and several years later when they took their finals, I heard that four of the six had got 1st class degrees. One is now studying for a Ph.D., two are studying law and one has yet to take his finals. I talked to five of the six graduates and here are their stories.

* * *

Science Graduate and Law Student

JAMES

Not having any qualifications whatsoever, I am always extremely impressed when I meet someone who has been to any university, let alone Oxford. It's not envy exactly but I'm sure no one thinks you stupid if you have a degree. Nice. So the idea that I was to meet five university students or graduates made me feel a little apprehensive and at a tremendous disadvantage.

My father was what my mother called a 'Scholarship boy' and got a double first at Oxford. Not that they're called scholarships or double firsts any more. But I'm sure it was this association with Oxford that made me, in a manner of speaking, sit at James' feet in his flat near Ruislip.

James is one of three children but no one else in the family is dyslexic. His mother recognized the problem when he was about seven. He was considered a laughing matter at school and given no support or encouragement. However, his parents helped him at home and he went on to achieve great academic success. He passed eleven O-levels and four A-levels with good grades, then gained a First in science at Oxford University, an impressive accomplishment. He was given a scholarship to law school and is now training to become a barrister.

* * *

I was born at home and it was slightly difficult. I had the umbilical cord wrapped round my neck or something slightly unpleasant like that.

I think my problem was found out when I was about seven or eight. It was my mother who guessed. She has a friend who is involved in a dyslexia association in Birmingham. She had been talking to her about dyslexic children and she thought that I was doing several of the usual type of things dyslexics do. So she referred me to an educational psychologist who did various tests, and they found out quite early.

I didn't have a huge amount of remedial help. Both my parents helped me a lot in learning to read and write. I had great difficulties learning to read. Poor Dad was working very hard with me at the time and he used to find it kind of unbelievable that I was so bad at it. I had a good relationship with my parents. We always got on very well. At that stage my reading was about two years behind my actual age. But it was really my spelling that was the

189

huge problem and still is. It's worse when I'm under pressure.

BULLYING AND TEACHER'S ATTITUDE

When my dyslexia was discovered there was one teacher who
was particularly horrible, she used to read my stuff out in front
of the class so that everyone could have a good laugh. It was
really a vile thing to do. Then there was another teacher who
used to get people, myself included, to write out things eight
hundred times.

I did the eleven-plus which I failed. But my parents were able
to send me to a private school, without that I would have been
really done for. So I left that school, and then with one notable
exception everyone was very good about it, by and large. They
basically took the attitude that they would just take the work
as it was and ignore that it was badly spelt.

EXAMS

Exams were not a huge problem. I did eleven O-levels but
it's quite funny because I got As in languages and English
and things like that, rather than other subjects, because they
accepted my spelling. I got four A-levels. I did biology, physics,
chemistry and general studies.

I didn't get extra time, but what they did is they said
they would take my dyslexia into account, which I think is
actually much better than extra time. Because I found that
the main thing is, to get the person who marks it to read
it slowly enough to realize that you have actually put down
the relevant facts they want. Once they had taken the view
that they were going to fairly much ignore the spelling I got
on with the subjects rather than spending all the time trying
to learn how to spell.

I wanted to be a scientist. I was fascinated by it, and still am, I still read round the subject. I read science at Oxford University. I got a First in my finals. Firsts are few, especially at Oxford. But I am doing law now.

I thought of doing law at university, but I was very much put off by the fact that my father was a lawyer. I was very keen not to be seen to follow in my father's footsteps and also like most lawyers my father always tries to persuade others not to become lawyers. However I found legal work interesting and was granted a scholarship to law school after Oxford. I'm doing bar finals this year, which means at the end of this year I'll actually be qualified. Then you do a year's pupillage before you actually start practising, so I am halfway to being there.

EMBARRASSMENT

My writing is pretty messy and my spelling still makes me look fairly stupid. The worst thing is knowing I have to write a letter that is very important and I haven't much time. In court work there are going to be times where I am going to have to be drafting something immediately. I can't just pick up my pen and write something down, and feel that it is something I could hand up to a judge without worrying that he or she might say 'Young man, have you ever seen a dictionary?'

Note taking can be very difficult. There's a lot of note taking. There's no problem doing it, but it will be embarrassing giving it to other people to read through, because my work looks as though I am completely careless.

SELF-ESTEEM

I don't think dyslexia has affected my self-esteem. To an extent it's always been that when I don't do particularly well,

191

I can say 'Oh, well, you must have been discriminating against dyslexics.'

The best thing about being dyslexic can be when people find out you're dyslexic, if they believe that dyslexia actually exists. Then they will always think you are pretty wonderful to have coped with it, so it can actually be quite an advantage!

MESSAGE

Certainly once you are older, word processors are pretty brilliant, I think, especially the ones with really good spelling checks. I think they are an excellent way of dealing with the problem. When you've got an important letter to write you can turn out something that's going to look impressive. *Don't worry about your spelling being perfect, concentrate on absorbing the knowledge and learning and developing other skills.*

Engineer

GEOFF

When Geoff started secondary school he couldn't read or write. He was the only one in the family to show any signs of dyslexia and was labelled sub-CSE. Geoff succeeded against the odds. He passed eight O-levels and five A-levels and gained a university place to read Mechanical Engineering, sponsored by Rolls Royce. He now works as a post-graduate Research Engineer in the Department of Engineering Science at Oxford University and is doing a Ph.D. there. Aside from his academic achievements Geoff is also President of the Oxford University hang-gliding club.

* * *

Neither of my parents are dyslexic and if they hadn't been doctors they would have assumed that they had a stupid child. I suffered from all the classic symptoms of dyslexia like getting my Bs and Ds the wrong way round, and speaking phonetically. When I was first diagnosed dyslexia was not terribly well understood and I think it is still being brought to the fore at the moment, being recognized.

When I was a child I could always write well, it's just nobody else could understand what I'd written. I never regarded it as a problem, it was others being too thick to read it. Once they learned to reverse the Bs and Ds and read it as though it was completely phonetic, then they could decode it. So far as I was concerned the people who mattered could read it.

My spelling was appalling and I didn't make any progress at all. I still couldn't read or write when I was twelve which was a problem to say the least. When I say I couldn't read or write, I mean when I was forced to sit down in front of a book I could figure out one word at a time. Then after I had figured out the words that comprised the sentence, I could say it again in my own head and then maybe it would occur to me that it had some meaning rather than just being a string of random words.

CHRISTMAS PRESENTS

To give an example I couldn't decipher a printed note from my parents. It was Christmas and there was a radio control gadget for a model aeroplane, it was very delicate and easily broken, so rather than leave it for me to unwrap at five in the morning while they were asleep, they left a note. The note explained that I had got it and that I would have to wait until they woke up. I remember reading it, and looking at it, just assuming that we couldn't afford it and I thought 'It looks like I'm not getting that!' I was eleven, I remember wanting to read that note, because it seemed so important at the time, but not being able to.

SCHOOL

The first senior school I went to was incredibly competitive, but I soon learnt that you can do just about anything if you want with hard work, and I still ended up coming top even though I couldn't read or write. I just learned to give very succinct answers to questions.

194

I couldn't do English, and French was a non-starter given that I had no grammar. But I had remarkable marks in things like history and geography which were heavily English based. I would do adequately in other subjects like metal work and technical drawing and just be correct in maths. Overall the ups would be big enough to cancel out the downs and I would still be near the top. It seemed quite normal at the time.

I didn't know I was dyslexic. I just thought I couldn't read or write very well. When it came to English that wasn't a particularly happy experience, to say the least. It was damned hard work. We would be given homework exercises during a lesson on say Friday and we had to have it done by Monday. Most people would do it by the end of the lesson, just dash something off incredibly quickly. I could never understand how they could move the pen that quickly. It always seemed astonishing. I would have to take it home, basically just to put down my thoughts and ideas and then write it, then get my parents to correct it, then copy it out neatly. I would spend three or four hours doing that. I wrote very slowly. One side of A4 every three-quarters of an hour. Then I would get perhaps fifteen or seventeen out of twenty.

It would be imaginative work for an eleven year old and it would be well done. It wouldn't contain many spelling mistakes, having been neatly copied out from a corrected draft, which would have been quite indecipherable to anybody who wasn't familiar with the code I wrote.

MARKED DOWN

Then of course you got the anomaly that the person who was obviously worst at spelling in the class was getting consistently high marks. It seemed rather unfair that the English teacher would then say 'Well, you have actually come 5th, but I'm going to mark you down to 20th because you have obviously been helped by your parents.'

EXAMS

My parents are both professionals. They have been to university and it was unthinkable for me not to go to university. I had to get O-levels to get A-levels to get to university. I got eight O-levels the first time round and then I think I picked up another one in the lower sixth. In the A-levels I got Bs in maths, physics and chemistry which wasn't too bad. It could have been better.

It never occurred to me to ask for extra time for exams. It strikes me that an exam is quite a good example of real life, because in real life you're not continually assessed. You coast along for three months and then suddenly somebody wants something tomorrow or somebody wants a big report or a presentation and they want it now. You have just got to do it, you can't say 'I'm dyslexic, can I have extra time?'

SCHOLARSHIP

Then someone showed me a little advert in one of the woodwork journals offering a Rolls Royce scholarship and it seemed like a good idea. It was a five years' apprenticeship. Technically you were employed by Rolls Royce PLC and worked full-time at Derby. In the middle of it you went to university for three years, coming back and working for Rolls Royce during the summer. Then you had a guaranteed job with them afterwards. You had another further year's training which took you to a recognized standard with the Institute of Mechanical Engineers which fulfilled all of your formal training and requirements for Associate Membership of the Institute of Mechanical Engineers. That's the most compact, compressed, quick way of doing all this training, all the requirements for becoming a chartered engineer.

Nobody doing the doctorate apart from myself, as far as I am aware in the Oxford Department of Engineering Science, has ever managed to become a chartered engineer on the strength of their work.

PARENTAL SUPPORT

At the end of my third year I had to do what's called a Third Year Project, it was twenty per cent of my degree, and that was hell quite frankly. I had to write three hundred typed pages. What I ended up doing was actually ringing up my dad to say 'This isn't working.' He took a week off work and slept on my floor, and he was re-writing bits for me and correcting spelling and the grammar. He obviously couldn't contribute to the content in any way. But he was doing all the spelling for me while I worked on the figures and eventually we got there.

Looking back now, it's so embarrassing because you could see which bits he did for me. But I got through, my father was the crutch because he basically shoe-horned me through. It was relatively complex, but he could say 'This is just total waffle, what are you trying to say here?' Then he could suggest how to do it and I would go away and try again, and then we got close enough to something which was acceptable.

My parents have been remarkably supportive. If I had had parents who regarded education as a waste of time, then I certainly wouldn't have got O-levels, so none of the rest would have followed.

ACADEMIC PROGRESS

My doctorate is on the cards pretty soon, in the next six months. That involved three years of research. It became pretty obvious that in a firm like Rolls Royce which is very specialized they weren't going to take any risks with me. I had an interview with the then Professor of Turbo Machinery Group in Oxford and I said I wanted somebody to take a risk and just chuck me in at the deep end; and he said 'Yes, we'll chuck you in the deep end and we'll chuck you straight out again if you're no bloody good.' I thought to myself, that's marvellous, that's the sort of attitude I want, and so I had a go at that.

I've been with the Turbo Machinery Group for three and a half years. The work I am now completing involves a £1.5 million project to mount a Rolls Royce turbine in a short duration wind tunnel. Due to members of the research group leaving unexpectedly, I became responsible for the project six months ago. I still find reading and writing difficult, but that does not change the fact that I am a good enough engineer to lead Europe's premier turbine research facility. I have just co-authored two research papers, and will present one of them this June in Amsterdam at the American Society of Mechanical Engineers, 33rd International Gas Turbine Conference, the most prestigious forum for gas turbine research.

My fiancée Caroline is very good at English. She is proof-reading my thesis for spelling and grammar which is hell for her. Honestly the content is completely dull, it's not as if I'm doing something in which she has any interest at all.

There are advantages of being dyslexic in that you never quit because you can't. Just keeping up with very simple things at an early age, you need incredible arrogance and a belief in yourself because nobody else has. You never quit, never. I have never taken time off school or work.

I remember I collapsed once at my desk and was sent home, but just because you can't do something doesn't mean to say you don't do it.

THE POSITIVE SIDE OF BEING DYSLEXIC

Once you have got to a level of public achievement in an academic sense, then the fact that you got there against the odds is almost an added bonus and you don't mind people knowing you are dyslexic.

It's strange how it's quite socially acceptable for people to be innumerate, but not illiterate. Saying 'I never was very good at maths' is socially acceptable, whereas if you say 'What does that road sign say, I never was very good at English?' that isn't socially acceptable.

We are in a society where illiteracy is regarded with horror and yet it is acceptable for people to be innumerate. I think it's just as important to be numerate.

NEW CHALLENGE

I have started to do something now which is almost absurd in view of my inability to spell and write. A friend of mine started a magazine for a particular group and I ended up writing factual articles for him which he is publishing. They are quite lengthy, two or three thousand words, and they are actually in print. I tend to get drawn towards the things I'm not very good at. When you can do things the challenge isn't the same. I would much rather do the written work for which I have absolutely no aptitude. To do that and still have it be good enough is very satisfying.

*　*　*

I also spoke to Geoff's fiancée, Caroline, who does a lot of proofreading for Geoff.

*　*　*

CAROLINE'S VIEW

Everything is proofread, although I have seen copies of things that were obviously just sent out to people without being checked – there's one on the spare bed which is full of spelling mistakes, very ordinary things, which I presume he sent out without having anyone read it. You read things through time and time again, especially reports, and it's very tedious. Having to read through this mass of papers is very, very difficult, especially when I don't know anything about engineering.

The other thing I've noticed is how impatient people are in the shops when Geoff asks the name to put on a cheque. They just look absolutely amazed when he asks 'How do I spell that?' He would just ask it quite naturally and I can see how impatient they are. It's written all over their face, 'Isn't he thick?'

Undergraduate

JOHN

What has been interesting is that in the main all the people I interviewed for the book have divided into three categories. Those who had dyslexia in the family and whose difficulties were hereditary, those whose birth proved an unusually difficult journey into the world, and those who were deaf or contracted meningitis or some other illness as babies.

John is a dyslexic who had a difficult birth. He was born a day late, a blue baby. He is the only dyslexic in his family, although his father has trouble with spelling. At school, the teachers thought he was thick at first, then lazy. John was eventually assessed as dyslexic and sent to a special school. He passed thirteen O-levels and six A-levels and is now in his second year at Christ Church, Oxford, reading mathematics. He is planning to lead an expedition to Venezuela to survey the dolphins in the Cazicara Canal.

* * *

I first went to a speech therapist when I was about three as I was very slow at learning to speak and pronunciation, although my hearing tests were fine.

When I went to my first school they kept me down for the first year and I had extra English lessons. That was fine and

I kept up with everybody else because of extra lessons. When I went to my next school I had to play rugby instead of going to English lessons because sport was more important to them. So I dropped down and down and down until after four years I was being shouted at by all the teachers. There was quite a bit of tension at school. As a child I was always good but as a teenager I was quite bad at school. Fights. Just a bit of a rebel.

THICK

There was one teacher who when I had just done a test for him shouted at me and said 'This standard of writing will never get you into the senior school.' The teachers said I was thick. After a while they realized that I was perhaps not so thick. So they said I was lazy, yet I would have spent all the night before going through and through my work with my mother. It was quite demoralizing. The English teacher there was very nice and she thought possibly 'he's dyslexic'. She took me to a psychiatrist and I was tested and told I was dyslexic and that there were a number of schools I could attend. So I went off to Grenville College and they put me in their dyslexic stream and I improved.

PARENTS' REACTION

My mother supported me, that was very good, but my father thought it was a middle-class name for laziness. He didn't actually say that to me. But I found out afterwards that he thought that.

I left Grenville College after O-levels, because it was thought that in the Sixth Form there, there wasn't enough competition. So, I did my A-levels at the local grammar school.

In my A-levels I got all As, although I had a place at Oxford before that. They had offered me a place on two Es as I had done an Entrance Exam. Then it's conditional on interview. I had an interview for about ten minutes.

I got extra time on the entrance paper. The teacher at school was a friend of the tutor at Christ Church and he said 'We've got this dyslexic person who wants to do the entrance paper. On A-levels he got ten minutes extra time per hour. Could he have the same?'

EXPEDITION

I am planning an expedition to Venezuela in July for one and a half to two months. It's an Oxford University approved expedition of which I'm team leader and we want to survey the dolphins in the Cazicara Canal which is between the Orinoco and the Orinegro. We are also building the electronic track equipment for dolphins and that's never been done before. The work is led by Jo Atkin and he is very dyslexic. He's at Kingston Polytechnic. He is a brilliant engineer.

We will be in canoes and we will have a long boat. Some of it will be done from the long boat. We are using hydrophones to pick up and determine the direction the dolphins are.

DISADVANTAGES OF DYSLEXIA

The worst part of being dyslexic is the lack of communication with people. You have to be able to write and be eloquent in speech, and I'm not. I'm not particularly good at expressing myself verbally.

MESSAGE

I think young dyslexics should have confidence in themselves and definitely keep going. There is always a way round problems. It's not so much a handicap. It's you, and you have got to work with it, and not against.

'Very good, Arthur, but you'd better let me write dyslexia.'

Environmental Consultant

LUCY

When my enquiries at Oxford all resulted in dyslexic men, I panicked as I thought I wasn't going to hear of any dyslexic girls. So I rang the novelist and playwright Angela Huth as her husband is an Oxford don and asked if she knew of any dyslexic girls who had been at Oxford in the last few years. The next day she rang back with Lucy's telephone number. But as Lucy is extremely busy, each time we made an appointment it had to be cancelled. Then I began to wonder if Lucy didn't really want to talk about her dyslexia. Eventually we managed a short telephone conversation one Saturday morning before she completed yet another report and prepared a speech for her work.

Lucy's academic career, once she got to fifteen, has been extremely successful. A first class honours degree at Oxford, then a scholarship to an American university. But at school the teacher told her mother that her work was poor and that she 'shouldn't consider further education'. This shows yet again that regrettably the teacher need not always be right.

* * *

Apparently my mum rejected me when I was born for about

205

seven months as my dad disappeared for a certain amount of time. Three out of five of us children have reading and spelling problems.

I don't know what happened when I was very little but according to my mum apparently I used to read and write backwards. I can always remember having very great reading difficulties and major spelling difficulties.

I remember vividly at school when I must have been about seven or eight, you used to have to learn about twenty words and the twenty words would appear on the page but there would then be a dictation with the twenty words hidden. My twenty words would be sitting there on the page and almost nothing else. Everybody else used to score about fifteen and I used to get minus thirty. It was so painful.

The other problem I had was reading out loud in class which used to fill me with horror. We used to have to read bits of a newspaper and I just couldn't begin. Certainly at that stage when I was little I was seen as having a problem. But I think when I went on to the next school it was better. It was certainly very painful when I had to read out of books and I used to stutter which was embarrassing. I don't remember actually having a stutter. I just used to get in a complete state when I had to read out loud.

IQ TEST

I was taken along to someone to test my IQ and they said I would be perfectly all right and as I couldn't spell I could be an engineer and so Mum didn't need to worry. I'm not sure but I think it was at that stage that something was instilled in me that I was going to be all right, because I could do science.

Then I did do science and I found that if you do science subjects it's not such a huge deal if you can't write and read well. So I stuck to sciences.

206

But I do remember the teacher who caused me most stress. I was upset when I was ten before I moved to the next school because the teacher said to my mum 'She shouldn't consider further education' which is such an awful thing to say to a parent. She thought just being at a normal school would be far too much for me and cause far too many problems. I don't know whether it was because I was dyslexic or being very left-handed and slow starting.

Until I was about ten I think I was considered to be stupid. I don't actually remember being teased. Certainly the teachers that used to get at me were getting at me unnecessarily. I think there were a couple of teachers who were very impatient.

THRIVING

Then between the ages of thirteen to eighteen I think I was described as almost anorexic. I was a workaholic for my exams. I did physics, chemistry and maths A-levels. I got two As and a B. I think it was the workaholic link doing the A-levels and having an incredibly strong will-power to stop eating things as well. Having got A-levels and having got into university it made things a bit easier and I just got out of it so it was no longer a problem. Also, when you go out with a couple of people who are very fond of you, I think it changes your perspective.

PARENTS

I had a very difficult relationship with my father, I think. My mother was very supportive and acutely aware of the difficulties. My father was not really around.

UNIVERSITY

I read metallurgy at Oxford. Looking back on it now I probably wouldn't choose it again. It was quite a high science and not a particularly creative subject. So I spent a lot of time doing drama and being with people who were doing history and English rather than having a passion for my subject. But whenever I had to do presentations I found them very painful.

The written work was no problem. But I think most scientists have difficulties writing prose. Certainly in the last three years having to produce quite snappy reports I don't have problems moving words round the page now, but writing doesn't come easily. I have always written in longhand.

SCHOLARSHIP

I got a First at Oxford. Then I got a scholarship to America. I went and did environmental law and it was a brilliant year. That was a very good year to the extent that all the classes were done by participation which was very healthy in terms of breaking down the worry about speaking out loud in class.

At university taking notes at lectures, if the lecturer was going too fast, I used to get in a state and be unable to write anything. I used to get completely stuck on words when I couldn't begin to think what letter they started with. I don't feel I have a problem now. I don't worry about things.

JOB

Having spent the year in America which allowed me to switch

from metallurgy to environmental law policy, I did a post-graduate course at London University, again more environmental policy law. There were plenty of jobs for anyone with a relatively good degree. So they lapped me up.

Ever since Oxford I have been reading more and more into policies, so since then I have been a scientist working in the policy end which has been very interesting. Most of my work for the last three years has been helping the European Commission develop policy and looking at the implications of different countries taking different actions.

At the moment I am working on a project which is developing a work product for the greenhouse effect and at the end of that they will then have priorities for action. So it's taking a science and interpreting what scientists mean and then doing further research. It's not sitting in a lab doing the very scientific stuff.

SELF-ESTEEM

I think my self-esteem is quite low. I think I have been battling along.

ADULT RELATIONSHIPS

Being dyslexic certainly does affect domestic life, because I don't have any energy left at the end of the week. Also it is all wrapped up in your head as well. Probably if it wasn't quite so stressful, one could actually just forget about it and leave it. I am sure it's all tied up.

I am now doing a diploma of international environmental law as well which is a little bit mad.

MESSAGE

I think in school it's the inflexibility of teachers that's the problem. Remember you can do it if you are not put under pressure.

Ask people to take and give you just a little bit more time.

In a number of cases you have to be brave to actually say something rather than just battle away. I normally say 'Can you spell that?' or 'Can you repeat that?' And I think people have to have the time otherwise you are just left with a mess if you haven't got the notes down properly or you don't know the correct name of the person you are meant to ring and so on.

Graduate and Secretary

'ANNA'

Finding the whereabouts and following the progress of possible dyslexic candidates for this book has resulted in a great deal of persistent detective work, as some dyslexics who were not keen to have their disability known went to ground.

But sometimes even when you have found the 'dyslexic achiever' things don't always run smoothly. On one occasion I drove a hundred miles to interview a surgeon only to receive a letter the following day asking me not to use the interview!

Luckily this has not happened too often. It has been mainly with professional people who, despite the fact they knew their testimony would be anonymous, felt they might be detectable, and feared the discovery that they are dyslexic would affect their working life.

I had a similar experience with some of the young ladies who have just come down from Oxford. Having agreed to be interviewed, they withdrew as they feared they would be thought of as fools rather than academics. Luckily 'Anna' only wishes to remain anonymous. She managed to get into Oxford on two interviews with oral exams then got 'chucked out' in her second year as the college did not make allowances or help her with her dyslexia. Nevertheless she stayed on with a private tutor and graduated with a 2.1. She is now working for a television

production company who do not know she is dyslexic.

* * *

At school I was perpetually being told that I was a poor student. I was very keen on history as a child, but I had a history teacher who would never mark any of my essays because there were too many spelling mistakes.

They discovered I was dyslexic when I was about fourteen, because I had a very good English teacher who spotted it. Until then, I had a fairly miserable time, everybody assumed that I was stupid, and that was quite tough. But she noticed that the quality of what I was saying and the quality of my writing and the way I was presenting it didn't match up, so she suggested to my parents that they had me tested, and they took me along to an educational psychologist.

DISCOVERING DYSLEXIA

I found being told that I was dyslexic a very liberating experience. I noticed a huge difference in the way people treated me. I don't know how real or imagined it was. But no longer was I labelled as a stupid child. I was labelled as a child with a specific problem which was called dyslexia and it didn't affect my worth as a person, which was wonderful.

Before then, there was some attempt to give me specialist teaching in the areas where I was weak, but I was very negative about it. I don't like doing things I'm bad at. I never really tried. I think it was seen as an incurable problem and just something that one had to live with.

My mother now she is working with dyslexics says she wishes that she had known what she knows now when I was small and she could have helped me.

212

EXAMS

I had a note saying I was dyslexic with my exam papers. I did worse at O-levels and A-levels than I was expected to. All my school reports said 'She is worse on paper, she performs badly in exams', and I did.

I think that even if people are supposed to be making allowances, it's very, very difficult for examiners to divorce the presentation on the page, the spelling and the scruffy writing from the content. I also write quite slowly which is an enormous pain in exams.

I got eight O-levels, all Bs. In A-levels, I got A for art and B for English, which I was very pleased about, and D for history and D for maths which is not so good.

GETTING INTO OXFORD WITHOUT AN EXAM

I think if I hadn't got to Oxford I couldn't have got into another university, because my A-levels were poor. But Oxford run this scheme where they will admit you on interview only and I wrote to all the colleges in Oxford and I said that I wanted to go to Oxford. I said I was dyslexic and I said would they consider giving me extended interviews instead of an exam. And they did, which was wonderful. So my papers weren't considered at all. I went for one two-hour interview and another one-hour interview and was asked quite detailed academic questions and they gave me an unconditional offer on the basis of that.

About four colleges offered me a place and I chose the one I thought the nicest. I went to Pembroke. You are only allowed to apply for one college.

COPING AT OXFORD

Although Oxford Uni\ rsity were quite disappointed when I told them my A-level results, they had already offered me a place. They had let me in knowing that I had a problem with exams and with written work. Then once I was in they did nothing to help me overcome it, which I thought was very strange. I suppose it's very typically Oxford. It's the sort of place where you tend to work by yourself.

I had quite a rough time academically at Oxford. I actually got chucked out. I got chucked out just before the beginning of my final year because basically my academic work was poor. They felt that I was lazy, which is true.

But because I had begun on my final year, I had the right to sit the finals. I was allowed to go to the lectures and I got a very, very good tutor from another college who helped me privately. He was a really excellent tutor and very sympathetic and understanding about my problem, and it all came together in my final year and I got a 2.1 which I was very, very proud of. I really felt that was quite an achievement.

DYSLEXIA AND RELATIONSHIPS

Sometimes I think being dyslexic makes some people condescending towards me. It's part of that thing about people laughing about spelling mistakes. And I think it makes me quite aggressive about presenting myself as someone who is clever. Because it makes me slightly insecure.

THE ADVANTAGE OF BEING DYSLEXIC

It's very difficult because it's very hard to separate what about you is caused by your dyslexia and what about you is in you anyway. I think it's probably a good thing. Any difficulty can be a positive thing because it makes you try harder. I think it makes you better in things that don't involve writing. I am fairly good at talking, for example. Because my written applications or essays have not been quite up to scratch I felt I had to compensate by getting to be good at talking to make a good impression.

JOBS

At my present job with a production company they don't know that I'm dyslexic. I thought about telling them but I decided that if I was interviewing someone for a secretarial job and somebody said they were dyslexic I just wouldn't take the risk. I thought I could do well enough in a job for them not to think 'My God, she's really incompetent.'

TRICKS

In the office I'm working in at the moment, there's a spell check facility on my word processor which makes it possible for me to do a secretarial job which would have been completely impossible otherwise. It makes life a lot easier. I wish I could have had one at university but I used to type to make things more legible.

CONFIDENCE AND SELF-ESTEEM

I think my self-esteem is higher now I know I'm dyslexic. Before I thought I was stupid but now I think I'm a person who has got a specific problem and I find that an easier thing to cope with.

215

MESSAGE

I think the thing about any disability or difficulty is that you should think about it in a positive way. You should not think 'this is a problem', but 'this is something that makes me different'. It's not good or bad, it's just different. I also think that what you should do if you are dyslexic is work out a way to do things which doesn't involve whatever you are bad at. For example, if you usually write letters to people about jobs, don't write letters, telephone them instead and then go and see them.

In truth deprivation can be a spur. First it makes you more conscious of other people's problems because if you have a problem yourself you can equate with other people who have got problems. Secondly there is that thing about human nature that makes one react (to a difficulty) and feel one has to do better.

Michael Heseltine MP
Politician

Michael Heseltine MP

POLITICIAN

I had been rather apprehensive about contacting Michael Heseltine, but I was persuaded by a neighbour that I should approach him as 'he is the most understanding of men'. So I did, and we arranged to meet in his offices the day after he had finished work on his latest book.

Immediately I was shown into his airy office, he expressed his concern for young dyslexics. He had spoken to a group of dyslexic children a short time before and he said 'I felt such a fraud. Everything had been comparatively easy for me, and seeing those children suffer to such an extent with their difficulties, I felt humbled and grateful for my own good fortune.'

Michael Heseltine became the Conservative MP for Tavistock, Devon, in 1965. He had already helped create, and later became the chairman of, Haymarket Publishing Group.

From 1979 to 1983 he was Secretary of State for the Environment. In 1983 he was appointed Secretary of State for Defence until 1986, when he resigned. He was awarded the Silver Medal of the British Association of Landscape Industries for his work in introducing Garden Festivals in Britain.

What is so remarkable about Michael Heseltine is that the nature of his work forces him to absorb daily an *ENORMOUS* amount of urgent information and Government papers, docu-

ments and reports, which would be taxing for the fastest of speed readers, let alone a dyslexic.

*   *   *

At school, I just didn't find it easy to develop an interest in the written word. I did read a good deal and I read very slowly but I always found it easier to absorb the spoken word than the written word. The word dyslexia never crossed anybody's mind. Nobody had ever heard of it in my childhood. So I just regarded myself as rather non-academic.

The whole concept of dyslexia as far as I am concerned is a matter of hindsight. People either had bad writing or found difficulty with their spelling or they didn't.

But when my son was going through school, in the late seventies, then the word was known and had got a sort of fashionable ring about it. People were concerned about dyslexia and everyone talked about it. He had some troubles and I identified with the things that he was finding difficult. He had the same problems that I had had, spelling and reluctance to read, and writing too, and to a certain extent, the transposition of letters – MI becomes IM. Those are very common characteristics, I think.

My writing is very bad and my spelling is now much better but it was very different. If I couldn't spell a word I would wiggle it and I knew what I meant. And if they didn't know it was rough luck, or I became extremely good at finding alternative words, and I am good at that now.

I didn't read to myself a lot and I think I learnt to read at about age seven or eight. I really must make the point that there is no way in which I was a bad case. Yet I am not at the forefront in the way my colleagues can absorb the stuff. I have huge amounts of paperwork every day. That is the way in which the public sector works, by the submission of written paper. The endless files – they are all about people putting their views to you on paper, and they all have to be read.

219

SHORT CUTS

I found that there were short cuts to the problems of the pressure of work I have to live with and some of them are classically known. The obvious Churchillian instruction is to stay on one single half sheet of paper, a message all ministers should carry in front of them. Let other people do the summarizing, let other people cut the thing down succinctly, as opposed to expecting you to wade through ten pages of closely written subclauses.

I was responsible for the road programme, which of course involved a very large number of public enquiries, the results of which were translated into files and submissions. They were extremely difficult to follow and complicated to absorb, but I simplified the process by insisting that my civil servants produced a map of the routes and got them to mark on the maps the homes of all the objectors, and then to give a number to each mark. Also to use a schedule with a summary of each objector.

So one very rapidly began to see much more visually the reasons for people's concerns, and the degree of flexibility there was in any of the proposals we were being asked to look at, because it was visually in front of you.

Then of course later, in the Department of the Environment, I introduced a system called the 'mini system', which was about management information. Giving much more clarity to what the department was all about – as opposed to relying on submission of prose, telling you what they were doing.

I got them to set down the information in columns and put costs to it in summary form. This was another way of imposing a discipline that suits me on the people I was politically responsible for.

SCHOOL REPORTS

I didn't have any difficulty getting into Shrewsbury. 'Could do better' was always the tone of my school reports. No doubts

220

about the ability but a great deal of doubt about the application.

I went to Oxford. I was the last person into Oxford University without an exam, because I had matriculation in the old school certificate. At that time you got exemption from university entrance exams and the college I went to didn't require a college exam.

I was always very good at maths and that showed in the early school reports. I think in one of the common entrance papers I got a hundred per cent, if not that I got ninety-eight per cent. My common entrance exams to Shrewsbury on the maths side were extremely good. I quite enjoy figures.

ACCOUNTANCY

When I left Oxford I went into business and became an articled clerk in an accountant office and then did my national service.

Accountancy is not just about maths, it's a very difficult course, accounts exams. I spent three years, got through the intermediate exam of the Institute of Chartered Accountants but didn't qualify. Then did national service. But coincidentally I had developed a business interest and after national service stayed with that, which is now the Haymarket Publishing Group. Today they publish about forty magazines, but there were then I suppose about twenty and they were specialist magazines – car magazines, gardening magazines, golf, hi-fi, cameras, medical, advertising, marketing, management.

I hadn't written books then. The books came after I left the government. I am MP for Henley.

I think that people really are born with a certain sort of energy factor and they have to use it up. If you've got a lot of it, politics is the right place to be because it's a very demanding profession.

221

SELF-ESTEEM

I think that now in a sense life has gone quite well and therefore there is the confidence. So if I can't spell something, I can't spell it, and if my writing is illegible, it's illegible. I don't feel any hang-ups about any of that. One is what one is and I suppose it's getting older as well gives you a certain maturity. You can't do anything about it, so you might as well enjoy it. I don't in any way feel any inadequacies as a result of it.

If you are constantly feeling inadequate it'll be the worse for you because you'll be less confident, you'll be less adventurous in your contributions and you will let it get on top of you.

MESSAGE

The main thing I think in the psychology of so much of modern therapy is that everybody has a contribution to make, and they should make it to the best of their abilities. Usually one finds it's one's own sense of inadequacy that is one's greatest burden. Other people don't feel that you are inadequate because it's not their problem. It's you personally who feel that you can't do something and therefore you feel other people feel that you are inadequate, which they don't.

I am always reminded of my dyslexia because whenever I have to write a letter, I get through a box of Basildon Bond just for one letter. I realize then that I can think, but I can't write straight off, even today.

Jenny Smith

Montessori Teacher

CLAIRE

Claire was approximately the seventeenth person that I had interviewed for the book, and one might have imagined that after so many interviews I would have become hardened, but as I sat on the sofa and listened to her battle for confidence, the joy of getting a spelling test right for the first time, and the sadness when her friends wouldn't go near her when they heard she was dyslexic because they thought it was catching, I felt tears coming to my eyes.

Claire is now a Montessori teacher, and because of her early difficulties she approaches her pupils with compassion and understanding. She said she always felt so upset for her parents, that they should have one daughter who was so clever, and one daughter, herself, who she thought was not.

* * *

My mother thought maybe she might be slightly dyslexic, because she remembers when she was at school she had a lot of trouble with reading and writing. But I am the only one who has been classified. My sister is not dyslexic. She is very talented.

Because I went to the same school as my sister, they thought I would be like her as she was very good academically. That is

224

one big difference between us. I was not.

REACTION TO MY DYSLEXIA

When the other girls in my school heard I was dyslexic, supposedly I was the first dyslexic they had ever had, they thought *that it was a disease* and *they could catch it*, so they were a bit dubious for about a month. Only two or three of my friends stayed close to me as friends. The rest would say 'I'm not going near her, she's dyslexic, I could catch that.' Eventually it was explained to them what was wrong with me, word blindness, and I had learning difficulties. They were told it was nothing you could catch, you were just born with it. Then they accepted me as normal, but the big thing was that they thought it was a disease they could catch. I always remember that because it makes me laugh now.

After two months or so, the children just said they realized dyslexia wasn't catching and I got back with all my friends. In fact I became a prefect of the school in the end.

I think it was after that when I became very conscious of myself and I lost all my self-confidence. I felt that I couldn't do anything right. Everything I did seemed to be wrong to me and felt twice as bad as it probably was. I just wasn't particularly happy. I gave up quite a few things which I really enjoyed doing like swimming – because I didn't have faith in myself.

As I lost all my self-confidence, my mother decided that my confidence had to be built up and also I had to be helped. So I started having remedial lessons outside school. The lady basically started by teaching me the alphabet again and was very helpful to me.

SUMMER SCHOOL

Then my mother found a summer school down in Romsey

run by Mr Lewis and Lee Pascall. They have been a major influence in my life, and all the teachers at that summer school. I went there every summer from about the age of twelve until I was sixteen, so I didn't miss a year. I was told there that 'to have faith in oneself is the most important thing', but I didn't believe them and I used to walk around with my head turned to the ground. I never used to look up. It sounds really silly, but I always used to look down at the ground and watch what I was doing with my feet.

Then a man called Steve Skidwell said to me 'You've got to look up, you can, no one is going to knock you down.' And he built my confidence up and that's where I learnt my confidence, at summer school. I think they were some of the best years of my youth. But I hated normal school so much.

Then I left my first school and went to another school. I stayed there for a term and a half. My parents decided to take me away because it didn't have a very good remedial centre and they were making me sit down and do Latin and French. At that time I was still trying to learn English. From what I can remember I spent months just sitting at the back in the corner by the window and staring out of the window all day, doing nothing. Some of the teachers used to leave me alone.

REMEDIAL HELP

Then my parents decided they had made a mistake and that it was probably best if I got out of school. So when I was twelve or thirteen my mother found a very good lady in the next town to where we lived, who used to teach me for two hours every morning, Monday to Friday – just English, nothing else. It was so enjoyable because we went through the Alphega Omega book and she used to teach me fables and I used to read fables and she would ask me to draw pictures of the fables and things. I remember we used to do the test and if you got one wrong she said 'Oh, don't worry about it, it's OK.' But I would feel bad myself because I always used to think 'I want to get better. I have got to try and do it.' The biggest moment was when I actually got to the test at the back of the book and I think I got virtually all the spellings right. I thought this is brilliant, this is great. I was so happy.

Then I went back to a school in my village again but I wasn't particularly happy. Then I had remedial lessons from a lady called Mrs Stockinbach. She used to always make us spell her name but I still can't spell her name to this day!

I failed my exams and I had decided then I wanted to do something with children because I like children. So I stayed on at school for an extra term to redo my O-levels.

NURSERY TEACHING

One day the Director of Studies took me into his office and said 'I know you like children. We can get you into the local nursery school and you can help out there on Wednesdays.'

So I went into the nursery school on Wednesday and realized that that was what I really wanted to do. I wanted to teach children but I was so horrified at how this old teacher there was teaching the children sitting them down at desks saying 'This is number one. You must learn number one', and literally drilling it into them. I could see even these five year olds were sitting there getting bored. She would say 'That's the naughty one, he doesn't pay attention' and I thought 'He's fine, how is he supposed to pay attention?' The way she was teaching, I'd have been bored.

I knew I couldn't teach that way. I had to find another way of teaching which I was going to be happy with. My mother was Froebel trained and she mentioned Montessori.

She applied for me to go to college. At the London Montessori Centre you only need CSEs to get in and not O-levels. So I was accepted at LMC to do my training.

227

The training lasted one year and it was combined with teaching practice as well. You spent all day in college and then two or three days out with children in a nursery school doing practical work. There was a lot of written work to do. You had to do four big files full of written work plus making things. The course was three ten-week terms and each half of the term you had to write two essays.

OUTSIDE HELP

I can't write essays to save my life and I still get all my tenses mixed up. So I used to write them out on a blank bit of paper and take them to my flatmate. She would read them through, correct all the spelling mistakes and my English. She would check with me what I was trying to say and then write it out for me.

I was petrified that I was going to get bad grades. We had to pass the exam at the end as well, to pass the course. The first essay I got back I got a C+ which to me was brilliant. It was a pass mark and I was really excited.

BEING PUT DOWN

A friend of mine was pleased for me too. But one girl turned round and said 'Anyone who gets lower than a B should leave the course now. Obviously it shows that they can't do it.' I sat there and I thought 'If you only knew what I've been through just to get here, just to do this, you wouldn't dare say it when I'm around.' But that did really make me determined to finish the course. And as it happened that girl couldn't cope and left the course!

I thought 'I'm going to get through the whole lot of it.' I must admit I am the worst person for exams and I don't do much revision. I have the feeling that if I don't know it already, it's too late. I am sure that stems back from doing all the exams at school and having tests and always coming bottom.

FLATMATE'S HELP WITH EXAMS

My flatmate sat me down and said 'You've got to revise, just five minutes looking through it.' She was the one who told me I could do it and she's the one who had faith in me and, well, I proved her right. I passed.

I passed my written exams which to me was the most amazing thing I have ever done because I never thought I would be able to sit in the exam and write an essay. They knew that I was dyslexic at college, so they understood a bit.

When I passed it was the biggest thing for me. It was brilliant. I was now a qualified teacher. It showed my parents that I could actually do something, and that I wasn't completely useless. I could do something that I wanted to do.

FEELING INFERIOR

In my own mind I always felt my parents were more proud of my sister than they were of me. She always used to pass exams and come home with wonderful essays with ninety-five per cent – and brilliant grades. I would come home, if I was lucky, maybe with forty-five per cent. It seemed a shame that they had one wonderful daughter and then they had me, who couldn't do anything right.

UNDERSTANDING LEARNING PROBLEMS

I teach two and a half to five year olds. It is the age I like because it's important to help to develop the child's manual dexterity when they are young, to do their co-ordination and give them independence. Also give them confidence because that's the thing I don't have much of.

Giving children at a young age the help and encouragement they need is so important. It's important to say 'You can do it', or 'Put it away for a bit and then come back and try it later.' It's wonderful to see their faces literally light up when they have read their first word. Even if it's only CAT. That to me is the best thing, as I found it so hard to read.

JOB

Two days before my exams I hadn't got a job. I had gone to lots of interviews but I didn't have enough experience. Then I went for an interview and the lady liked me and said I would fit in well with the school, so she employed me. I told her I was dyslexic and she asked me about it. So I explained that it was a word blindness and then she said 'If you've got through this course, surely it's not going to affect your teaching the children two and three letter words?' and I said 'Only if I have to spell "orange".' She looked at me and I had to explain why – I still can't spell orange and I write it virtually every single day. Now if there are words I can't spell, 'penguin' for instance, I just go and ask one of the other teachers and they are more than willing to help me and write it down.

If I have a blank on how to spell a very short word, like 'frog', the children look at me and say 'You've forgotten, haven't you, Miss Pearce!' and laugh because it just shows that I'm not one of those teachers who knows everything. I have to think. Even at five they can understand and realize if a teacher can forget, then it's all right for them to forget, but not too often!

AN ADULT REACTION TO DYSLEXIA

When I told a friend of mine that I was dyslexic he said 'Oh, isn't that sweet' and I just felt so humiliated. I thought 'Don't patronize me, it's not sweet, it's an actual problem and you wouldn't like it, so why say it?' It was the worst thing he could have said to me.

MOST EMBARRASSING MOMENT

The most embarrassing thing was having to read out loud at school. One English teacher I had never used to let me read out loud because I was so bad. But then another teacher decided that was going to change, and he stood me up in front of the whole of my year and handed me a book which I had never seen before in my life and said 'read'. I stood there for about two minutes completely silent, looking at the words and then I tried and did about half the page and burst into tears as I couldn't do it. People in the class were shuffling around as they knew what I was going through because they knew I was dyslexic.

ADVICE

It's nice to explain to people you are dyslexic and get it across to other people who can understand it. The amount of people I have told who have been interested in it and asked me more, especially the other teachers, also business men when I was working in Australia. I just say 'Be patient with dyslexics, if they want to do the job well, they will do it.'

231

The worst thing is having to write a letter to somebody for a job when no one's there to help you, and you are not too sure of the spelling. Not knowing if it is right or wrong. I've been so desperate that I wondered if I should find someone in the street who could correct for me. That's the worst thing.

MESSAGE

Have faith in yourself, it's the best thing to have. It's very hard when you have been knocked down to say 'I know I can do it.' But it is important to have confidence in yourself. If I had had confidence in myself I am sure I could have done a lot better. Have confidence in yourself, and try and *get your parents to understand* that even if you have problems with them you're not going to be useless. You will be good at something, but you have got to find it in yourself what you want to do. If it's important to you, then do it. If you are not happy in something, then you aren't going to be able to do your best and prove yourself.

I am always trying to prove to myself that I can teach, which I have done, and I feel happier in myself for doing that.

Cabinet Maker

CHRIS

Many of the members of Chris's family are dyslexic. His two brothers are dyslexic, his fiancée is dyslexic, and his mother, Jean Augur, teaches dyslexics. She was the first specialist teacher I met (shortly after I had been diagnosed dyslexic in the early 1970s), when I was fronting a programme about dyslexia for BBC's *Horizon*. In *If You Knew Suzie* Jean was the teacher who taught Suzie the 'Star Dyslexic' of the show, in real life and on television. After the programme was shown in 1975, the BBC's telephone lines were jammed and letters poured in. It was the first time that there had been a programme covering this subject which at the time the public knew so little about. In fact if you said the word 'dyslexic' then people thought you had a skin disease, or were anorexic or autistic.

Chris had great problems at school and has coped with them stoically. The teachers were not kind to him and he always felt in the shadow of his eldest brother Roderick, who despite his dyslexia now has a Ph.D., and his younger brother Nigel, who is also in this book. I met Chris through his craft when we needed a cabinet maker. He designed and made our beautiful bedroom furniture.

*   *   *

233

When I was at junior school, I think Mother knew there was something wrong, but I kept getting put in the bottom classes with all the 'thickies'. I was also treated for a lisp which I didn't actually have, but they were prepared to do anything to try and help me. So at about seven or eight, Mother decided that she must do something about it and I was diagnosed by Dr MacDonald Critchley. After that I went for two hours a week to the Remedial Centre.

INSENSITIVE TEACHER

The very worst bit was when a teacher, Mrs Smith, read out my essay on 'Our day at the Commonwealth Institute'. She had ringed everything in red and put great big red marks on it and really belittled it in front of the class. She read it out loud and basically said it was a load of rubbish and that it wasn't a proper report on the day, it was more like a story. That's the bit I hated most.

I suppose I was immature in the writing aspect. I couldn't write a report – I didn't know what a report was.

I remember Mum photocopying it and using it as an example of the way not to treat a child. She actually rang the teacher at home and they had quite a do about it.

I was always getting into scraps, because the kids kept saying that I had to go away to 'Spastic School' as I used to go for an hour every day for remedial help, but I got used to that. It was at the beginning that I couldn't cope. Junior school was the worst, both the teachers and the children. I had some pretty nasty teachers.

Certainly when I went to secondary school it didn't bother me at all what people said, I was used to it.

BROTHER'S SHADOW

I think that my brother Nigel and I were both in the shadow of Roderick, my eldest brother, and Nigel was nothing like Roderick and I was supposed to be either Roderick or Nigel, and I was actually me. The teachers couldn't understand that. They would say 'You are not like your brother' and if I did something stupid I wasn't like Roderick because he was clever, and if I did something naughty I was like Nigel. There was never me in the middle, and that was quite hard. I am the youngest and they had both gone to that school before me.

As regards the dyslexia, it was really only a problem at school when I had to read aloud, otherwise I could keep it to myself or between me and the teacher. I was once accused of using it as a get-out, when I tried to explain it to a teacher because I felt she didn't know about it, and she accused me of using it as an excuse. All I wanted was to be sure that she understood the problem. When Mum went to the parents' evening the teacher actually told Mum that I used it as an excuse, which I didn't. She just didn't give me a chance to explain.

EXAMS

I took my O-levels and CSEs. I got five CSEs and two O-levels. I got unclassified in chemistry because they changed the teacher and he was Australian and I couldn't understand him.

Physics I got a B and I did that course on my own. I got one of those key facts learning books, because the teacher couldn't control the class, so if I was going to pass I had to do it on my own. I literally memorized the book from beginning to end and got a B. I got an A for design technology.

COLLEGE

I left home and went to live in Finsbury Park when I was sixteen years old, which Mother didn't like, and went to college. I went to the Mount View Theatre School and trained in a stage management course for two years. The only time dyslexia really affected me there was reading scripts and reading stage directions.

I remember doing *The Importance of Being Earnest*, my first book at college, and having to go to the read-through and actually being in a cold sweat, because I knew that the first thing that was going to happen was that I was going to have to read stage directions out loud.

But I can tell you some stories about prompting! I hated that. I was so bad at it. I was stage manager for the summer season, and one actress who was the theatre manager's wife needed more prompts than anybody I can remember, so the policy was to prompt. You really had to shout them out. You even prompted on the night. The trouble was trying to read the script and being able to come up with the right words – but I could never find the place!

Then I worked for Bernard Delfont – that was all practical stage management – *Swan with Topping* in the West End, pantomime and the summer seasons.

I did several jobs in theatre until I finally got discouraged at Northampton, because the people that worked there weren't interested in doing shows. They were only interested in overtime and paying the mortgage.

CHANGING PROFESSIONS

I have always wanted to make furniture and I just decided that the time was right. I read an article in a magazine and

I just went down to Bideford in Devon, because there was a cabinet maker there called David Sedgewick who had written articles in magazines and who also offered courses. So I went to see what it was like. That's where I ended up for a year. I paid him to be in his workshop, paid for his time and the use of his machines.

STARTING A BUSINESS

I didn't have any money. It just turned out that there were two other chaps on the course who lived in Bideford and were going to make furniture, so we decided to go into business together. We had no idea of business or anything.

We just muddled through and the problem of bookkeeping was absolute murder. Now I have decided I don't like doing it, so I pay an accountant to do it. It costs me but it's worth it.

AWARD

One of my pieces won the pre-professional woodwork of the year award – that got it on to the cover of a magazine. I won £1,400 worth of equipment which went a great way to helping me start the business. The only thing that happened after that was they said they would like me to write an article on how I made the tool cabinet. Making it was all right, but writing an article on it is something else! And they paid me to write it too!

Photographer

GEORGE

One does not hear a great deal about numeric dyslexia. But I do sympathize with dyslexics who are numerically dyslexic, as although this is not my main problem, I made a perfect fool of myself when having to present a cheque to a pools winner some years ago. I was unable to read the cheque correctly and the poor man thought he had won £690 instead of £690,000 (over half a million). Telephone numbers are another problem. A friend of mine, Felicity Kendal, who has contributed to the Parents section, says she always finds it impossible to remember the number and dial at the same time, and finds she often dials or writes the number down in the wrong order.

George is a photographer, yet his life has been tremendously affected by being numerically dyslexic.

George is the only dyslexic in his family, and found school such an ordeal that he ran away on several occasions. He finally left at thirteen and joined his sister working in a photographic studio where he showed a natural talent for photography. Determined to be his own boss, George moved to London and set up two businesses of his own. Both times the business went bust because he couldn't add up or read the paperwork. He has now started

a third business, this time successfully and with a co-director to handle the accounts.

* * *

When I went to school I did find it difficult, much more difficult than the other children. It was a private school with a very strict sort of regime. It was run by an upright Victorian sort of lady who had run the school all her life. She was no youngster.

I seemed to get into more and more difficulty at school. The reports got worse and my parents got more and more worried. But I was never diagnosed as having anything at all.

My parents took me away from that school and put me into another school. That had a much kinder regime and I think it was probably a better school. There was more patience and understanding around and whilst I never excelled, I went along comfortably. It was no longer hideous to think about school on Monday morning. There was a war and I went off to the country as an evacuee and that certainly didn't help educationally. The teachers were not very good teachers, some of them weren't really teachers at all. We tended to sing hymns in the morning and then we painted a lot and that suited me fine, because I became quite a good artist and I think really that my knowledge of colour and interest in photography began here.

RAN AWAY

I opted out of school at about thirteen and a half and was really rather a tearaway. In fact my sister was about the only one who could really handle me. School was never a very happy place for me. I ran away from school. I ran away from where I was evacuated because I was being put down by a couple of children of the house I was living in. I just cleared off and I thought if I go away perhaps people will worry about me. It was a good way I suppose of getting some attention. I

remember I slept the night in the woods. That was terrifying.
I gave up the following day.

FIRST JOB

I wanted to be a farmer but there was no way my father
was going to buy me a farm. However, I had a sister who
was a photographer and she said 'Well, why don't you come
and work with me? You like painting and you like art.' It was
a very, very good studio and I went there and I just enjoyed the
whole thing. I didn't have a very good track record at the time
and they weren't sure whether to take me on as an apprentice
but I fell into something I happened to feel I was good at.

I think there is nothing to get wrong about visual things.
You know, it's there and you see it, and that's it. I enjoyed
the success of photography immediately because I could do it.
We used to have meetings and discussions about portraiture
because it was one of the old world studios where everything
was very, very artistic and a lot of thought went into all the
sittings.

BANKRUPTCY

But one thing in photography, it's never any good working
for anyone, you have got to be your own boss because there's
not too much money around and certainly if you work for
somebody then you can't make any real success. So I came
to London.

I did in fact have two or three businesses and it was
because of the digits that I went bust and that was all a bit
traumatic. I don't know how much one could attribute that
to dyslexia but I certainly wasn't very good at keeping figures.
Artistic people do tend to shy away from that. That's how I've
always looked at it. Now I have a co-director who does look

after the digits. I am quite methodical and with the years I have improved, so perhaps I could look after them myself now.

Nurse

'LIZA'

I met 'Liza', who is a sister in an intensive care unit for premature babies, many years ago when I was researching *The Maternal Instinct* about infertility and the extent to which women will go to have children. In her care was Amanda, the first child of a couple who for fifteen years had been unable to have a child. Of course Liza has a tremendous responsibility for all premature babies, but it must seem even greater when the baby in question is the couple's one and only chance of ever having a family. I'm happy to say that with Liza's loving care the baby left hospital and grew into a bonny girl.

Liza knew she was dyslexic from a young age but hoped she would grow out of it eventually. After school she trained as a nurse and has now been promoted to sister in charge of the special care unit in a top teaching hospital.

* * *

I discovered quite early on that I was dyslexic because I couldn't learn to read. I was severely dyslexic. Luckily my father was in the medical profession. Not much was known about dyslexia when I was a child, but my father had some knowledge. I wasn't given extra tuition or remedial help, as

242

they didn't have it then, but I was told that I had this thing and that I would probably grow out of it.

My father described it by saying that the messages were not being sent properly from the eye to the brain. That's an over-simplified version of what actually happens, but somewhere, he said, the message gets muddled up and that's how he explained it and that it was nothing to worry about and that I would grow out of it when I was about thirty. We were brought up in that very matter of fact way. So I accepted it.

GCEs

But I did try for my GCEs saying I was dyslexic, and eventually got them and got into a top London teaching hospital, which was wonderful. It's very difficult to get into the top hospitals and I did my entrance exams declaring myself to be a dyslexic. But it was a strain and I had to work incredibly hard.

I still can't spell very well. But I can read perfectly well, but slowly – I'll never be a speed reader.

NURSING

Being a nurse, or rather a sister as I am now, is a very responsible job. Looking after ill, premature babies in the intensive care unit, though I say it myself, is very skilled work. And being dyslexic makes me doubly careful.

I write my own notes. But they are very medical and there's a kind of medical shorthand that I know, so that's not such a problem. It's a *very* fulfilling life, specializing in looking after these tiny premature babies that are in need of such very special care.

I'm grateful that, despite the struggles I've had, I'm actually able to do a job that I really want to do and that I enjoy it so much.

243

Egyptologist

RICHARD

Quite a number of the dyslexics in this book have written the most eloquent and impressive letters. Richard is no exception. The letter may have been written and discarded many times, or it may have been written with the aid of a spell checker and computer. All I know is that the letter that arrived on my doorstep is in a far grander form than any that leave this house, unless of course they have been typed by my secretary, Janine.

Richard wrote and told me about himself and his son, Paul, who is also in this book. Early one Saturday morning they both came to the house and Richard told me how the discovery of Paul's dyslexia had such a profound effect on him that it resulted in a series of nervous breakdowns as he relived his own terrible experiences as a young boy. Richard is involved in a programme to help young people.

* * *

In retrospect, the first indications that I had a problem were that I was highly sensitive to sound, noise, changes in temperature. Certainly on one occasion as a young child when I was bathed I blacked out completely, a kind of sensory overload.

My parents were certainly aware that I was very, very

irritable, very, very tense, very, very edgy – even the clock chiming would upset me. I was sent to a private school and this school was fortunately so tiny that I was almost able to obtain individual tuition. The methods of teaching that I received there were the same methods that my son received when he went to the Dyslexic Institute. If it hadn't been for that early education I would be far, far worse than I am now.

You could meet my dyslexic father, who is eighty and was only diagnosed a few years ago. He will tell you of my grandfather who was, as far as I can tell, also dyslexic. One thing I know, the problem does not become easier as you get older. I have found great encouragement from the work undertaken by Harold Levinson in the U.S.A. He is convinced that dyslexia is a specific organic problem. I must in all honesty say I concluded the same thing years ago.

HYPOCHONDRIA

People began to realize I was hopeless at games, very, very clumsy, couldn't tell the time, couldn't tell left from right. I felt all mixed up. I dreaded games and I became quite a hypochondriac, developing the most fascinating conditions to get out of games. I would do anything to get out of games. Then at the age of ten I was moved to an ordinary state school and I almost seemed to collapse educationally.

I suddenly realized that in a class of fifty I couldn't take things in. My parents began to realize there was something wrong. My spelling was atrocious, my memory was bad. I used to come home every evening and my father would often lose his temper and storm at me. I don't think they began to realize anything was seriously wrong probably until much, much later, but I was the one who realized it.

I went into nursing. I had wanted to be a doctor but somehow I just couldn't memorize things and I began to be very concerned that I couldn't remember faces, I couldn't

245

remember names, I couldn't read a lot although I enjoyed reading. Eventually I got my SRN and I left nursing.

Literally, I would walk onto the ward and while I would know everybody's diagnostic state, I wouldn't know their names, I wouldn't recognize them.

I then began to realize there was something wrong. I didn't know what it was. I used to ask my parents if there was something wrong with me. I just didn't know what it was. I used to fall down a lot.

RELATIONSHIPS

I didn't get on with people. I tended to be very arrogant, which was a defensive mechanism.

Then I met my wife and I suddenly found here was someone I loved and trusted. Whereas normally I have a singular distrust of people, I have absolutely no distrust of my wife.

We have been married now for twenty-eight years.

BREAKDOWN

All seemed to go well at first, I got into selling, I got a good job with a pharmaceutical company and then things really began to erupt when Paul was born.

Something rather strange began to happen after Paul was born and started to go to school. He began to fail at about ten, and I started to wake up at night often in tears or trembling, strange things happened to me, strange memories that I couldn't quite explain. Then eventually about eight or nine years ago I had a complete breakdown and ended up in the bedroom crying what's wrong with me, I can't understand it. I then had a course of hypnotherapy which eventually helped me to deal with my own problems.

I could then see that I was reliving experiences – like when

246

someone said to me 'Why can't you copy that off the board, are you stupid, can you see it? Why have you put the wrong word down in your book?' and with forty-five people looking at you, you wanted to die.

OPEN UNIVERSITY

Then in 1982 I decided that I had got to come to terms with myself intellectually. I knew I was intelligent. I knew that I was bright but I felt stupid, I felt thick, I felt clumsy and I decided I would go to the Open University and get a degree.

I told them I thought I had a learning problem. They sent a guy up to screen me. By that time we had come to realize that Paul was dyslexic and this guy said 'You are riddled with it as well, my boy.' Then I suddenly realized that I was dyslexic, but I didn't know until I was in my early forties, so I had been dragging the whole thing with me.

A man wanted to hire a horse so he went to a priest who gave him a horse but warned him, 'The horse only obeys these instructions – it's "Alleluya" to STOP and "Thank the Lord" to GO.' The man set off on the horse saying 'Thank the Lord, Thank the Lord.' The horse went faster and faster, then the man saw they were approaching a cliff edge! He was trying to think of the word to stop and just five centimetres from the edge he remembered and said 'Alleluya!' The horse stopped. The relieved man shouted in joy, 'Thank the Lord!'

Wendy Barton, Bolton

247

Car Sprayer and Restorer

PAUL

Richard's son Paul is severely dyslexic. His parents were aware of his dyslexia and enrolled him for remedial classes. Unfortunately these did not help much and he left school at sixteen with no qualifications and in a state of despair. However, he has found a job he loves – car spraying and restoring – and is now planning to start adult literacy classes.

* * *

My parents were aware that there was something wrong. I was hyperactive. When I started school, my mother thought I would be the first person to be expelled from kindergarten as I was very violent and anti-social. They were aware that I just couldn't concentrate.

My parents tried everything they could. I went to a place at Chester and they put me on amphetamines, but you can't keep children on amphetamines. They tried everything, hypnotherapy, homoeopathy, zinc, every avenue they could think of, as my parents were told I was *not* dyslexic. Then eventually they took me to the Dyslexia Institute at Sutton Coldfield and they confirmed I was dyslexic when I was about eleven or twelve.

I was in middle school at the time and for about a year

248

somebody would pick me up after dinner time at school and I would spend an hour at the Dyslexia Institute.

UNHAPPY

By that time everything was a total block. I didn't want to learn and I just hated school. So I had more remedial classes, but the teacher was teaching me one thing and the school was teaching me another. So I went to a special block in the school that was totally remedial – it was the lowest of the low, and my ego just collapsed completely. I was really unhappy. Very deep down I knew I could do better than the people who were in class with me.

I used to go into a shell and just switched off. It was a continual state of despair and unhappiness.

TEACHER'S CRUELTY

I left school at sixteen. I was determined to get an O-level in art. I could do art with no problem. We had to put all our pictures up on a board so there were probably about at least fifty boards with fifty of us putting our art display up. When the art teacher came up, he thought my artwork was done by somebody else because it was so good. My father had been teaching me advanced watercolour techniques, but it was all my own work.

So I got the lowest grade you can get because they wouldn't believe me. It was my one chance, but I didn't say anything to my father until afterwards.

I think that was the cruellest thing that happened to me when they wouldn't accept it, because I was hoping for an A and I was so disappointed to get a Grade 5 CSE.

249

JOB

I am very interested in cars. I have been car spraying since I left school. I do restoring as well now. We restore old sports cars. The cars come in completely rusty and our job is to make them A1 again. I have been in this particular job about three months. The people are nice there and the boss is very understanding. I think my artistic side has been helpful.

E.S.P.

I don't know whether it is connected with my dyslexia, but I have got tremendous E.S.P. – extra sensory perception, right from being a child. For instance, the Japanese plane crash when the plane hit the hillside. My parents were going to Egypt and I was very concerned because I thought I had seen their plane go down. Then we confirmed the details that evening on television. When they said everyone was dead, I said no, there was a little girl alive, *and they found her the next day.*

The horrible thing is, though, you actually see the thing happen. I saw the plane crash.

Another time we were fossil hunting at Whitby and we were working on some rock and I just said 'Come away, Dad, come away, please come away,' and Dad said 'Don't worry, there is nothing wrong.' But I insisted 'Come away, please come away,' so we walked away and started to walk along the shore, and the whole cliff just caved in. So I'm a handy chap to have around!

Electrician

BARBARA

It is interesting that some dyslexics have amazingly brave hobbies. But hang gliding, abseiling and going up the Amazon seem tame in comparison with sky diving, which has to be the most daring of pastimes. Yet Barbara has completed 313 jumps and intends to make many more.

Barbara is the youngest in her family. Her father is also dyslexic. She caught flu as a baby and was deaf for three years. This led to speech problems at junior school. Later, she was teased at school because she was dyslexic. She passed six CSEs and then served a four year apprenticeship as an electrician with London Transport, the only woman on her course. Barbara nearly gave up because she was so nervous about the college work she was making herself ill. However, she persevered and now works in the fault-finding section. She is also a skiing instructor.

* * *

I don't read, I can read but I don't get any enjoyment out of sitting down reading a book, and I hardly read the newspapers, it's too much effort.

If I pick up the newspaper to read an article or anything I have to make a marked effort to get through it and I can't be interrupted at all or I totally lose where I am, so I don't bother.

251

BULLYING

I was always teased but I was a fighter. I used to fight. I fought down at junior school. When I got to senior school I didn't need to, because one of the boys I beat up came with me to senior school. He was one of the bullies and if anyone started bullying me he stopped it. I don't know why but he was very protective of me. Probably because I beat him up!

We had quite a few battles over my dyslexia, like we had quite a few teachers who didn't believe in it and all that. I had special tuition, my mum made sure of that from the start.

OLDE ENGLISH

When I was still at school we went round to my cousin's. We had some fun. She was doing a degree or something and she had an olde English book with olde English spelling, and I could read it and she couldn't. So I was over the moon, but the spelling just made sense to me, not all of it, but most of it. My mum couldn't believe that I could read it. I said 'It's spelt as you say it.' That's the way I write.

I left school at sixteen. I did CSEs. The practical ones I got on all right with.

APPRENTICESHIP

I wasn't going to become an electrician, I was going to be a sheet metal worker. For my CSE I had to design and make a lamp out of sheet metal. I did that and thought right that's it, I want to become a sheet metal worker. But when I went for the interview

252

they suggested I did electrical work. So I did four years' apprenticeship in Acton at the London Transport Apprentice Centre.

I had a lot of problems. When I left school I decided that was it. I wasn't going to learn anything else. When I started my apprenticeship I was told that I would have to go to college, and I near enough threw it in there and then. But we started at the Training Centre where you just did all practical work, which I love. Being the only girl, in the electrical section I had no one to talk to. So I always got down to it and got the work done and I found I could get on with it.

COLLEGE

At college they always went at too fast a rate for me and the blackboard used to go round every time I got the first couple of lines down and so I became ill. I was always off college. A couple of days at college and then I was too ill to go.

My doctor said it was just me not wanting to go. I just got worked up. We used to do a fortnight in the Apprentice Centre and then a fortnight at college and a week before I started college I started working myself up so much that when I went to college I just became ill, too nervous or stomach pains and that.

My Governor wanted to fire me because I was always off sick. But the unions were on my side and his secretary had a good go at him, because she was a friend of the family, and they arranged for me to go on day release.

Once a week I went to college and then I worked the rest of the week, which I found a lot easier. I'd just think I'd just got to get through *one* day.

PRACTICAL WORK

On the practical work I was ahead. I could whip through

253

practical work. I just seemed to be able to do it.

In the end I started to help the boys out at the Apprentice Centre, helping them with their practical work, because I was so far ahead. They caught up in the end and they started doing my college work for me. They used to copy the notes down and photocopy them and give them to me to take home to copy. They knew I was dyslexic. I told quite a few of them, I thought it best to be open.

EXAMS

So luckily enough I got through my exams until the third year, which I failed. Then at Christmas I had to take it again, doing one evening a week at college. I was the only one to re-sit it. But I passed. That was a miracle. I've found reading drawings is the hardest thing in my job as an electrician. Because they are nothing like the electrical work – the layout of the electrics you're working on. Once you've cracked them, you are all right but they take a lot of time to crack.

There are certain jobs that have to be done on the trains. Every day is the same, the same routine, tips have to be checked for gapping and cleaned, brushes in the motors have to be changed. I said 'I'd like to take that job over, I wouldn't mind coming back and doing that.' None of the electrical fitters liked the job because it was routine every single day. But it suited me, so the foreman saw the Governor and I got the job down there. They made a job for me which wasn't there at the time. I liked it because it became routine, and I knew how to cope and so I really knew what I was doing every day. But it became boring. So I slowly got into fault finding for London Transport. I had a very good foreman who is like a big brother to me now. He started teaching me how to read drawings but it took him two years to get it through to me!

I think being dyslexic makes you grow up a lot quicker. I don't know if it's me but I could never get on with kids. Even when I was a child I could never get on with children my own age. I always got on with the teachers at school, like tea time and dinner time I used to go and talk to teachers. I hardly had any friends of my own age.

I liked very sensible conversations and I could never compete with words. I always found the kids talked too fast for me.

HOBBIES

My hobbies are sky diving and skiing. Sky diving is like parachuting. Parachuting is where you jump out of a plane and your parachute automatically opens. Sky diving is when you jump out, do different things in free fall and then pull your own parachute.

I've done it 313 times at the moment.

You can join up with other people. You speed up to 120 miles per hour for about the whole thing. You start slower than that and then it speeds up and then you're going faster.

It's like swimming really, just move your arms and that to get across, and your legs. It's basically helping the air flow across your body to move yourself.

I did have problems with co-ordination. I can't catch a ball to save my life. I can't kick a ball. It took me a lot of time to get to know which way to move parts of the body to get in certain places. It took me longer than most people. I have a lot of determination.

I go up to the parachuting centre in Peterborough. You've got to get through a category system to become an experienced sky diver. It means you have to show that you can do basic things in free fall.

There are quite a few girls. We are catching the fellows up. You can't start until you're sixteen and can go on to about fiftyish when people stop. There was one seventy year old. You have to get your doctor to sign a medical certificate before you start.

SCARED OF HEIGHTS

The joke is, I'm scared of heights which sounds stupid but most sky divers are. Climbing ladders and that scares me, but that's because you can see the ground. But when you're up there it doesn't look real, it's so far away.

An Irishman and an Englishman were walking along a hillside.
The Irishman fell down a hole!
The Englishman knelt down and yelled,
'Is it dark down there?'
The Irishman replied, 'I don't know – I can't see!'

Sarah Housden (13), Peterborough

Flautist

MARTIN

Despite the fact that I love music I passed all my music exams without managing to sight read properly and have sung in three musicals. I have never moved in 'music circles' so it worried me greatly that musical dyslexics were not going to be represented in this book. Then suddenly in the same week I met and interviewed a singer (turned singing coach), whose story appears later in the book, and a flautist, Martin.

I was giving a lift to Martin's mother and asking about her children's careers when she said one of her sons was a flautist. Out of the blue I asked, 'Is he dyslexic?' and she answered, 'Well, as a matter of fact he is.'

Martin, who suffered tremendous bullying and unhappiness at school, didn't take up the flute until he was sixteen, and has always found reading music difficult. He studied at the Royal College of Music and completed his musical education in West Germany on a German Government Scholarship.

As a founder and leader of the Feinstein Quartet, and as a soloist, he has broadcast for BBC Radio and given many performances at major venues, including several appearances at the South Bank Centre and the Wigmore Hall.

Martin is a member of the contemporary group Ensemble

Modern and has recently toured France, Italy and Germany with them.

* * *

I don't remember exactly when I learnt to read or write. The problem was exacerbated by the fact that I went to a lot of different schools as my parents moved around a lot. Certainly I remember being about ten and having great difficulty in stringing words together. People just couldn't understand it because I was very articulate and it seemed to have no correlation. It was very frustrating for me because people thought I was dumb and I wasn't dumb. It was just that I couldn't do this particular thing. I had an inability to take things in from the written page.

My spelling was hilarious. It still is. But now with the aid of a dictionary I'm all right. But in those days I just wasn't aware of the fact that what I was spelling had no relation to what I was supposed to be spelling. I did it all phonetically. Reading was a problem too.

I am surprised my father didn't cotton on because he is a scientist, but he didn't realize what was happening. Nobody knew what was happening. I used to steal, and I wet my bed until I was eleven or twelve. There were many problems of that kind.

BOOKS

I think my mother realized there was something strange going on because I was very interested in literature. I understood the books well, but when it came to writing about them I couldn't put pen to paper. I would come up with a three sentence boring banal thing about some book which I had really very much enjoyed. And my mother could never understand that.

I often wonder if I didn't read partly because my mother kept pushing these books at me. I remember at a ridiculously young age she tried to get me to read *A Farewell to Arms*. I was about six and obviously I couldn't do it.

My relationship with my parents was difficult only because they were worried that I was not doing academically well, or rather that I was doing appallingly badly. They couldn't understand why because they are so academic themselves. My father probably was dyslexic. He was a very late developer. My mother is certainly not.

DIAGNOSED DYSLEXIC

I went to a very good comprehensive school. I was doing very well in science and things like that, until I had to write, at which point I couldn't do it. I just didn't have the energy to go to the trouble of trying to write down words because I couldn't. I knew I would get them wrong and I would get a big red S written through it. Then when I was about thirteen or fourteen, a very clever lady at my school realized what it was and diagnosed it as being dyslexia. The headmaster also realized there was something worth looking for in me which no one else had bothered about.

I went for special lessons which were basically calligraphy – just forming my letters slowly and thoughtfully was what partially solved the problem for me. The problem is still not solved in that my handwriting is appalling and my spelling is still very erratic, but things certainly improved with the lessons.

TEACHERS

I have never got on well with teachers. I have had so many teachers. There is something terrifying about sitting at the back of the class and having somebody ask you questions which you know you will never be able to answer. Day in day out, you are not going to be able to answer, not really having the smallest grasp of what's going on. So they become enemies, the teachers, but they became more friendly as I improved.

BULLIED

I was bullied a lot, it was awful. I was a rather strange and introverted person. I liked to be alone all the time which is exactly the thing which brings out the worst in children. I was academically very, very bad, beyond the pale, and I presume there were other reasons for it as well.

I did the eleven-plus. I was in the middle stream. I did well in O-levels because I did sciences. I also did English language, which I passed. I don't know how because my spelling was so bad.

MUSIC

I was interested in music when I was relatively young, about eleven. I started playing the piano and I did the occasional thing in pubs which earned a little bit of money. I didn't learn to sight read music until I got past the problem of not being able to take things in from the written page. I started to sight read at the hilariously late age of sixteen and still find it a problem. Nobody believes me when I tell them, because I went to the Royal College two years later.

I did the grade exams in a mad rush. I did Grade 5 after six months and Grade 8 after a year. I solved the problem of not being able to keep up with people, but obviously a lot of background was missing because I had missed so many years. I didn't start playing the flute until I was sixteen so it was all very late.

I went to the Royal College of Music for three years, which is the normal course, and they filled in all the background, but it was so late to start. I had missed out on so much.

It was very difficult to get in. I just scraped in. I actually did very well when I was there and I was among the best flute players there, but after I had been there for three years, I realized that what I really needed was to get a proper training. That's why I went to Germany.

SCHOLARSHIP

I got a scholarship to go to Hamburg for a few years. I was very lucky I got this scholarship. It was a German Government Scholarship to study with a famous flute player over there called Carl Heinz Zeuler, solo flautist of the Berlin Philharmonic Orchestra. The German way of teaching is so thorough. They went over all the groundwork I should have done. My first job was with the Hamburg Symphony Orchestra.

RUNNING A BUSINESS

When I came back to England the first thing I did was to look at the situation here and think, 'Yuck!' So I formed two chamber groups, a quartet called 'The Feinstein Quartet', and a duo with a guitar called 'The Light Fingered Gentry'. I got on the Government Enterprise Allowance Scheme because it was the only way to get money out of my bank manager.

I now sit at my word processor and type letters because musicians have to write to promoters and to arts councils for grants. I also write to composers to commission works and to the South Bank to get dates and things. All these letters have to be written and spelt correctly for a start. You can't write a letter to a promoter that's not written properly and is not articulate. It was a great struggle at first. It's that kind of work that I find difficult but I do a lot of it, funnily enough.

The satisfaction when I got back my first brochure which I worded myself, was tremendous – a glossy thing with my words on it. My mother says I write well – she should know, she's a writer!

ADVANTAGE

An advantage of being dyslexic is that it makes you a 'go it alone' person. The disadvantage is that I lost so much time. I would love to have learnt to read music earlier. I regret that. All the literature I could have learnt, who knows what would have happened. You never can tell.

MESSAGE

Once people know you are dyslexic your problem is solved mostly. The message is to try to notice when there is a very obvious lack of correlation between intelligence and ability. It really could easily be dyslexia. I am sure it often is.

Now that there is a note of respectability in being dyslexic, it's far better to be diagnosed as having something wrong with you, rather than not being diagnosed. Because you then have a title to your problem that gives you respect – because you are not lazy, stupid, inattentive, and people will be more compassionate.

Anon

Health Visitor

DIANE

As I have said, many dyslexics seem to be drawn to professions which help others. As a child I desperately wanted to be a nurse, but I didn't manage to get Latin O-level (or any O-levels except art, for that matter). In '*my day*' Latin O-level was a must if you wanted to take up nursing.

But Diane was so determined to be a nurse that she mastered Latin and was accepted at a teaching hospital to train as a nurse. This is all the more surprising as Diane was called 'Dunce' at school as she was so behind. She was made to stay with her nose pressed against a little mark on the blackboard for hours on end for not being able to read. She failed her eleven-plus. And although she failed her entrance exam into Barts she nevertheless managed to get into a top teaching hospital and qualify as a nurse and a midwife.

* * *

My aunt and cousin were dyslexic. My father feels he might be because as he gets older his problem with reading and writing seems to be getting worse. My brother is fine.

Not until my aunt, who is very interested in learning problems, saw the sort of work I was doing at fifteen did anyone realize something was wrong.

264

I was very happy at school until the age of six, and then we went to Sheffield and I remember very well reading classes. I hated them. I can't remember much about my writing but my reading was awful. I would pretend that I was reading but I always turned the pages over too quickly and they used to ask me what was in the book and I would never know.

In Assembly we were meant to be able to read the hymns and I couldn't. I would always be behind everyone else and then I would end up miming.

THE TEACHERS' CRUELTY

My teachers were particularly nasty. One used to ridicule me in class. So from being a very quiet child I became what she would call a chatterbox. I would try my best at spelling tests. She would say it was appalling. I would then play up and be sent out of the class for making a noise.

Or the teacher would take me up to the blackboard, say I was a dunce and draw a little mark on the blackboard and put my nose on it. And I would have to stand there until the next break. I could stand there for half an hour or an hour. The children would laugh at me in the actual class, especially when I started to have to wear glasses.

I failed my eleven-plus but I got into the comprehensive school. I was so unsure of myself and finding life very difficult and nobody knew about dyslexia. I was struggling with my work, my parents couldn't understand as my brother was quite bright. I seemed to be able to say what I wanted quite intelligently but I couldn't write anything down. My spelling was appalling and my maths was just awful. The numbers 3, 5 and 8 were impossible for me.

I went through the adolescent rebellious stage. I did go through an awful time. Although I actually tried very hard to go to all lessons, there were a lot of lessons I was sent out of.

I used to stand outside the headmistress's office – I did a lot of standing in my school life. But I was one of her key sports people and so one of her favourites.

CAREERS ADVICE

I went to see a specialist. I had a day of tests because I didn't know what job I was capable of doing and my parents were very worried about where I was going and what was going to happen to me. I wanted to do art, I wasn't that talented, but it was the only thing I had any interest in. After the report, they came out with three things I could do, a PE teacher, occupational therapy and midwifery.

So I qualified as a nurse and a midwife and then went on to do health visiting. I went into nursing not really knowing how hard the exams would be. I failed my entrance exam into Barts, which was the hospital I wanted to train at, so I had to go somewhere else.

PARENTS' GUILT

My parents feel very guilty now for the things they have said and done with me, and my father is very remorseful now. He never took much time because he was so involved with work himself. My mother just didn't realize and they feel very guilty now, it's very sad to think back on the things they said to me then.

SELF-ESTEEM

I think my self-esteem is very poor. I think the things you go through as a child give you very little confidence, and no matter what people say, 'Of course you can read, of course

266

you can do this', you still feel it. You know underneath that all the anxiety is there.

In a meeting at work I would be given a report, and they would say 'We'll discuss it later', and I would be thinking 'I'm not going to read this in time.' Everybody else would sit through this and speed read, and so the anxieties are always there.

COURSE

I went on a two day course on group work. One of the things you had to do was to write about yourself, things you most liked and things you didn't like. I wrote that I thought I was 'conscientious', but I couldn't spell it, I knew it had a lot of i's and c's in it and it turned out it was completely wrong.

I think good spacing and large writing is far more easy for the brain to absorb. The thing that still really upsets me is looking things up in alphabetical order, like the alphabet. I still don't know the order. To look things up in an A to Z or the telephone directory takes a long time.

MESSAGE

Although we all have different skills, recognize the skills that you do have. Actually acknowledge those skills and see them as much a talent as being an academic.

Because of the knowledge we have of dyslexia in our own family we are particularly concerned about young children whose problems have not yet been identified and who are therefore labelled stupid or lazy while their true ability still goes unrecognized.

Her Majesty Queen Anne Marie of the Hellenes

Henry Winkler

FILM AND TELEVISION STAR
AND PRODUCER

Henry Winkler, the much loved actor who from 1974 to 1984 played The Fonz in *Happy Days* is also a successful film and television producer and director who, despite his dyslexia, runs his own production company in Hollywood. A busy man whose career has won him a series of nominations for Emmy and Golden Globe Awards, he is also known for his personal commitment to helping children. This would certainly seem to be the case when I telephoned him as he spent his only free moments during his break in directing to share his experiences. For his work with children he has been awarded the United Nations Peace Prize and the Norma Zarky Humanitarian Award from Women in Film for his tireless effort and devotion to the 'improvement of the human condition'.

* * *

When I went to school in the fifties, dyslexia was not acknowledged or even known about. So I was the person about whom everyone, including my teachers, said 'Oh, he's so smart but he's just not living up to his potential. He must be lazy, he must be goofing off, he's not doing his homework. If he would just apply himself.' But the truth of the matter is that I could have

269

applied myself from now until doomsday and it wouldn't have made any difference. When we were studying Greek history it was all Greek to me. I underlined everything, I highlighted it all in yellow and blue and pink, I did everything they taught me in study class and it was just not computing in my mind.

It wasn't just maths that was hard, it was reading, comprehension, being able to spell, being able to write without leaving words out of sentences. Now I always have to order double the amount of my own stationery because I have to rip up so many letters.

PARENTS

My parents of course wanted me to do better, never knowing what the problem was. I know it was not their fault, but there was a tremendous amount of conflict in our home. I would be grounded and not able to socialize with my friends for six weeks at a time, because they thought I was goofing off [not trying].

I was under terrible pressure from my parents. To define the word pressure, look in Webster's dictionary and look for Henry's parents under pressure! My parents are European so I would write a letter home and my father would send it back corrected. One day my American history teacher said 'Winkler, if you ever get out of high school you're going to do all right.'

BEING THE CLOWN

I was teased at school so what I did was I became the 'class clown'. I compensated for everything by being the clown. I was good in the plays, I won the dance contest. But then I learnt that there is more than one way to skin a cat. So my thinking process became very highly tuned. I was then able to reason things out and that combined with my intuitive skills got me through.

GRADUATING

I was not able to graduate from High School with the rest of my class because I was still taking geometry. Geometry is a course that is taken in the 10th grade in the second year of high school, and I was still taking the same course in the fourth year at high school when I took the exams to get into college. You get 200 points right off the bat for spelling your name correctly. I got 159 points over my name. I was in the lowest three percentile in math in America!

EXAMS

The emotional damage done during day-school years was so severe that I kept asking myself how could I be so stupid. I'm being told I'm not stupid and yet the results say that I don't know what I'm talking about. I have studied for this exam, how could I not know this stuff? You get so frustrated, it makes you nuts.

UNIVERSITY

I was finally accepted at a university in Boston, Massachusetts, called Emerson College and I had four wonderful years there. In my second year at university something clicked in and I started to be able to use the logic in my intuitive self to do well. And then I was able to go on to Yale University and get a Masters degree in theatre. That helped a little bit with my self-esteem.

YALE

When I got into Yale, which is one of the finest universities in America, I threw open the windows, I yelled to the streets of Boston that I had got into Yale, I rushed out of the house to tell my friends that I had been accepted and locked myself out – it cost me $28 to get back in my own flat.

JOB

After three years at Yale University studying history, drama, theatre studies, movement and voice, I was one of three students out of twenty-five to be asked into the professional repertory company. So from 1967 to 1971 I did about seventy plays, from one act plays to full length drama.

STUDYING LINES

Learning lines for a series or those plays was not a problem. The concentration I needed when I was younger and did Peer Gynt, which was very difficult for me, was tremendous as I had to read and keep track of all those incredible monologues. But if it's important enough to you, you concentrate. Also what happened was another system of compensation came up and I was able to instantly memorize. I developed a photographic memory, out of necessity.

RUNNING A BUSINESS AND DIRECTING

Now I am running my own company. First of all you hire great people, who do their work very well. Secondly all the

272

people know to come and tell me only what's important. I would assume other people do that. But the volume of work! I mean I have so many scripts that I have to read now that I direct. But you know I think that my dyslexia has helped me to be a better director, because it forced me to solve problems and a director's job ultimately is to solve 200 problems a minute. So the process to me then is like a duck taking to water. But the best short cut is to hire great people.

COMMUNICATING

I am distraught at the fact that I can't spell. Sometimes when I'm writing something, I would much prefer to talk to somebody either in person or on the phone because verbally I'm more adroit. If I don't have somebody around who can spell for me or there is no dictionary around or whatever, I can never write what I want to say, it's very irritating.

My daughter is also dyslexic but we discovered when she was very young and she's now in the third grade and has made incredible strides. My stepson, too, is dyslexic and we discovered that in the third grade and he is now going to university and he's an A student.

THE POSITIVE SIDE OF BEING DYSLEXIC

I think being dyslexic has been an advantage in my life. I look at it in the most positive way it has forced me to use other parts of myself that otherwise may have lain dormant. I'm humbled by my dyslexia. Sometimes I do make the wrong choice, but I am proud of my intuitive skills.

But I never want what happened to me to happen to anyone else. I really believe that letting people know about dyslexia does help. It is very important. Dyslexics are very intelligent. Dyslexia has nothing to do with intelligence.

Cher has dyslexia, Tom Cruise has dyslexia, Nelson Rocke-feller had dyslexia. Einstein was terrible at math.

It doesn't mean anything! All it means is that you've got to find another way to solve a problem.

SELF-ESTEEM

Sometimes my self-esteem is down around my ankles! It has taken me since high school, and I'm now forty-four years old, to get it up at least to my sternum.

MESSAGE

If you will it, it will not be just a dream. There is more than one way to get where you want to go. And it doesn't always have to be the conventional way. But you must prepare yourself in the best way you can. You must focus! You must train yourself in those things that work for you. Being dyslexic does not mean in any way, shape or form that you are stupid or that you are not intelligent. It just means that parts of your brain are not working and one out of five people have got a similar problem.

Interior Designer

JANE

**Running your own interior design business requires organi-
zational skills which are often very difficult for a dyslexic.
Anyone who has redecorated a house knows that organizing
painters, stencillers, upholsterers, carpet layers and curtain
makers can be exasperating. It is all too easy to misspell or
misread material names or (worse) mismeasure and land up
with a large headscarf hanging over your window instead of
a curtain. Yet, despite Jane's dyslexia she has run her own
interior design business for seven years and successfully solved
her clients' problems.**

**Jane is an example of how once dyslexics have found the job
they really want to do they will cope with their difficulty and
do it. Yet school was traumatic for Jane and she spent hours
writing out spelling mistakes as a punishment and suffering the
cruelty of her English teacher.**

* * *

I started school at five, which was a nightmare. I had a
twin brother and it was patently obvious that he could do
things that I just couldn't do. We would sit in a row to recite
the alphabet and I could go 'A, B, C, . . .' and then nothing.

275

Just panic. I remember feeling panic as it was approaching my turn to recite and I just couldn't do it at all.

Then I changed to another primary school after a term, where there wasn't any pressure put on me. We just did exactly whatever we fancied, really, which I think just put off the evil hour and didn't actually solve any problems. They weren't actually trying to teach me how to read or how to decipher books. I just couldn't do it so I concentrated on other things which I found I could understand like painting, drawing, practical things.

I was very interested in science and I was very good at maths. I could do maths with no trouble at all.

TEACHERS COULDN'T HELP

I went to secondary school after I had failed my eleven-plus and was sent to a large comprehensive school. I had gone from a tiny primary school which must have had seventy or eighty children, to a vast comprehensive school. I was just completely lost. We were streamed according to our ability to do English, which was hopeless, so I was in the bottom set, the dregs, and you really felt that all the teachers just looked on our class as being no hopers. There was nothing that they could do for us. Our class used to reduce two teachers in particular to tears in half an hour, just being totally objectionable and disruptive. There was no remedial teaching, there was nothing. We just moved from one class to the next class and we just ran riot really.

NEW SCHOOL

I was then sent to a small convent school which was kinder. My first English teacher was kind. I don't think she understood at all but she didn't victimize you at all. But I then moved on to another teacher because I moved up the school. I got a horrific teacher who would just hand back my work and say 'In the first

276

five lines you had twenty spelling mistakes, go away and write out each spelling mistake twenty times. I will not mark work like that.' And that went on for about a year.

Eventually it was O-levels but I was not being put in for them and my parents said 'Jane is just as clever as Magnus.' But the school wouldn't put me in, so that was fairly nightmarish.

PARENTS' ATTITUDE

In the end there was a massive row and my parents actually noticed what was going on in school. I think they had looked at the school and home as being quite separate. They didn't ask how I had got on at school and ask what the lessons were like.

My father is a great reader, he loves playing with words and I think he was just so frustrated that I didn't, could not, would not – he would just shout at me 'Why don't you understand, it's so simple, it's perfectly clear.' I couldn't do it. I just couldn't, I couldn't understand it, I couldn't see the logic to it at all. I would say again and again 'But why or how?' and he would just shout at me. So I just stopped asking him. I would rather go and ask my brothers – they could spell and they would just do it for me.

My mother, I think because she was a teacher, didn't want to appear to be interfering, which was a bit stupid, I think. But at O-levels they realized that I wasn't doing the same as my brother and that was the point at which they suddenly said to me, 'But, Jane, why haven't you said?' – but, they didn't notice that I was thoroughly unhappy at school, they had totally ignored that for the last five years. I suppose it was partly because when I got home from school I just got on with something that I would rather do.

EFFECT OF CRUEL TEACHER

I used to be quite angry, I think, really frustrated. I suppose it

277

was because there were lots of things that I was interested in, but I had to spend so much time trying to write essays which were just a nightmare and which still tie me in a knot. I think I blame that on my horrific English teacher, she was definitely a spanner in the works. Because up until then I would write things perfectly happily. I may not have been right. It may not have made any sense to anybody else, but at least I would write it. It made sense to me. It was really after her that I didn't want to pick up a pen.

EXAMS

I did take O-levels and I passed geography, biology, art and I got U for religious instruction from my convent school which must have got thoroughly up their noses, I think! I just didn't agree and I was just bloody minded. I got extended time for the exams.

I WAS NEVER REALLY TOLD I WAS DYSLEXIC

When I was at the comprehensive at eleven, and was streamed in the lower stream, I did lots of tests. I suppose at that stage they had decided 'Jane is dyslexic.' But it was never really discussed or made an issue of. I was never told 'You're dys-lexic.'

I had private coaching for a while when I was twelve when I moved from the comprehensive to the convent. I used to come home and get down to the nitty gritty of reading and remembering, learning ways of remembering. How to get Bs and Ds and things the right way round, and all those sort of things.

278

ENCOURAGEMENT

The only teacher in my whole school life who helped me was my geography teacher. I don't think she could understand why I couldn't spell, I think she was as frustrated as everybody else, but she could see that I was clever. I could do a multiple choice and get seventy per cent or whatever. She would say 'You can do it. You are doing better than half the people in the class. Just concentrate on what you can do.' She actually encouraged me just to stick at what I could do and apply that throughout everything. If there was something I was interested in and could do, just hang on in there.

UNIVERSITY IN AMERICA

From doing my O-levels, I actually went and did A-levels. I did art and biology, and I got those. I only just got the biology. Then I went to Farnham Art College and did a foundation course and then I felt at the end of that, 'What on earth am I going to do?' and got a chance to go to the States. The Dean of Syracuse University was over and he was looking at portfolios and he offered me a place over there on the strength of my drawings. No writing, just my drawing! So I went out there for a year and did fine art and ceramics.

I thought, 'How refreshing, how encouraging', because it was so different from the education system over here, where you have to do this, you have to do that. You've got to have such and such, so many O-levels, before you can do anything.

Whereas I would go in with an idea about ceramics and say, 'I've got this idea' and they'd say, 'That sounds very interesting, but I don't actually know how you would go about doing that, but so and so knows something similar.' So off I would go, and see them. It was just so encouraging that I came back and felt I could really do whatever I liked

279

if I just set my mind to it and look for the people who will help.

WORK

Now I run my own business. My turnover is good and I am quite happy with it. I go into people's homes who want to rethink the decor. I will go and choose the materials, have the curtains made up, have sofas covered, drag the walls, stencils – I do all those sort of things. I use my practical talents which I have got. My self-esteem has risen, I suppose.

Dyslexia has affected my work because I still hate writing. I send out the bills, I can manage that. But I hate writing estimates, I absolutely hate them and they do become a nightmare. Now at last I have actually worked out a system of how to do it on a computer.

MESSAGE

Don't let nasty people get at you. Just be determined. I think I am lucky that I am pretty big headed and I am not going to be put down. I think partly because I have two brothers and I was not going to be pushed out of anything. I could see that I was just as clever as they were.

I don't think anyone can understand the fear that reading aloud imparts in people.

Beryl Reid
Actress

Physiotherapist

'MARIE-ANNE'

In what little spare time I have I am a keen water skier, but needless to say I am at my age a little out of shape for this strenuous sport and so on my infrequent trips to ski it occasionally results in my pulling a muscle or whatever. In one way this has been rather fortunate, as I discovered one of the physiotherapists who works at the Physiotherapy Centre is dyslexic. I eventually persuaded her to talk to me; she agreed as long as she remained anonymous.

'Marie-Anne' is adopted and so has no idea if anyone else in her family is dyslexic. She was considered bright at school but had problems reading and writing. Her essays didn't make sense. Things got worse and Marie-Anne was told she had little hope of getting an O-level English. Much to the surprise of the teachers she achieved six O-levels, including English. She then trained as a physiotherapist and later qualified as a Master of Science. Marie-Anne now teaches students and is involved in research work.

*   *   *

I think my first recollection of things being odd was when I was about seven. I had written what I thought was a brilliant essay and the teacher actually called my parents to the school and said 'I'll let Marie-Anne read this essay to you.' My mother is in fact a teacher and she said 'For a seven year old I think that is very good' and the teacher said 'Now I'll read it to you,' and in fact it was rubbish.

What I had done was I had written words backwards, put all sorts of vowels in the wrong places to the point at which I had even left things out but I knew where they were supposed to go so I could read it but nobody else could.

The one thing I could do was maths and that just stood out all the way along the line. If people put algebra on the board or mathematical problems I could always do them, and yet with English it was just absolutely hopeless.

I just ticked along, nobody ever said anything to me and I just carried on assuming that was just normal and I was just bad at English.

The one thing that stood out was the fact that I would go anywhere and do anything except read aloud. I would give any excuse under the sun to get out of that one thing. I knew that I was doing it wrong. I go word by word so it sounds like a five year old even if I get the words right, and I can see the audience yawning. When it comes to reading things in church or prayers or anything, I just avoid it like the plague.

DISCOVERING DYSLEXIA

I passed my O-levels. I don't think it ever really dawned on me that there was anything wrong at all, *it was just that it was difficult*.

Surprisingly enough the first time anybody noticed that I was dyslexic was after an interview on the radio many years ago when I was eighteen. My mother who is a teacher listened to it and suddenly recognized that that was what I had been doing all these years. She rang me up when I was at college and at almost the same time I had an essay handed back, I hadn't been there long, and the lecturer had said she thought

I was dyslexic. So it came at me literally in the space of a week.

PHYSIOTHERAPY

I wanted to do medicine and in fact I had angled my way towards physics and chemistry. But it didn't really work. Whether that was because of the reading I don't know. I failed to get in so that's why I ended up in physiotherapy.

After college I went to work in a private practice for a doctor. I worked there for a long time and became interested in research. I decided to apply to do an M.Sc., never thinking I would be able to do it. I think part of it was I had no confidence in my ability to do it.

I had no idea that I was able to achieve what I could achieve. Prior to that, if somebody had said to me 'You'll be doing a Masters,' I just would not have believed them. And it was through the support of a doctor I was working with that I started to stop thinking of myself as being thick and stupid.

DOCTORATE

I am now studying for a doctorate, which is a thesis that you write based on your research. I am doing my doctorate part-time because I am a full-time physiotherapy teacher.

I think because I am dyslexic I am probably more receptive to verbal information. When people speak I probably pick things up more easily, whereas colleagues who have gone through Oxford or whatever and who are very academic, would probably miss things.

MESSAGE

If you've got the mental ability to do something, there's nothing to stop you doing it. *It's finding a way of doing it that's the biggest hurdle.*

Recognizing the problem as dyslexia is half the battle, the other half is making the public aware so the problem can be solved.

Whoopi Goldberg
Actress

Greg Louganis

OLYMPIC GOLD MEDALLIST – DIVER

To give an idea of how many hours and days were devoted to contacting dyslexics for this book, I will tell you how I tried to track down Greg Louganis.

We were in Seoul for the 1988 Olympics, and I had been told by the American head of the Olympics Swimming Committee that as Greg Louganis is dyslexic he would introduce me to him during the lunch break the following day. But due to a series of mishaps such as the Korean officials not allowing me into the competitors' area although I had a pass, the introduction never took place. I spent many hours watching Greg Louganis dive, although I didn't see the notorious dive when he hit and cut his head open on the diving board and could have been killed.

Hours later when I finally managed to get into the competitors' area Mr Hamlick who was to introduce us had gone, and although I stood next to Greg Louganis for some time during the lunch break, I was too polite or respectful of his need for privacy to say 'Hello'. I felt that chattering about *dyslexia* just before the Olympic finals was not the best way to get into his good books. That afternoon he won his fourth Olympic Gold, which was wonderful. But I still had not managed to talk to him. So it was arranged with his coach that I would call him at his hotel that night.

When I called, his manager made it clear that (even if I did know the head of the USA Olympic Swimming Committee) it wasn't possible to talk, so 'Please write'.

I kicked myself for not making use of the earlier opportunities to speak to him. Despite being next to him all that time, all I could do now was write. Three months had passed and my letters had gone unanswered. There were only another five months before the book had to be finished and there were another forty people to see. Days being taken up with finding ways to contact my 'Stars' were becoming all too frequent.

Eventually I was given Greg Louganis' home telephone number, in California, although I had heard that even Greg's mother could not get to speak to him. Every time I called, his manager always had a reason why I could not speak to Greg. In the end, he wished me well and said words to the effect: 'Greg is concerned for all dyslexics and Goodbye.'

So, I called his coach Ron O'Brien in Florida, who, when I told him my difficulties, suggested I try another number, adding 'Good luck!' I tried with no luck!

By now I was desperate, not for myself but for the dyslexics who would be encouraged by Greg's story. So I sent more letters to his manager, his publicity representatives, his agent and of course to Greg. A polite bombardment of letters and telephone calls across the Atlantic. But no answer.

Finally with the help of Hamilton Bland, Neil Allen, Lavinia Scott Elliot, Susan Schulman, *Sports Illustrated for kids* and Pat Jordan of *Gentleman's Quarterly*, I have put together Greg's own story myself.

* * *

Greg Louganis, greatest diver in the history of swimming, won a silver medal at the 1976 Olympics at the age of sixteen. He then won two Gold Medals in the 1984 Olympics and two more in the 1988 Olympics. Not to mention nine world championship titles and forty-three United States titles.

He won the James E. Sullivan Award for the best Amateur Athlete in the World in 1987.

288

In 1960 Greg was adopted by a Greek American and his wife, Peter and Frances Louganis in San Diego, when he was nine months old. He was the son of fifteen year old college students, an English-Welsh-Irish mother and a Samoan father.

* * *

'I started dance and gymnastics at eighteen months old. By six I was tap dancing. When I was nine I was doing tumbling moves off the diving board. My mother said I should learn to dive right, so I began taking lessons which was fine, but I was ashamed of my dancing. It was a sissy sport.

'I was skinny and stuttered. I guess I'm still shy. I was put into speech therapy, because I stuttered so badly. But getting over it was difficult. When Mom asked what I wanted to eat, my sister would answer for me. Despina only wanted to help. I could visualize the word but I couldn't get it out so Despina would say "Greg wants potato chips, Ma."

'At school when I read, I saw the letters in the wrong order, to me the word WAS looked like SAW, and ITS looked like SIT. I would work hard in the English class and still get a C or D. I excelled in diving, though, so I thought that was more important. But now I think education is more important than diving!

'Because I couldn't read, the kids called me stupid and retarded. But, in college I realized that I'm dyslexic and not retarded. That made me feel good. The kids teased me and called me nigger because my skin is tanned.'

TEACHER'S PET

In order to compensate at school Greg became the willing horse and offered to clean the blackboard, empty the waste paper basket, close the curtains, do anything that would ensure that he would not be asked to read aloud, and read 'Dog was a god', instead of 'God saw a dog.' This willingness in class resulted in his classmates calling him 'teacher's pet', as well as 'nigger' and 'retarded'. He was regularly beaten up by the other boys, so when he arrived home with yet more bruises, he used to tell his mother he had fallen.

TRICKS TO AVOID BULLYING

By the time he was a teenager he thought of himself as a 'freak' and a 'wimp'. His dyslexia still had not been diagnosed and he was still being badly bullied. He had no choice but to outsmart the bullies by ingratiating himself. He said 'I became a trained seal for them.' He told them to bet their lunch money with other boys as to whether or not he could do a particularly difficult backward flip. When he had successfully performed the flip, he and the bullies split the winnings. In order to survive he kept in with tough teenagers and smoked and pilfered beer and wine with them.

'I didn't want to be different, I wanted to be like everyone else. So I learned the advantage of role playing. I kept all my lives separate. I kept my diving and my dance classes separate from my drinking friends, and my drinking friends from my dance and diving friends. It was bizarre really.'

DRINKING

But eventually he was so unhappy when he was at junior high school that he says, 'I kept a bottle in my locker. I was drinking before lunch.'

When he was thirteen, he found himself in juvenile hall. That night he had been in a fistfight with his father. Afterwards he went to his room and lay down. When he woke, two policemen were standing over his bed. They handcuffed him and took him away. The counsellor said that he was going through life with the attitude that if his natural parents didn't love him, no one could. Then Greg became aware of children whose parents really did not love them and he began to realize how lucky he was. After that, he became closer to his mother.

DIVING

Fortunately, despite these problems at home and at school, Greg was still diving in his pool in the back yard and competing. 'I'm a little wary of heights, but I don't fear heights as long as there is water underneath the board, then I'm OK!'

The first time the Korean Olympic diver, Dr Sammy Lee, saw Greg Louganis dive he was ten years old and Dr Lee said, 'There's the greatest diver in history if he gets the right coach.'

Then a few years later, when one of Dr Sammy Lee's divers had beaten Greg in a competition, Greg's father talked to Sammy Lee and the next week Sammy Lee started coaching Greg.

UNIVERSITY

Despite Greg's dyslexia, he went to the University of Miami and in 1984 he says 'I majored in theatre. I grew up there, and I kept my diving friends separate from my theatre friends.' After college, at twenty-three, he gave up drinking.

He is the only diver to have received perfect scores of ten across the board from seven judges on a single dive. But when on the rare occasion he dived less than perfectly he laughed good naturedly.

'I find things humorous. I am up there and blow a few dives, I can't afford to do that, but I did it. When people say I'm unbeatable, I disagree. I've always been beatable. I never know how I'm going to dive? It's fun because I never know until it's over.'

291

THE FUTURE

'I've been diving now for eighteen years. It's time to move on. I'm looking forward to pursuing a career as an actor. Film, TV, theatre, I'd like to try it all. I'm realistic about dancing. I'm starting up a little late for a career in that. That's a physical obsession. I'm going to leave one physical obsession and I don't want another one. Although acting is an obsession, I've been studying it for nine years, it's more emotional and intellectual.

'After I hit my head in the 1988 Olympics I didn't sleep all night I was terrified I would hit my head again.'

But he didn't and won his fourth Olympic Gold Medal.

Hands up – he's got a gnu.

Mural and Trompe-l'œil Painter

COLIN

Many of the people who are in this book wrote to me after hearing on BBC Radio's *Start the Week* that I was compiling a book to encourage dyslexic teenagers.

It was very fortunate that Colin, a much in demand mural painter, wrote to me, as not only did he give an interview for the book, but also solved the problem of an ugly blank wall at the top of my stairs as Colin painted a trompe-l'œil of an open door going into an imaginary room for us. This humorous painting makes people smile when they see it and has become the talking point of the house. Once again it shows that dyslexics have a strong visual sense.

* * *

I went to an ordinary primary school where they had remedial classes for backward children. They thought I was slightly backward, so I knew something was wrong, but there was no name for it then.

At school, when it came to the eleven-plus some of the staff thought I had cheated in the maths exam because the English was so dreadful and the maths so good. They couldn't understand that there was a child that more or less came top of the maths group and bottom of the English written work.

293

ASSUMED STUPID

Just trying to get anything down on paper was difficult, writing was just impossible and I suppose reading as well. Reading was very slow. At the age of twelve, I was told that I had the reading age of a five year old. I think the worst thing about it was that the teachers never understood. They seemed to assume that I was totally stupid.

READING ALOUD

I remember one embarrassing situation in the class when I was about twelve or thirteen. Each child was asked to stand and read a few paragraphs. I was trapped in that class and I was absolutely terrified. My stomach turned over because I just could not face standing up and reading aloud. So I had to make an excuse to go to the loo and I stayed in the loo long enough for them to have passed me by. Then I went back and just hoped they weren't going to come back to me. Again, even then I had this way of getting by somehow, by talking a lot.

It was very frustrating with subjects like history and geography which obviously I was very interested in. At the end of each lesson you were asked to write an essay about this or that. Homework was just torture.

The other children in the class were nice to me, but the worst memory of that period of my life was feeling inferior.

I went to the secondary modern school. That was strange because I went into the lowest form in the first year, and as I went up the years to the fourth form I went across the stream so by the time I got to the fourth year I was in the fourth year A stream instead of the B stream. Obviously my ability to write and read had improved.

I think the school was just confronted by this person that they realized was fairly bright. But nobody really took the time to say, 'Your written work is just peculiar.'

I used to entertain the other prefects in the prefects' room doing impressions – Frankie Howerd and various comedians, *Round the Horn*, I think I could do every character from *Round the Horn*, even to the extent when one day, the Deputy Head came in and he just hit the roof. He knew it was me because I was standing on the table using it as a stage and there were fits of laughter all round. He closed down the prefects' room – no more prefects' room, so we had to hang around the corridors.

The English teacher wrote on my last report something to the effect that he hoped to see me on the stage, because he knew that I used to do take-offs. I used to take-off the staff, and I think he overheard one day when some other student said to listen to Colin doing Miss So-and-so down in the hall . . . and I think I made him laugh. I never pursued a stage career because I thought, well, I can't read and write, and you have to be able to read and write.

LACK OF PARENTAL SUPPORT

I was a really nasty little goody, goody child. Whereas the others could muck about and still get away with it, I couldn't handle the fact that if I mucked about I did bad work. So I tried hard, I tried and tried, until my mother despaired when I tried to do homework and I finished up in tears, because I couldn't really do it efficiently and I would worry so much about it so I would get terribly het up. Not that my mother was very aware of anything, quite frankly, and my father wasn't around from the age of three.

When I did well in the maths, my mother actually said, 'I don't believe it.' I was obviously so hurt by that that it has remained in my mind. I don't think she actually believed that I could come top in anything and I think it was partly because she never really encouraged us in anything. She tried her best in her own way but my father was even worse. We had absolutely no encouragement from him whatsoever. My mother wasn't very academic, she didn't understand.

WINNING PRIZE AND BUYING BOOKS

Because I am thirty-nine now, we are talking about a time when employment was very easy to find, and at school I showed great ability at metal work. I was making things at the age of twelve and they just couldn't believe it – a genius. I couldn't describe it in words but I could make it, so it was naturally assumed that I would go straight into engineering, which I did when I left school. I think that was an escape route because I knew I could do it.

But when I won the first prize for metal work, what did I do? I went out and bought three poetry books, much to the annoyance of the metal work teacher. He thought I should buy a Morris Minor or something. He wasn't very amused by that. But I genuinely wanted those books. I bought three very slim volumes of poetry. I don't know whether I just tried to read them but I think I actually did read them – in fact reading wasn't such a problem, it's the recall, so I used to read.

EXAMS

Obviously when I left school I wasn't qualified to go to art school because even then you needed three O-levels, and I think I got two, one for technical drawing and one for metal work.

I just went to pieces in examinations. I could not get anything down. But I think it was because my recall was so hampered by the fear and stress of doing exams. So even if I did know anything I wouldn't be able to get it down.

I was just terrified and I would physically go to pieces –
my stomach would churn, I would feel nauseous, I would feel
sick. Now, as I have got older, I can write and read perfectly
well, but then certainly if I was put on the spot, especially in
an examination, any minimal skills that I did have would go
out of the window.

APPRENTICESHIP

However I was offered three or four apprenticeships, which
was quite remarkable.

I took one as a design draughtsman and I stuck that for
about two years, from sixteen to eighteen years. But the story
was very familiar, I didn't really spend much time doing the
work. I had a drawing table with drawers in it and I used to
have all these art books – Van Gogh, Gauguin, and spent my
time looking at all the paintings. Then my mother, in fact,
found an advert in the local paper for evening classes by a
guy and his wife who had started up a private art school in
Cheltenham. I went along, and to cut a long story short, he
accepted me.

Then I applied to Gloucestershire College of Art but they
wouldn't give me a place because they thought it was certainly against their regulations because I hadn't got the academic
qualifications.

ART SCHOOL

Then I moved to London and took a job in a pub, part-time,
and applied to the City and Guilds School of Art in Kennington.
Kennington is partly local authority and partly privately run.
They accepted me on my portfolio of work.

But I didn't have a grant, so I worked part-time. I was
a singing waiter, I was a barman. The singing waiter was in

297

the Tottenham Court Road, really cockney, and we did more singing than waiting and Equity moved in and we were thrown out so that was the end of that.

Then I worked in the film industry for a few years doing modelling, doing the sculpture bits for the sets and that sort of thing.

Then I found that you could see your work thrown away in the skip because the script had changed, and my ego couldn't cope with that. So I gave that up because in a way I would have wanted to be the director. I started up my own business doing trompe-l'œil paintings.

In recent years I write letters for my work and I also write to the MPs all the time, one lot was about sex education in schools and all sorts of other things like poll tax. I have had letters read on the radio and I had one letter published in a magazine last month. My letters are very short and very brief and I think that is why they are used! Years ago, I wouldn't have dreamt of writing to anybody, I was too ashamed, but I don't care now, I just write what I think.

If you are dyslexic, I believe, you are born with a wonderful advantage. Because once dyslexics have found what they want to do in life, they'll usually have an extra quota of determination and energy to enable them to do it. They will be more determined to succeed. I think for me it was a plus – otherwise I may not have been an actress or written six books. It has made me determined not to be at the bottom of the pile. *Hard work sometimes counts for more than qualifications.*

Susan Hampshire
Actress

Opera Singer and Singing Coach

IAN

I met Ian Adam when I was sent to him for singing lessons before I started rehearsals for *A Little Night Music* at Chichester. At my first lesson, in order to put me at my ease, Ian told me that he was also dyslexic. So not only was he a great singer and great vocal tutor, but also a great dyslexic.

Ian prepares great singers, and also 'non-singers' for their roles in musicals and operas. Michael Crawford, Jonathan Price, Roger Moore, Terence Stamp, Siân Phillips, Tom Conti, Michael Ball, Felicity Kendal, Barbara Dickson, Elaine Paige, Gemma Craven, Liz Robertson and Sarah Brightman are just a few of his 'students'.

'My father was very musical,' says Ian, 'he played the violin, and my mother had a pretty voice. My grandmother also had a very pretty voice. As my father collected records, I listened to all the great singers, the Carusos and the Giglis, and the Nellie Melbas. So I lived in that atmosphere and it was no problem actually to sing.'

Ian Adam was a child prodigy and at eight he had already made his debut in Scotland singing Mozart's *Exultate Jubilate*.

From then on he sang in concerts and oratorios. He worked with wonderful people like Henri Bataille in Munich and Ivor Walters in London, and with Maggie Teyte, who was a great interpretive artist.

After studying in London, Paris and Munich, his career opened out into international opera, recital tours and major festival performances. He sang with many of the leading orchestras and conductors, including Sir Malcolm Sargent, Sir Adrian Boult, Benjamin Britten and Leonard Bernstein.

Ian is now much in demand for his direction and master classes both in Britain and abroad, and is frequently required by the National Theatre, Really Useful Company and Royal Shakespeare Company, and has just presented a major television series about his work. Despite being put down by teachers as a child, Ian feels his dyslexia has helped his work.

* * *

Even when I was very small I was one of those rather terrible, advanced children that spoke too soon and did all sorts of things it seems too soon. I even arrived into this world too soon. I was about a month premature and I was only about two and a half pounds in weight – just like a bag of sugar. My father was rather of the opinion that I had to sleep in a little drawer by the side of the bed.

It was interesting because my mother became sick and very ill when I was born. They were much more concerned to save my mother than they were to save me because I was so small and like a little rat and I had everything possible wrong with me. I arrived with measles and I was ruptured under the arms and in the groins and everywhere.

Then when it got to the point of taking me out in the pram my father used to walk a bit behind, because he used to be ashamed what people would say about the new baby. He was embarrassed about it. That's how life began so perhaps I am very lucky not to be blind or all the things I could have been.

301

MOTHER'S LOVE

It was incredible love on my mother's part. She wanted me to live so she looked after me day and night and I grew rather healthy and rather sweet, and was apparently one of the most gentle dear little creatures that's ever been. And so a great deal of love was lavished upon me and I spoke very early. I sang when I was about two and a half. I could hold a melody and remember the words.

My mother thought it would be a good thing if she taught me to read before I went to school. She was the one who noticed I would reverse words. I would jumble them around. And I suppose it was a bit of a worry but people didn't really know much about such a word as dyslexia. It was just that you had a problem and I suppose it must have been a fearful thing.

They knew I wasn't a slow learner because I had learnt these songs from my mother singing and of course I had this phenomenal way of picking up a tune and remembering the words elsewhere.

But when my mother taught me to read I would get the words all upside down. She used to say I was very quick at learning if somebody *says* it to me. So my mother had taught me by speaking rather than by looking at the page. I had that extraordinary ability to photograph a page. It's only when I am under stress or very tired, or very nervous, that I will jumble it all up and it will be absolutely like an upside-down cake when I am in one of those conditions. They don't happen often but when they do happen most of the people whom I love and work with, feed me the word to put me back on the right road without even acknowledging that I have a problem.

SPELLING

It always affects my spelling. I still can't spell. I have a terrible problem spelling. But again I have a photographic mind so if I see the word I can remember it. But if it's a word like kaleidoscope or something that I'm not familiar with, I have a terrible problem spelling it. If it's a word I have seen a lot I will remember it totally. People always laugh. I do actually take a great deal of bother in writing a letter to get the spelling right.

CRUEL TEACHERS

My teachers were appallingly unkind about my spelling. They would write lengthy comments against what I had written. I was very good at essays because I had a feeling for writing. They would say 'The line is very flowery but please learn to spell it. It's a good idea but when you can put it together and spell it properly, then maybe it will be better' – things like that.

OVERCOMING SPELLING

Again I had a way of learning spelling. I started at the beginning of the dictionary and tried to learn thirty words every day. Of course some of them were very difficult.

That's how I learnt French as well, and it stands me in good stead today.

Teachers at school were very tough about my singing career. They would say 'This boy sings so well, it's a pity he can't learn.' I would have been off singing in something the night before which everyone was awfully pleased I was doing, except perhaps the French mistress the next day as I hadn't done my memory trick of learning the thing by heart which of course I always had to do.

I wasn't naughty or deceptive. I just got very grand for a period and awfully spoilt. I thought I was really the cat's whiskers because I could do so many things that other people couldn't do.

MUSIC

When I was at school all my music teachers thought that I had an amazingly unusual voice. In the north of Scotland on Sundays when people have been to church and afterwards lunch, you then often had a singsong and my mother would sing and somebody would play the piano. My aunt played the piano quite brilliantly, so we would have that kind of atmosphere. So it was never a problem for me to perform music.

CHILD PRODIGY

Then my music teacher at school who had been a choral master at York Minster picked up on my talent and because of him perhaps, I became a child prodigy singer. He must have known I was dyslexic as well, because sometimes I would jumble up words in the middle of a song, get them all backwards or round about, or sing the word before it, if it was an easier word. People say, 'Do you get the word backwards?' Sometimes one *does* get the word backwards, but sometimes one gets the next word right and the word half right and the next one mixed up with it. It's not a set pattern.

LEARNING TO READ MUSIC

My master of music at school taught me to sight read. He said it's very simple – when you try to read the hymns, they are sometimes very difficult because of their range and the melody. But he taught me through *intervals* – that's looking at it in a different way. It's not looking in an elongated way at the notes, but in steps. So in a funny way, vertically it's

304

not so bad as it is horizontally. That's how he taught me to read the music. He'd say 'Take a simple hymn – you know the tune already, now that's a fourth and that's a third, and that one's the same, that's a semitone. Practise those like "Doh re mi fa so la ti doh." ' I never actually did tonic solfa. I think he knew that would be really difficult for me. But he said 'Look, that's the interval – that's easy' – so that's how I learnt to read music.

It's the same pattern playing the piano with both hands, but I spent a long time practising. I used to go home with him and his wife, and they took me to concerts and interested me in all sorts of avant-garde music and the modern music of the period.

When I was singing professionally it was fine because I have got a tremendous memory. I knew something like 240 songs from memory and I rarely forget them today.

AUDITION

The first audition that I went to do in a theatre for a speaking part was a terrifying experience, because I thought they're going to give me a piece of script to read and I am going to come unstuck and they are going to think this is an absolute imbecile that has arrived. It was pretty frightening. But I seemed to cope with it rather well, and I actually got the job.

This was the audition for the second tour of *My Fair Lady* and I thought I would like to sing the part of Freddie. I didn't even tell my agent I was going. I was a very callow youth and I arrived to do my audition and a voice said from the stalls afterwards 'That was really great, that's the nicest singing I have heard all day, what's your name again? Would you like to take a little piece of the script and read it to us?' I thought 'My God, this is where it's going to fall apart,' and because he gave me a minute, I could remember it, and then I amazed him by just doing it from memory and he said 'Have you seen this before? Do you know this scene?' And I said 'No, I haven't seen it before.' And he came down and shook hands and said

'You've got the job of Freddie.' Alas, in the end I couldn't do it.

TEACHING

In Scandinavia they call me the wizard of song which is very commendable and very nice, but I think when teaching the first thing you've got to do is watch and listen, and try to become part of a person's development. You have got to find the way that is easy and natural for that person to develop their understanding and technique. You can't say 'You've got to do it this way.'

I do try and find it through love, but of course I can be tough if somebody is not bothering and not learning and not making progress as they should. It's their life but on the other hand I have enormous patience and hope to see, and love to see, what that person can attain.

HOW DYSLEXIA HAS HELPED TEACHING

I was singing with Scottish Opera and I was doing lots of concerts around the country. I was also teaching. It always seemed when I was working that people would ask me to teach them because I had the patience and I would work it out for them. Maybe it's the dyslexic thing because you have to take a thing apart to put it together. Maybe it's a great deal to do with it. Maybe it's a gift, a hidden gift upside down. I believe very much in a healing power of love, that if you are willing to love and understand enough there is so much added to what you are doing. It's never done by shouting and screaming. I don't think that produces the best results. When I was singing in opera or singing in a concert or wherever it was, even when I went to work with Sona Ardontz who worked for a time with Montserrat Caballé as a historian, she said 'I don't know how you can sing for five hours. You are never tired. You have such an ability to do this, I would like to come and study singing with you.'

So it's not anything to do with how clever you are, it's to do with opening a door for someone. It's a dual relationship, it's a love affair that you have with people you work with. You have a compassion for one another, they know you want them to be good. They know that you want the best for them. But if someone is throwing away their gift, it is your duty to call them to task and be compassionate enough to have them back when things may not be going well!

SELF-ESTEEM

Maybe you don't come over as bright to people sometimes when you are making *faux pas* and mistakes. I think dyslexia has helped me in my life, because I remember names, for instance when I'm abroad and I have to speak to people. They are always utterly amazed that after the first day I can remember every single person's name. I remember fifty people in a class. I think that's to do with dyslexia and also because I want to remember that person's name.

I hate those people who say 'You in the green frock, you in the red shirt, you in blue trousers . . .' – the type of director who doesn't bother to make a person feel like a person. I remember if it's a name like Henning, I think of hens, I think I see hens, and then there's something on that 'ing', so I put the name together that way. I do it from a picture point of view.

MESSAGE

I think the message would be that I believe that to be dyslexic is not a malady. *It's something you can turn totally to advantage* because you have pictures and things that other people don't have. You have the ability to remember things sometimes because of the very training you have to do. Other people do a play and forget it the next day I've sung an opera and I remember every word of it today. Or I sing twenty, forty, sixty German songs and can remember every word, the same as French songs, because I put the extra factor into it.

An Englishman, Irishman and a Scotsman were on a train. They passed a cow. The Englishman said, 'That's an English cow.' The Irishman said, 'No, it's an Irish cow.' The Scotsman said, 'No, it's a Scottish cow – it's got bagpipes under it.'

Iain McArthur Stone(12)

Steven Redgrave

OLYMPIC GOLD MEDALLIST – OARSMAN

I first saw Steven Redgrave row in the 1984 Olympics. It may appear that I'm tracking down all these brilliant dyslexic Olympic Gold Medallists at one Olympic Games after another. But Eddie, my husband, is a sports fanatic, and also Chairman of the Sports Aid Foundation, so through him I have had the opportunity to meet great sportsmen and, fortunately for the book, four of them have been dyslexic.

Steven has a dazzling collection of medals for his rowing achievements. His success story began in 1978, when he won a gold medal in the National Schools Junior Coxed Fours, and since then he has achieved victory after victory, including two Olympic Gold Medals at the 1984 and 1988 Olympics. He was awarded an MBE in 1987 and is widely regarded as one of the most outstanding oarsmen of all time.

* * *

I was very slow at reading and writing and the headmistress at my infant school, Mrs Clunk, thought I might be dyslexic. So when I was about ten, she did a few tests herself and decided that I was slightly dyslexic, and basically it's been left at that. So my parents did know about it, but it was at a time that

309

nobody really knew what dyslexia was and nothing was done about it.

When I went to Great Marlow School at twelve, I was still struggling in the English classes, so I was given extra writing and special reading classes, but nothing to solve the dyslexic problem itself.

All the friends around me were helpful. When we had to take dictation down in class, I used to try and take it down as best I could or I used to copy off the person next to me. There were probably around thirty in the class. Dyslexia has never really given me that much of a problem, because I excelled at sport at an early age. The only times that it has really worried me is when you are suddenly put on the spot to write something or fill in a form. Then suddenly your mind goes blank and you have problems doing it. What you put down just doesn't make sense.

I did very poorly in exams, but I was always very good at crafts and things like that, so in CSEs I got very good marks in the practical side and not very good ones in the written side.

Both reading and writing were affected equally. If one's bad at one, it's difficult to do the other one.

ROWING

I have always been surrounded by people who have been very helpful and, being involved in rowing, most of it is done in crew boats, so you are always with somebody else. You nearly always have a coach with you, especially at major championships, so there's no chance of not reading something properly letting you down. Every crew has its own coach so you are virtually told that there will be a bus at this time and you've got to be on it, and I have never really had any problems like that.

I think it may have been an advantage that my sisters

310

were older than I am; my eldest sister is nine years older than I am and the other one is five years older than I am. So there is quite a big age gap. They saw me develop dyslexia as a child. Had I been a couple of years older, they might have taken the mickey. But like my parents, knowing I had problems they really tried to help me to go in the direction I was trying to go.

PARENTS' HELP

Homework. I can always remember doing it with my mother. We used to have dinner and I used to sit down and my mum used to help me do it. We used to do it together. I can never remember doing homework on my own, because I just couldn't cope with it.

I think my parents were very worried about my dyslexia at first. They are very, very supportive. Once they saw that I was doing very well at sports, and once I took up rowing and they saw that I wasn't very good academically at school, they encouraged me to go into sport and probably that's how I have achieved what I have achieved really, through my parents encouraging me. My mother actually went to work as a driving instructor so I could carry on rowing and I could continue to do sport to the level I wanted to do without really worrying about finding a full-time job when I left school.

I started rowing when I was at school. A lot of kids go through a craze of trying to skive out of sports, but I really enjoyed sports, probably because it was something I was good at and I could show everybody else that I was good at it, so I liked doing it.

So when I had this chance to row during school time I thought this is fantastic, going down the river in school time – this has got to be good, and it just sort of started from there.

Very, very quickly I got hooked on sports and within a

311

few years of being there, there were people saying 'One day you are going to be a world champion, you are going to be very, very good.' But it doesn't happen that easily, you have to work very, very hard.

I think competing at top level, you have to be very alert.

LEARNING TO SPEAK IN PUBLIC

The sponsors that sponsored me the last four years, Dale and Duff, sent Andy Holmes and me to a guy that coaches people in after-dinner speaking. It was an all-round exercise to improve the way we put ourselves across and to cope with the media as a whole.

One of the things that he asked us to do was to stand up in front of a video camera and read from a script. Being put on the spot like that, I had great problems with reading. Because you know you have got a problem, you can cope with the embarrassment. But other people who don't know and suddenly find out in a situation like that, find it very embarrassing.

After the next Olympics I can never see myself going and doing something which is a nine-to-five office job. My life has never been like that so long as I can remember. I have always ruled what I have done. I have had a free hand in what I do, really. My wife is a doctor. We are planning to open a Sports Injuries clinic, so I will be involved in that in some way. I could go into coaching in the sport, or expand into other sports as well.

DAY-TO-DAY DIFFICULTIES

When I get directions on the phone it's quite difficult getting them down when you can't write very well. So I find the dictaphone excellent. So many times I have tried to write directions down, and you try and remember what was told as well as trying to work out what you have written. But the dictaphone is very simple to work, just press two buttons to record. I am very good with mechanical things anyway, so things like that don't worry me.

Steven's wife Ann adds, 'I have to act the secretary. I write all Steve's letters. We have bought all sorts of gadgets like his dictaphone and a computer memory for telephone numbers, so he doesn't have to dial them.'

Owner of Recording Equipment Business

ANDREW

When I met Andrew's wife at the opening of the Dyslexia Institute extension in Staines she told me that her husband had been told by his teacher at school that 'all he'd make is a good dustman'. Such remarks make one realize what an enormous responsibility teachers have and what a profound effect their comments can have on people's lives. It says a lot for the tenacity of youngsters whose fragile egos overcome this type of brutal dismissal, especially when such damning remarks are put in a school report. From what I hear, this cruel and dismissive approach happens far too often. Although one knows it is mainly because so few teachers (as yet) have a proper understanding of the learning-disabled.

Although Andrew was told he was useless and would make a good dustman he now runs his own business supplying electronic equipment to recording companies. When he was a boy, despite his parents' persistence, no one, not even the headmaster, would accept that he was dyslexic. So he suffered all through his school life and his confidence was shattered. Nevertheless he used his wits to great effect once he had left

school and he was soon making his way up the ladder of the company for which he worked and was appointed as a director.

* * *

At school I was beaten every day because I made more than three spelling mistakes.

When I was about twelve I was one of the first children to go to the Word Blind Centre in London when they used to have a portakabin near Regents Park. I came up there for assessment and did a lot of tests. I used to come up from Cheltenham on the train.

Then we came up one day and the portakabin had disappeared and my mother couldn't find them after that. The whole thing had just shut down through lack of funds.

Then my mother tried to get some special tuition for me but really by the time I was thirteen or fourteen I was well gone. I had lost the incentive to learn. One of the things that I am very, very enthusiastic about with my son, who is also dyslexic, is that he is so keen to learn. It's important that he doesn't get frustrated by any slowness of his ability. We are trying to help him a lot *now while he's young*.

SCHOOL REPORTS

I had the stuffing knocked out of me at school by being told in my reports 'He would make a good dustman.' I always remember my reports saying I was useless, and that my parents were wasting their money sending me to this school.

315

MOTHER'S DETERMINATION

My parents reacted to my dyslexia very sympathetically. Both my parents are university graduates. They are both quite bright and they definitely took a view that there was something wrong with me and something needed to be worked at, and they investigated it. They knew a lot more about it than the teachers did at the time. They tried to educate the schools and the teachers and say 'Look, there are ways round.' In fact when I was going to sit my CSEs my mother managed to persuade Buckinghamshire Education Authority that I should take my CSEs verbally and have them dictated and they were going to do this as an experiment. About two weeks before my exams they called it off. It would have been an interesting experience for someone to try.

Towards the end of my private school, the headmaster of the school began to realize that what my mother was saying was true but he wouldn't admit it in public.

I failed all my CSEs but one. Nobody could read them really. I got woodwork. You don't have to write anything for that.

When I left school my parents and the school sent me to one of those recruitment places. I had a hobby of playing with tape recorders and trying to make music. I went for an interview. I said 'I would like to go into the record industry and make records.' So they got me an interview at EMI, which I was very pleased about. But it was at the record pressing plant in Hayes. I said it's not really what I had in mind. I would like to get a bit further up the chain than actually pressing records out of a machine.

USING YOUR WITS

Eventually I got a job as a mail boy for a fellow selling records, just running around the streets of London with records and master tapes. Most of the chaps that were doing that job wore jeans and a sweat shirt and that was it. But I took a slightly different view and I was a bit smarter and I used to have this sales line. I used to go round to all the cutting rooms and things and say 'I couldn't get a messenger today, I had to bring it round myself.'

One day a chap in a record studio said 'Well, if you're not a messenger and you come in every day saying you had to bring it, what do you actually do round there?' So I told him. One day he offered me a job and that was it.

So I got a job as an engineer in studios and did quite a lot of recording for some quite well-known people. But I found that I wasn't that good at it because I was a little argumentative with the clients and I used to upset some of them. But a lot of musicians in those days would say 'I would like to do a bit of recording at home, could you help me?'

So I started to help them and then I started to sell equipment and then actually get equipment from different areas, and build systems, and then from that my business developed.

Our business supplies electronic equipment for recording studios and broadcast television companies and we are quite good at it really. We supply the BBC, Thames Television, Yorkshire TV and all the major television companies and we also build studios and supply the equipment for most of the professional musicians. We have supplied equipment for George Michael and people like The Shadows and Paul McCartney.

TELEPHONE

The nice thing for me in this business, and I suppose one of the reasons I have ended up in it, apart from having a slight technical bent, is that musicians and professional music people are not that interested in paper transactions. They pick up the phone and order £150,000 of equipment over the phone, and we say yes we'll do that – deliver it tomorrow – deal done.

Whereas so many industries require miles of paperwork, we don't have memos here. Anybody caught doing a memo in this building gets into trouble.

We have bought two companies in the past four years,

317

which is very difficult because you have to deal with lawyers and solicitors and millions of letters. You should see my files – they are huge, but my wife reads it all to me. I can read words, but as soon as I get to the end of the page I have forgotten what the beginning page is all about.

THE EFFECT OF DYSLEXIA

Adult relationships are very difficult. Part of it is to do with being dyslexic, because one of the things I have is an inferiority complex. I always feel very inferior about myself and I always think everybody else is doing ever so well and I can never understand why I can't seem to achieve. I seem to have a lack of fulfilment about my own achievements which I find very difficult to live with. My ambition has an unhealthy edge to it. There is a constant feeling of underachieving all the time, no matter what I do. My wife finds it extremely hard to live with.

THE IMPORTANCE OF THE RIGHT PARTNER

But I am very fortunate that I have a wife who can work with me. She reads for me, digests it and then spits it out in a language I can understand. She's wonderful. I've started two companies with her. I'm not very understanding, I'm afraid, but I am learning. I am desperately trying to learn now to give her something back. If I had to sit down and read something myself, forget it. It would just take me so long, and also you spend so much energy actually trying to read the words that you don't actually take on board what it is saying.

It's because I never did achieve as a child, I suppose, I was never given the satisfaction of achievement so I never experienced it. I don't know how to behave when I get there. I like to achieve and then when I get there I fall flat personally. Everyone pats you on the back and says 'great', 'wonderful', and you get on the front page of one of the magazines in our industry and then I go home and instead of enjoying it I think, well, now what do I do?

I get very annoyed with myself because I can become a bit grumpy and a bit miserable and I think this is ridiculous. Before we started the new business I had this fall-out with my old firm. I was sitting at home feeling unbelievably sorry for myself. Then I saw this programme on television about this poor boy back from the Falklands all burned, I burst into tears. He really helped me in his own way, because I just got off my behind and thought I've got to go and deal with this. I haven't got any problems at all.

GO FOR IT!

All I know is that I know an awful lot of dyslexic people that have achieved. Now whether they would have achieved even greater heights had they been normal or whether they have achieved because of the fact that they had underachieved in the past and it has goaded them on, I don't really know. I feel that I have a level of intelligence and ability and if I could do 'the other bit' I would be even better. So I don't necessarily think that being dyslexic has helped me. I have a natural willingness to want to do something and do it well. And go for it.

There are a lot of nice things in this world and I want to be part of it. The only way that I can see of doing it is to work my butt off and go for it. But I'm not money motivated in any way whatsoever. A lot of people get very greedy about money. For a lot of people we work with, money is vital to them. It's not at all to me. I don't even have a cheque book. My wife pays all the bills and that's the end of it. I don't worry about it. I leave the entire thing to her.

319

FORMS

Form filling – forget it. I mean I know how to spell my address to a point but sometimes if I get into what I call a dyslexic flurry, which happens to me occasionally, all sanity goes and I just can't.

RESOLVING PROBLEMS

Everybody in the company at the management level knows that I am dyslexic. I don't hide it from anybody. I have given up hiding it. There is no point and if people want to call me an idiot I fire them!

I write badly and blame people's inability to read my writing rather than my bad spelling. I used to have a cheque book and I used to have all the spelling of all the numbers written on the back of the cheque book because I could never spell 'eight', for example, and a lot of others, so I used to copy them.

MESSAGE

Don't be put off. Go for it. There's room for everybody and I think that the wonderful thing about the human body is when you have a disadvantage other senses seem to take over – if you are blind, you can walk around in a dark room.

Most of the dyslexic people that I've met admitted that they have a wonderful way of thinking three-dimensionally rather than very flat. They can look at problems and see them from many different angles which a lot of 'normal' people can't do. I have seen dyslexics when they are doing business deals. They can sit down and assimilate a deal, look at all the problems involved in that deal and solve it far quicker than anybody else.

Why should we all be made to feel we *should* be the same. Some people are good at sports, some at art. Because of this whole thing of conforming in society you have to learn to read at eight. If you don't, there's pressure. That can sometimes make a child's life a disaster, because it can make a child feel a failure. It's the same as the fat boy who can't get over the horse in the gym. People have different talents. Why should we all be the same?

John Tramper
Actor

Actor

JOHN

It is always interesting to talk to another actor and hear exactly why and how they became actors and what method they prefer for learning their lines. John, unlike me, likes to use a tape recorder to assist his line learning. I have never used this method but that's probably because I'm terrified I'll press *record* instead of *play* and wipe the tape!

Not too many actors or stars want people to know they are dyslexic. I have written to a fair number in England, Australia and America for this book. Only a few replied and I'm sure it's not that they can't write but more that they feel being associated with a handicap is not good for their working life. Sadly, of this I can vouch, which makes me doubly grateful to the actors who felt strongly enough about their fellow dyslexics to commit themselves to print.

But, when he was ten the teacher told the whole class 'Look at this boy, he's a fool, he can't read.' John was very fortunate in that, as in so many success stories, his parents were very supportive and understanding of his early difficulties. Now John is a much in demand actor. He has toured the world playing Shakespeare and has performed in the West End. He is also a wonderful photographer.

* * *

I was very happy within the home. My parents in a way learned to accept my early problems although they didn't understand why I couldn't read, because I was quite bright. There was nothing that could really be done at that time. Nobody understood. My parents would go to teachers and to the headmaster and say 'Why can't he read?' They were told that there were lots of children that couldn't read in the school.

SPELLING

I still can't spell. Well, I can spell phonetically. I felt a lot better when I learnt that in Elizabethan times they used to write phonetically anyway. So if it was good enough for Shakespeare it is good enough for me.

I can remember sitting on my father's knee and he was reading with me and I wanted to read and the words started to swim. He got upset and threw the book on the floor, and I can remember feeling miserable for him. Not awful for me but upset for him, because I couldn't do it, and I would have liked to have read for him. But they were really wonderful parents and very supportive and always said I could do whatever I wanted to do and they wouldn't care what I wanted to do as long as I was happy and enjoyed it.

READING ALOUD

I went to prep school in Suffolk at the age of ten. I'll never forget my first day there, in a geography lesson. There were about twenty children in the class – everyone had a book in front of them and we had to read a passage. It came round to me and I just couldn't do it, and the words just swam and I stuttered and I couldn't talk. I felt all hot and terrible and the teacher, who was a right bastard, just laughed and said, 'Look at this boy, he can't even read, he's a fool.' And the whole class just roared with laughter.

SCHOOL FRIEND HELP

I told my friend what had happened and he took me to the headmaster's study and said 'he needs somebody to teach him to read', and could he fix it up. He was only ten and a half or eleven at the time. The headmaster said 'yes', and I started having remedial lessons with a woman called Jill Cockrell in Bury St Edmunds. I used to visit her every Wednesday.

I started to learn to read with very short little words like cat. But I found it very difficult and I would reverse figures and reverse symbols, whether it be writing or arithmetic. Particularly, I found that when I was tired or when I was under pressure it would happen more. If I managed to really cool myself down and relax and just cover the whole page with a blank piece of paper and just look at one line, it wouldn't be so bad. But when I was presented with a whole page, it was like trying to read the whole page at once and it would swim. I just couldn't even look at the page in the end.

When I was at prep school they used to have this marquee and the theatre was outside in the garden and it was only the boys that were academic that were allowed to do plays. So I used to just take the tickets and watch and I thought I could do that. I could say that line, I could move that trunk, I could do this and that.

PLAYS

So when I went to the next school, this dyslexic school,

Brick Hall House, there were lots of boys who were dyslexic and they all seemed to excel in their own thing, whatever it was – sport, or drawing. Most of them had some kind of talent. I was asked to be in a play and I was delighted. I then realized that I'd have to learn to read so that I could learn the lines and understand a bit of what was going on.

HAVING A REASON TO READ

When they told me I was in the play, it was wonderful. It was great. From then on, with every single play that they did, and they did a lot there, I was in it. That helped me enormously and gave me a lot of confidence. I had something to really go for and a real reason to learn to read. Because I was surrounded by people in the same position as me, we could share our experiences and traumas and realized that we weren't actually stupid or thick, but just couldn't read symbols on a page. Simple as that.

WHY SHOULD WE ALL BE MADE TO FEEL WE SHOULD BE THE SAME?

Some people are good at sports, some are good at whatever; it's because of the whole thing of conforming in society that you have to learn to read by the age of eight. If you don't there's pressure. That sometimes can make a child's life a disaster because it can make the child feel a failure. The same as if there's a fat boy that can't get over a horse in the gym. People have different talents and why should we all be the same? We're not. But as soon as I had something to inspire me it was a lot easier to go for it and to get confidence in it.

DRAMA SCHOOL

At RADA I used to tape; a friend of mine, Guy Manning, used to tape my lines and I used to learn them from his reading. Now I can actually read I work on it every single day. Sometimes it would be for ten minutes but sometimes it would be for an hour, by myself. I find that reading aloud is a lot harder to do straight off, and I think that's also because of the psychological thing of reading to an audience and going back to my past when I was young and I couldn't do it.

I love dictionaries now and looking through and finding words. It's a great joy to actually be able to look at symbols and be able to distinguish what they are and what they mean and what they can give you.

THE POSITIVE SIDE OF DYSLEXIA

I think being dyslexic has given me understanding of people who have problems, whatever they are. I can relate to people with family problems or those who are blind or deaf or handicapped or a little bit mentally unstable. I find that it's easy to relate to those people and understand their problems and what it's like to have something like that.

The disadvantages of being dyslexic are when you're not working as an actor and you want to do something else to earn some money. If you don't have qualifications to do something else that can be a problem and that I suppose is really a disadvantage. But I don't really think about that.

SWIMMING HELPED

I used to be incredibly clumsy, I've got better now. The teacher would say 'Oh, don't knock over that pot of paint,' and I'd go and knock it over. I just would somehow knock it over, I used to break things a lot. But when I started to swim I found that helped. Then I took up karate and learning different moves and after that I could catch a ball. I could hit a ball with a bat and I could do things that I couldn't do before.

MESSAGE

Once you accept dyslexia it isn't actually a problem any more, you can then do something about it.

I think confidence has a lot to do with it. Once you get a barrier and you say, 'I'm dyslexic, I can't do it' you are in a sense stopping yourself from going forward. Say to yourself that you are dyslexic and that you reverse things occasionally and find it difficult to read, but also say that you can get a little bit better every day. Not just think that you have to conquer it by tomorrow.

It's only when you come out of the closet that these things will actually be dealt with. It's very scary that society has such a strong hold on the norm that if you have something that is slightly different you don't dare talk about it, amazing.

Richard Rogers
Architect

Richard Rogers

ARCHITECT

Richard Rogers, who has more letters after his name than there are in the alphabet, and has won no less than eighteen architectural awards, was so unhappy at school he contemplated suicide. He was told as a boy that all he would be good for was 'a policeman in South Africa'. Now he runs his own extremely successful architectural firms in London and Tokyo.

The first time I became aware of Richard Rogers' work was when I was working in Paris and the controversial Pompidou Centre had just been built. Later I met him in person at the opening of another very controversial project, the new Lloyds of London building, for which he did the design. But as his dyslexia takes the form of a complete blank on all names and faces, he probably won't remember meeting!

* * *

I had tremendous difficulty at school, partly because I was foreign. But I am British because my great-great-grandfather was British and we kept our dual nationality when we were abroad.

I think I had three problems really. One, being Italian in 1939 was not a good thing. Two, I came from a very Italian spoilt upper middle-class background, when a single son was

God. I was sent to England to a little private school where I had to be a boarder; where a little Italian child was a right pain and had to be dealt with like an animal. Three, it soon became apparent that I had a learning difficulty which they thought was stupidity. I had to go to a boarding school because my mother became ill and the three problems together created an absolute crisis.

MEMORY DYSLEXIA

My form of dyslexia is a form of memory dyslexia. I can't work out what memory dyslexia it is, but I have great difficulty in remembering when I see people I know quite well, specifically with names. I have real difficulty with names. I have no memory for any lines, of poems or songs, I can't spell, and they are all the things you have to do at school. Without those you are lost. I learnt to read, I suppose, when I was about twelve, which in an English prep school is just not accepted. I therefore became terribly depressed and by ten I was really seriously considering suicide. I remember standing on a roof top, it's hard to say if I would have jumped. I was very muddled by then and I couldn't talk. It would go in waves, but I got so muddled up at some point that I couldn't remember what I had done two minutes before, which is obviously a form of nervousness.

NERVOUS BREAKDOWN

I suppose I was somewhere near a nervous breakdown. Because when people asked me 'What did you do before?' I couldn't remember and I would get beaten for it. But I couldn't remember. My mind got so completely muddled up.

I was moderately large, I was tall and I could look after myself physically so I didn't get bullied, but I was extremely unhappy.

PARENTS

At about eleven or twelve, the only consistent thing was my parents. I was a boarder at this place which I couldn't stand, somewhere where physical and mental punishment was the rule of the day.

But when my parents came back, they supported me continuously. They always have, I am very close to my parents. They never had doubts that their son was OK.

When I was about eleven, I remember I was dragged off to have an IQ test and that gave them a cheer, because until then everybody said I was daft, and I was still seeing psychologists. They would ask me questions such as 'Don't you think you should leave your school?' I would say 'No', not because I didn't want to leave my school, but because the unknown was more fearful than the present torture. That's one of the problems as you lose perspective, change is actually more threatening. But luckily in the end my parents decided they just couldn't cope any longer, and at about twelve I was sent to a very small school for sort of drop-out kids.

UNABLE TO LEARN

There were many incidents at my first school like people saying 'You haven't learnt that poem, you will therefore stay in to learn it.' Well, I cannot learn a poem. If someone said tomorrow you have to learn this poem or be shot, I would be shot. It's like someone asking me to fly. Where a thing is so specific to the short-term memory, there's no way out of it. I just couldn't cope. I got a little better with tutors and my parents' help. I learnt to work very, very hard.

NEW SCHOOL

At the next school there were kids who lived nearby who were drop-outs and hadn't fitted into any system. That was tremendous, as for the first time I found people who were worse than me. I had always been bottom of the class. The other children were less able to learn, more distraught from their upbringing conditions, etc., I guess. There was about a teacher to every five children, so it was a very small unit and like heaven for me. It was unbelievable.

I went in as thick as could be and in the two years I picked up two years, so that I actually took the Common Entrance and got into my public school.

SPORT

Up to then I had been totally unable to co-ordinate in sport, I suddenly became good at sport. This actually saw me well into the future.

It did me an unbelievable amount of good to gain confidence. To me it was an amazing event that I could do this thing.

Then I went to a medium sized public school where because I was quite good at sport, I was looked up to, so things went quite well at first. But the real problem when I look back is I don't think I ever improved. I didn't actually learn anything else when I went to public school, so I was back to square one, I lived off the fat of the previous school for a while. I was actually running as fast at fourteen as at seventeen. I never got better. Swimming too, I could always swim moderately well.

So when I went to public school things started well, but then got worse and worse. By the time I was coming up for School Certificate it became clear that I was going to break the school record. No one had ever failed the School Certificate before in 400 children. I was the first ever to do it.

Of course as you get older, you tend to cope a bit better. But I was in trouble and back to being beaten by the school, tutors and students and so on. I was always moderately rebellious and there is no question that I was quite strong.

PARENTS

I was always strongly pushed by my parents who gave me tutorials galore. I have always worked through holidays, it was the Italian system to do that. Although they weren't particularly well off, education is the top thing in my family. So whatever they had, they would give up basically for education.

My wife always cracks jokes that when my father and I walk down a street, only he and I, and probably my mother, can understand what we are saying. We have to miss out every fifth word because we can't use names, but we do it perfectly well. It is a bit like a school language. My father, who is a doctor, did get through his exams, but he said it was a great strain.

I think both my parents were probably dyslexic but of course it was not recognized as such then.

CAREERS OFFICER

At about sixteen I took my School Certificate and failed. Luckily they changed over to O-levels where you could take them one at a time. I remember then seeing a Careers Officer and after spending a couple of hours with me, he said 'Mr Rogers, it is quite clear you have no academic abilities whatsoever.' I didn't have any. Then he said 'What about going to South Africa and being a policeman?' I thought that's a very intriguing view, even more so because I am a pacifist!

Immediately the war was over, we would go to Italy every summer. I had forgotten my Italian during the war because it

333

was convenient to forget it. But I picked it up again.

I got quite a few O-levels, to my surprise. It does look as though there are moments when I can actually learn. Having completely failed the School Certificate, I then proceeded to get eight pretty reasonable O-levels – maths, English, biology, all the sort of normal subjects.

LEAVING SCHOOL

Then I had no idea what I wanted to do. It was clear that I couldn't do what my father and grandfather did, they were basically doctors, because I didn't have the academic qualifications. I went into the army to do National Service. I was unbelievably unhappy. I was totally unsuitable to be a soldier, because you do the same damn things as you do at school. You have to do things which I couldn't do.

They give you IQ tests like you had to put a padlock together – I couldn't put it together, it's not my type of thing. So they put me into the typing course. I think I was the only Private in the British Army who couldn't pass a typing course, because I couldn't work out where the letters were.

BECOMING AN ARCHITECT

So in absolute despair the army sent me off to Trieste by mistake, I was meant to go to Germany. I spent a year in Trieste, which is actually where my parents come from. One of my uncles was one of the leading Italian modern architects, I came under his influence and I got on very well with him. He made me realize that architecture is obvious to me. I am very interested in social problems and I enjoy very much modern art. I have always been interested in history as it combines the scientific and art elements and sociologist elements.

334

Of course then I didn't have any of the right things as I have never done drawing, my maths was medium, but I got into the architecture.

FINDING ARCHITECTURE DIFFICULT

I can't say I took to architecture very easily either, I loved it, but I had a lot of difficulty. It's a five years' course plus two years out.

Again I began to come across all the usual problems of exams, which I had difficulties with, and by the third year I was being advised by the principal that I should give up architecture and do furniture design. But the big thing I learnt, with the help of my parents, was to persevere. I don't actually believe in what people tell me. I just have to keep at it, it's my nature.

YALE

In the fifth year I began to know what I was doing, I came across the tutors at AA who were very influential. I was very fortunate. I was all right by then, and in the last eighteen months I blossomed. I then went to Yale University in America. At Yale, some of the problems appeared again because a Masters Class has a lot of yes/no type tests that I am no good at.

Even now I probably know architectural history better than a large number of people and certainly I am an authority on Italian history and architecture. Therefore, I know my dates.

But I don't know any telephone numbers. I only know two telephone numbers, my home and office, that's all I remember.

HARD WORK

I am practically never beaten by anything. I'll apply myself until I do it. I work very hard, I think, and certainly when I was young I worked extremely hard. I expected to work all my holidays, even when I was a teenager and everybody else was out, I would work to try and cope with the fact that I was so far behind.

Also, I believe in what I am and go for it. People say, well, of course dyslexia gives us special knowledge, and maybe it does. I can get to the heart of problems. *But life must be easier without dyslexia.*

The worst thing about being dyslexic is the fact that I have to go through a semi-charade, because I can't memorize anybody's names. As you get older you have a support system, it could be called tricks. I never go into a room first. My partner goes into a room, so he can do the introducing for me. My secretary, my wife and my children check my spelling. Everybody knows what I can't do and therefore they help.

CONFIDENCE

I think I am rather a confident person. I am an optimist, so I suppose that's related to self-esteem. I have become an optimist. I don't think I was optimistic until I became quite a lot older. But I feel strongly about the ethical position about the individual and I don't retreat easily. Anyone who innovates is likely to be criticized, but it doesn't exactly put me off from what I am doing. And so I suppose in a sense maybe a sort of hardness does come out of the fact that having been criticized all one's life, you realize that most of the criticism seems to have been way off the mark. I have a vision about what things should be.

Being the fastest reader and the quickest at comprehension would be nice, but is not required for success and happiness.

Neil Bush
Oil Exploration Executive
(Son of President George Bush)

Conclusion to Interviews

For every dyslexic cited in this book there are a great many who have not been lucky enough to have either strong parental support, an extra quota of determination, or the good fortune to fall into the care of the right teacher who has spotted their potential and given them encouragement before their confidence has been irrevocably broken down.

There are many professions that dyslexics do extremely well in, but which have not been included in this book. That does not mean that they have been overlooked, simply that an encyclopaedia of careers suitable for dyslexics would have made a very long book for dyslexics to read!

Nevertheless, the fact is that, if you can't read and write, you don't have a fair start. Family support, Determination, Inspired Teacher and a Persistent Mother are still the essential ingredients for a dyslexic's survival. That is, until the Government has assessments and the correct specialist teaching in every school, for all children with learning difficulties.

PART TWO

Parents

Our daughter, Dorothy, works full-time, but she'll still have to sit with her arm around her children, the way I did, and read to them and listen to them and care about them. I think a lot of our problems are because people don't listen to their children. It's not always easy – they're not always so brilliant that you want to spend hours with them. But it's very important to listen.

Mrs Barbara Bush
First Lady of the United States
Honorary Chairperson of National Advisory Council
of Literacy Volunteers in America
Reprinted with permission from *Parade*, © 1989

Parents

After my son was born I thought, 'This is the most important contribution I shall make to life.' Not the actual birth, but my role as a parent. I imagine this kind of high flown idea is common after the elation of child birth!

Maybe some of this feeling was due to the endless patience, perseverance, love and determination of my own mother who, although she feared I might be mentally retarded, willed me through school, and gave me positive encouragement in my every working hour. She propelled me into working life with the *belief that I could do it*. This brought home to me, long before researching this book, that a mother's role as far as a dyslexic child is concerned is a demanding and extra special one.

My own case was unusual in that my mother was also the principal of the school as well as my teacher. Later, I was taught by my sisters too after they had matriculated and left school.

As a small child I was severely dyslexic, but my sisters and my mother were totally wonderful in their complete kindness to me, and due to their sensible help I didn't drop out, become a delinquent or a tormented soul for the rest of my life. But like most dyslexics, I live with the constant nagging uncertainty that everything will be wrong and lack of confidence in my ability!

This is what needs to be understood. Dyslexics fear at all times that whatever they do will not be right. A pattern set up in those first years at school when even saying the alphabet in the correct order is bewildering. Fear of failure is in all of us, but even more so with dyslexics who have been conditioned at an early age to think of themselves as someone 'who always makes mistakes'.

Research has shown that on the whole, the dyslexics who fare the best consider their mother's help as the single most important factor for their survival.

So this section is devoted to parents – mothers talking of the fight, the despair and even the guilt when faced with their child's dyslexia. I hope this chapter will help other parents who are coping with young dyslexics. Without the amazing fight mothers (and some fathers) have put up over the last two decades, some dyslexic children would still be labelled 'mentally retarded'.

UNDERSTANDING AND PATIENCE

Sometimes being parents of a non-handicapped child can be confusing and exasperating and stretches the patience to its limits at the best of times, so coping with the difficulties, and finding the extra patience needed to understand a dyslexic child is inevitably more demanding and tiring.

But it can be very rewarding too. I received a letter from Anna several years ago when she was fourteen. She wrote and told me that it was only her father's help and encouragement that had changed her school life for the better:

The thing that I feel has helped me the most, from being called lazy and a dunce, to being someone with a difficulty (the school will not use the word dyslexic), was my father. After many years of tears and arguments, my father could not understand why I spelt the word 'paint',

343

'panit' and then did not see what was wrong with it. When he finally accepted I could not read or spell he did his best to help me. And help me he did. In fact it worked almost completely.

Every morning for about two hours in my summer holidays (which were eight weeks) he worked with me, teaching, making me learn what sound each letter of the alphabet makes. I learnt a whole new alphabet. I still use this alphabet now to break down words into bits. I can read by saying all the bits of the word. Eventually, I learnt the sounds of groups of letters, like 'oo' and 'ou'. And then the rules of sounding words, such as the rule of the magic 'e' making a vowel sound its name.

I think of these eight weeks as the eight weeks of my life when I learnt to read, write and spell. Using picture cards and visual aids to make the time more interesting, I actually enjoyed learning. The only thing I now wish is that I had a wider vocabulary. It is getting bigger as I now like to read books. It is better than television, because every time I finish a book, I feel a sense of achievement although I read each page twice, because I get lost and forget what I have just read!!!

(N.B. The spelling in this letter has been corrected)

When I wrote to ask Anna if I might use her letter in this book, she wrote back 'letter perfect' and told me she is now doing GCSE's and then hopes to do physics, chemistry and biology A-levels.

TIREDNESS

A dyslexic finds everything tiring and it is important for parents to take this into account. It takes twice as much effort for the dyslexic to achieve the same results as a non-dyslexic.

They find homework, reading a book, remembering to pack their tennis shoes or writing a letter, twice as much effort as anyone else. Even adult dyslexics find many of these things tiring.

For a dyslexic everything is an effort, whether it is looking up a telephone number, reading directions, deciphering a form or looking up a word in the dictionary. And even the thought of doing it can be tiring. It is hard for a non-dyslexic to imagine how such simple things can be so difficult, but parents should be prepared and allow for this tiredness.

BEHAVIOURAL PROBLEMS

Behavioural problems resulting from their experiences are not uncommon in dyslexic youngsters. Although I would have considered myself fairly lucky on this count, I did, in common with a number of the famous and not-so-famous dyslexics in this book, have the problems of bedwetting after kindergarten years. But many dyslexics preferred not to mention this, or indeed, any of their behavioural problems, like stealing or cheating.

Many problems may start as early as the moment the dyslexic realizes that spelling simple words like THE, SO, BEFORE or OFF is going to be impossibly difficult for them.

Parents should be prepared for problems due to the strain of concentrating and the frustration of underachieving. There can be even a reluctance to go to school, in some cases truancy, but more commonly temper tantrums before school. I have been in despair and furious at times when I am writing. It is not being bad tempered, it is being exasperated with oneself at still being unable to do a comparatively simple task like rewriting a paragraph without making the same mistakes again and again.

I talked to one father about his son's behavioural problems when we met under rather strange circumstances. We were both on a waterskiing course, and as we stood on the dock in

345

dripping wetsuits and freezing cold, awaiting our next ski, he told me about his son:

> When my son was thirteen, unfortunately he had lost his confidence so badly that unbeknown to us he was in with a bad lot and experimenting with drugs.
> It went from bad to worse and eventually we had to tell the police, and he went to court at seventeen for selling drugs and was bound over for eighteen months. I gave up my job and for the next two years. They were tricky, I fought with him and for him and helped him to get his confidence back. Now he is farming. He always loved animals, only really felt at home with them. He's off drugs, out of crime and he's wonderful on the farm, and in some ways I feel I can take the credit. But loss of confidence is a terrible thing.

The difficulties often begin at school when dyslexics are classified as stupid, slow and lazy. Barbara Bush, wife of President Bush, sent this message, saying:

> As the mother of a learning disabled child, I know the worry and concern a parent can feel. I also know how important love and support from a child's family can be at a time when the child is so vulnerable. There is help available, but parents need to be patient and persevere as they advocate for their child. They need to constantly assure their child of his value and intelligence. They need to know that there are wonderful success stories everywhere. They need to know they are not alone.

Dyslexics may always see themselves as failures. Well, they should not, and they need not. Mrs Bush's own son Neil is a good example. From eighth grade, Neil Bush knew that he had a learning problem. He just could not keep up in school – and what really came as a shock to his parents – was that he hated to read. But Mr and Mrs Bush gave him as much love

346

and support as possible and found schools and teachers who could help him. Neil's own courage and persistence helped him the rest of the way through an MBA programme and on to a successful career in the oil exploration business.

EDUCATIONAL AUTHORITIES

Today dyslexia is a subject for television serials and even in Channel 4's *Brookside*, a poor frustrated mother has to battle with the school, the local authorities, and even the child's father, to get the educational system to provide help. Just as in real life some schools are of little help, and the mother is left to fight alone and sort out her child's educational rights with the local authorities.

In a few areas unhelpful authorities still remain a problem. I have had letters from parents alleging that their local education authority still doesn't provide the necessary help for dyslexic children in state schools, and so the parents 'have had to go privately for remedial help, which costs about £80 a month for two afternoon sessions a week.'

Another mother wrote and told me that her local authority had been most unhelpful and could only suggest 'a boarding school for maladjusted children', instead of specialist teaching in the day school, for her son who had been diagnosed dyslexic and had an IQ of 115. Distressing letters of this kind pour in all the time, and I am sure that until there is adequate help in schools throughout the country, they will continue to do so.

Mrs Charles Dance, who has a dyslexic son, has also had first hand experience of unhelpful authorities. She and I were first in touch some years ago after her son was first diagnosed as dyslexic, and she told me:

Had it been left up to our local authority I don't know what Oliver's reading age would be now. They said if we wanted him assessed it was absolutely up to us, although the Council would be happy to arrange it, but they didn't feel there was any need. Then the report came back saying although he wasn't brilliant at reading and writing, there was nothing wrong! How wrong they were!

If my son had had to go to a comprehensive school after being assessed dyslexic, I think he would have sunk like a stone. He would have just given up and hung out at Wimpy bars and he wouldn't have tried. So we have set about trying to build up his confidence but he is still terribly wobbly. The slightest thing will make him visibly retreat and draw back and another little layer of defence goes up.

Mrs Jackson also had problems with the authorities, as she wrote and told me:

I was forty-two when I realized what was the matter with me. Divorced with three daughters, my eldest at eighteen could hardly write her own name and address, one of fifteen who was causing havoc at home and at school and the youngest, twelve, who had a strange hearing difficulty, which added to her learning problem. I had reached a point very near to a complete breakdown. I knew for certain that Kay (my eldest) was dyslexic, yet the school denied it.

Since 1979 I have been on a lone crusade trying to get my daughter's problems recognized. A typical response has been 'Oh yes. Well, dyslexia is now well known so your daughter can't be one or the school would have found out.' What I think of my local education authority is unprintable. It was known Kay was in difficulties and I was 'blocked' whenever I tried to find out what her problem was. She was a 'mirror writer' at primary school, left handed, and I was always telling her teacher that *I* could not spell or add up. The teacher would then change the subject rapidly. If I had known it was possible to inherit dyslexia, I might have saved my daughter the years of torture at school, and appalling emotional turmoil, both at home and at school.

My mother certainly had all the dyslexic difficulties but would not admit it, an affliction of the brain was not to be thought of, so she denied that I had any problems too. She thought my behaviour as a child was just to spite her.

You will understand my terror as I found my childhood being recreated in my own children. I thought I was going mad. If I had not read your book or Professor Miles' book I am sure by now I would have been in a mental hospital (I won't attempt to spell ci-kee-at-ric).

(N.B. Some spelling in this letter has been corrected)

Although it must be stressed that in some parts of the United Kingdom the educational authorities are not helpful, in other areas the situation is improving and there is good will and they are becoming more co-operative and supportive. Indeed some local authorities are even subsidizing private specialist help as there is no help available in their schools. But it is a matter of luck depending on where you live as to whether your child is helped or not.

PARENTAL SUPPORT

The value of parental support can never be underestimated, and the following testimonies add credence to the belief that children who are fortunate enough to have this support fare better than those that don't. But not every young mother is as dedicated as Mrs Christopher Cazenove, who, better known as Angharad Rees, is not only a lovely actress, but also a very special mother, and her son Linford is the perfect example of a young man who has been guided back into the main stream by his mother's devotion.

When Linford was little, he was enormously bright and interested in everything, he loved books, always wanted me to read books like little encyclopaedias, as bedtime stories. Yet he wasn't particularly interested in learning to read.

One day I suddenly thought 'Oh my God, I wonder if he's dyslexic.' He was not quite six. I took him to Dr Bevé Hornsby who used to run the dyslexia unit at Bart's Hospital who did all the tests, and discovered that he was very, very bright, he was in the top two per cent of the human race, but was severely dyslexic. They put me on to this wonderful teacher that we went to just two mornings a week before school for an hour. We went to North Kensington which was miles away from us, but it was worth it. For two years, including holidays, we left the house around 7 a.m. two days a week for special lessons.

Every night we did our little homework from the age of six, every single night before he went to sleep, and that was a little bit of doing whatever he had done with the teacher. The terribly important thing was to keep it fun so that it never became a drag for him, but also for it to become a discipline, a habit, so that it would be a natural part of his life, so that bit by bit over the years he would pick up and learn to read.

He was a perfect candidate because he is a very self-motivated person. Once he got the reading and writing sorted out, the next thing he worked on then was speed. And working quicker. By the time he got to his final year, he was taking his Common Entrance. He always won the academic prize in his year and still does. He passed out of Sussex House top in his year.

But at one school it was terribly frustrating. The headmaster and two of the teachers were very unfair to him. One teacher continued to call him slowcoach and keep him in from games because he hadn't finished his story.

It's like making a cripple run. It's just as cruel. They hurt us terribly and they hurt me terribly. There's nothing worse than knowing that somebody is hurting your child and they did. Still, after all these years there is this one teacher, this male teacher, I would give anything to punch on the nose!

BEING IN SYMPATHY WITH THE TEACHER

Another actress, Felicity Kendal, has the experience of dyslexia in her own family. Like Angharad, she feels very strongly that all dyslexics should be given the support and help they need.

When I sat in her dressing room after seeing her brilliant performance as Anna, the dying wife in Chekhov's *Ivanov*, she made two very important observations:

The child should be sympathetic with the teacher. If the child is not sympathetic with that teacher, it won't work. It's no good saying this is the teacher who teaches dyslexics and that's it. If the child is not sympathetic with that teacher, it's a waste of time. It must be someone the child gets on with, and who understands that the child is not only having to overcome being someone who is having a problem, but also the learning problem itself. Otherwise the *teacher* can become a new problem.

Secondly, having seen and understood a child who is dyslexic, I now understand dyslexia doesn't go away, you just have to manage with it. I know that dyslexia should not be treated as a simple reading problem where children are made to 'memorize' in the conventional way. It is unbelievable when you actually know a child has dyslexia, that the child can be treated as a fool by the teacher, and that you, the mother, are treated as a neurotic parent! I don't know how many years it will take, but eventually dyslexia will have to be accepted everywhere and dealt with for the children's sake. It's something I feel very strongly. If the little one I have now is dyslexic it won't worry me as it would have done in the past. The point is I know about it now. The sad thing is when people don't know.

H.M. King Olav of Norway has similar views. I had heard that there were several dyslexic kings in Europe, H.M. the King of Sweden and H.M. King Constantine of the Hellenes, but King Olav, it was said, had dyslexic children and grandchildren. So I wrote and asked if he would see me as I was sure he could give encouragement to dyslexics and their parents. Being the warm hearted man he is, and concerned about dyslexia, he granted me an audience, although 'as a general rule His Majesty does not consent to being interviewed'. So in the warm January of 1989, I walked up the hill to the Royal Palace in Oslo. No snow on the ground, but sunshine in a bright blue sky. To my surprise only His Majesty and myself were present at the meeting and I was allowed to take a tape recorder and ask questions. His Majesty commented:

I think that like so many other things, the more open it [dyslexia] is, the better it is for everyone. There is no point in shutting someone up in a closet and leaving it at that. In my day, I don't think they knew about dyslexia and if you had a handicap you weren't shown about much. You were kept out of the way.

I don't think I was a very fast reader as a child, about average, but when I was small I had a certain amount of difficulty with spelling. It's still difficult. I had tutors until I was sixteen and then I went to a normal school. I suppose there was a certain amount of slight irritation from my parents as I don't think they knew about it.

My youngest daughter has five children. They have all had difficulties, especially the two youngest, a girl and a boy. My youngest daughter had a little difficulty with writing herself, but not as bad as her own children.

It was the school that noticed her children's problem but they said they were retarded, that's because they weren't sure what it really was. Then they realized, as

352

it developed, that it was dyslexia. That's why I think it's important to discover dyslexia as soon as possible. To find it at an early age, I think, is one of the most important things. And then of course to be able to do something about it scientifically. Confidence is very important, too, in this sort of thing. There's no point in being told that you are just a nitwit and then leaving it at that.

LISTENING TO YOUR CHILD

It is often during the quiet special moments before sleep or when children are ill that parents get to know more about their children. Charles Dance discovered his son was unable to read while sitting and reading a bedtime story with him. 'He was memorizing all the words!'

Mrs Barbara Bush discovered her son couldn't read quite by accident. She said in *Parade* (© 1989 *Parade*):

I will never forget the day I discovered that one of my children was hiding the truth. It was the kids' spring vacation, and Neil, my third son, was recovering from chicken-pox. I put my arm around him and said 'Let's read'. Neil was in the second grade and he was the sweetest little boy. I mean he just smiled up at me so sweetly. But if I hadn't sat with him in bed, as a mother does, I would never have found out that Neil *could not read a word*! I called Neil's teacher, and she said, 'Of course your son can read. He's getting all As in reading. You come to the school and I'll show you.' So I went to school, and the teacher called on Neil, and he smiled, and the kid next to him began feeding him words in a whisper, and the kid on the other side did the same. You know, people who have reading disabilities learn to fake. And Neil really had learned to fake.

353

A PARENT'S REACTION TO DISCOVERING
THEIR CHILD IS DYSLEXIC

There are many different reactions to discovering your child is dyslexic. Different parents react in different ways. Jo Dance, who earlier talked of her problems with the authorities, says:

> When we discovered our son was dyslexic I felt terribly guilty. I can actually remember sitting down and crying. Charlie, my husband, didn't feel it was his fault, but it made me think about being perfect and realizing one isn't perfect after all. In fact I felt less than perfect. I really did feel 'Oh my goodness, have I done something wrong?' The school sent out a questionnaire asking 'Did you smoke when you were pregnant?' 'Did you drink when you were pregnant?' and it was almost too much. I have to say I didn't fill in the questionnaire because I didn't want to be pigeon-holed. But his being dyslexic did make me feel guilty.

Yet another response to knowing your son or daughter is dyslexic is that of Mrs Day whom I met in America. She told me:

> Finding out that John couldn't read and didn't seem able to learn to read was without doubt one of the most traumatic events in my life. I don't quite know when this creeping panic began. Some teachers have a way of making you, the parent, feel that you are simply neurotic and over anxious. But if you've had other children who have learned to read and write so easily, you know when something is wrong. I didn't want to appear neurotic and so I tried to seem calm until it just became impossible to deny my feelings any longer. There was just no way that this little boy was going to learn despite the fact that he loved books

354

and spent many hours poring over them, turning the pages and pretending to read.

I find it difficult to remember what I found frightening. But, by the time he was six, his teacher was already beginning to write him off – a failure at six! Of course I felt that it was my failure, that I had failed to be a good mother. I steeled myself to accepting that he might simply not be very bright and took John to a psychologist to find out if he was stupid or if he had other problems. John was diagnosed as dyslexic.

Faced with an irate teacher who told me that 'this child has no prospects whatsoever', I changed John's school. His new teacher was gentle and caring and knew about dyslexia. She gave him extra help after school and he slowly began to improve. The change in him was very gradual. It literally took years and years.

In fact he passed ten GCSEs with virtually all A and B grades, and he is now studying for his A-levels and a place at university. Despite John's achievements, the worry and feeling of terror in the pit of my stomach never quite goes away.

A CHILD'S REACTION TO DYSLEXIA

In the same way parents react in different ways to the discovery of their child's dyslexia, so children react in many surprising fashions to being dyslexic. One mother told me that her son felt that it was 'his treat' to be assessed to see if he was dyslexic, as both his brothers were dyslexics and in his eyes it was rather special to be the same:

When it was confirmed he was dyslexic, he said, 'Mum, thank God, I couldn't be that bad at spelling if I wasn't.' So he was pleased. His brother was always going round saying to people 'Are you dyslexic?' as if it was something lovely, and they would say, 'No, no, but could I be?' – in hopes of also having a special teacher!

This reminded me of a carol concert where I was giving a talk to raise money for the Dyslexia Institute Bursary Fund, and I mentioned people in the past who had been dyslexic. At the end of the speech the conductor said to the audience, 'I wish I was dyslexic so I could be associated with such great men!' It is far better, to be proud of your handicap, if you can, rather than ashamed of it.

When I was in America talking at the Orton Society annual conference, the feeling of being ashamed was brought home to me when I met a mother who was trying to cope with the deep shame her daughter had of being dyslexic. I was signing copies of my book *Susan's Story* after giving the talk, and in the queue were two smartly dressed black women clinging to each other and crying. As they made their way towards me their emotional state increased. I rose and they immediately swept me into their arms, hugging me with such affection I was overwhelmed and I felt tears coming to my own eyes. The next thing I knew, the older of the two women slipped a silver bangle with a gold buckle from her wrist and pressed it into my hand. Still hugging me, she sobbed, 'My daughter is happy now she knows her troubles are like yours – she's dyslexic and she needn't be ashamed of it, you're not.' They both cried some more and after a final warm embrace, the mother and daughter suddenly disappeared.

Today the bangle is a treasured reminder of all those who have lost heart or feel ashamed of having this difficulty.

PRACTICE TIPS

We have talked of the importance of love and encouragement. As I said, my mother willed me through school and always managed to praise me for anything that I was good at. So encouragement and praise come very high on the list of priorities to help dyslexics.

But there are a couple of important don'ts which have been brought to my attention in a piece written by Helen Arkell, who has her own centre and was one of the pioneers in the dyslexia field in the early days, along with Wendy Fisher, Dr Bevé Hornsby and the late Kathleen Hickey, all of whom did so much to put dyslexia on the map.

DON'T ridicule or point out each and every mistake a dyslexic makes. This is disheartening. It is better to point out only a few mistakes then add that this word is nicely written, or that answer was very good. Also, never compare a dyslexic child unfavourably to his brother or sister, as this will result in an even greater loss of confidence.

There are a number of ways in which parents can better understand and help their children. Dr Nata Goulandris, a qualified psychologist, who has taught children for ten years explains:

PRACTICAL SUGGESTIONS FOR PARENTS

If a child is having unexpected difficulties learning to read and write, he will need parental support right from the start. Once parents become concerned they should go straight to the child's teacher to discuss why the child is not learning adequately. There are many reasons why a child may not be learning to read apart from dyslexia. The child may have poor hearing or vision, he may have attended many schools and not have settled down yet or he may still be quite immature. Your child's teacher will almost definitely have an opinion about why your child is not progressing satisfactorily.

If you still feel that you need to pursue the matter further you should try to arrange for a psychological assessment with the school's educational psychologist. This is your statutory right under the provision of the 1981 Educational Act. Alternatively (or for a second opinion), you may wish to pay for a private psychological assessment but this can be very expensive. Your doctor may also be able to help by referring you to a specialist paediatrician. *Every* child has a statutory right to an assessment under the provisions of the Education Act 1981. It is worth remembering that it is helpful to have an assessment to send to the authority when exercising your legal right.

It is worthwhile contacting the British Dyslexia Association (BDA) who can give you the phone number of your nearest local dyslexia association who will offer advice on the many problems parents may be facing, can put them in touch with parents of other dyslexics and also of suitably trained specialist teachers.

CONFIDENCE

It is vital for parents of dyslexics to give their children abundant love and to foster their self-confidence. When a child is worried that he is not as good at school work as his peers, he is likely to worry that his parents may be disappointed in him. It really makes a difference when the child's parents rally around him – helping him when he has problems rather than chastising him. Sometimes parents become over-anxious and this anxiety is passed on to the child. It helps if parents can remain calm, even if they are troubled and cannot get the authorities to listen to them.

Encouraging the dyslexic to develop all his talents, for example, music, drama, drawing, sport, computing or more academic interests, is essential for helping a child 'feel good' about himself.

There are practical ways you can help too.

GETTING ORGANIZED

A dyslexic child often has difficulty organizing himself. He may forget to take his swimwear if he is going swimming or takes his English books to school on the day he needs his history books. Although all children forget sometimes, the dyslexic forgets routinely.

It can be helpful if you sit with the child and the two of you make a schedule of the child's week and the things he ought to remember each day. The aim is to teach him gradually to become more organized and to take responsibility for himself.

You should also check that he knows the names and order of the days of the week, the months and the seasons. You may find that he knows only a few of the names for each category and is confused about the order within the categories. So the idea of 'time' may be very confusing for him since he cannot make sense of it – for example what you do on Wednesday compared to Sunday. He may even be uncertain about the terms morning, afternoon and evening. Help him by teaching a few items at a time, beginning with the days of the week. Try and associate each day with an event if possible. For example 'Monday' may be swimming day and 'Tuesday' may be the day he generally visits his grandmother. He will eventually need help telling the time using a conventional clock face.

LEFT AND RIGHT

Many dyslexics also have 'left and right confusion'. This can be improved by associating one hand to one of the words. If they wear a watch on their left hand, for example, 'left' is the side on which they wear their watch. If this also happens to be their writing hand all the better. Girls sometimes enjoy having their 'right' hand marked with a pretty ribbon. Eventually the mnemonics (memory aids) are no longer needed.

READ TO YOUR CHILD

It is important to read to all children, but especially to dyslexics so that they do not miss out. Read any books the child likes, particularly books his non-dyslexic friends are reading. It is more important to convince the child that reading is great fun than to worry about the quality of the book. Read anything the child wants to hear, even comics can help a child learn to enjoy and value learning to read. There are also books on tapes and Talking Books schemes. Don't ever let reading become a battle ground in which the tables are turned and the child is suddenly obliged to read. Never force him to read or story time will be a threat rather than an enjoyable experience. If the child has been assigned homework by the school or the specialist teacher that should ideally be completed well before story time.

B/D CONFUSION

Children who muddle the letters b and d can become very anxious about this problem although most children grow out of it as their reading and spelling improve. It is generally considered a *naming* problem as children are not sure which name goes with which letter. Children can be helped to deal with this confusion if they are allowed to refer to a mnemonic which can be drawn on a card. A parent can make a 'bed' card in which the 'b' is the head of the bed, the mattress forms the middle letter and the 'd' the base, see fig. 1. Another mnemonic used regularly by specialist teachers is the cricket bat and ball which illustrate how a b is constructed, see fig. 2. First you make the bat, and then draw the ball. If the class teacher does not mind, the child can take the card to school and refer to it when he needs to.

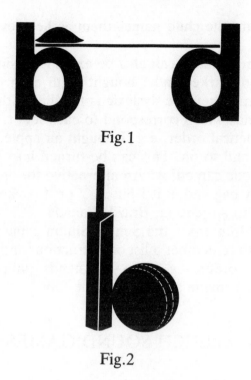

Fig.1

Fig.2

MEMORY

Many dyslexics forget instructions because they have poor short term memory, which means they cannot remember more than a few items. Names, numbers or instructions are forgotten all too quickly if the list is long. Memory games may help to increase the child's short term memory and are best played with other children who are not markedly better than the dyslexic.

Kim's game can help improve the child's memory for objects which are seen. Place two or three items on a tray. Let the child study these for ten or fifteen seconds and then cover them up with a cloth. If the child always gets it right it is too easy. If he always gets it wrong it is too difficult and he should be given fewer items or more time to study the items. Later you can use pictures or plastic letters instead of objects but make sure the child names them as he tries to remember them.

Short term memory can also be extended using games such as 'I went to market and I bought' with each person adding another item. When the dyslexic is familiar with the alphabet and the sounds which correspond to each letter, the items can be in alphabetical order, e.g. I bought an apple, bread, a cat, a doughnut and so on. This can be turned into a family game which everyone can enjoy. An alternative for older children is 'I packed my bag and in it I put . . .' or 'I packed my bag and then I went to Argentina, Brazil, Canada . . .'

Many children enjoy the Simple Simon game in which they are obliged to remember a list of instructions and execute them in the correct order, e.g. 'Clap your hands, jump up and down twice, recite a rhyme and hop on one foot.'

SPEECH SOUND GAMES

'I spy' games are useful because dyslexics often have great difficulties hearing the sounds in words and doing this is crucial for understanding how letters correspond to speech sounds in writing. Usually you play 'I spy' using the sounds at the beginning of words but when children have become good at this you can try 'I spy something which ends with . . .' Rhyming games are also extremely useful. It is fun making up silly rhymes. Both you and the child can try seeing how many rhyming words can be used in one sentence, e.g. 'The fat cat had a chat with the rat.' There are also rhyming snap games available and you can make or buy domino games using pictures of rhyming objects.

TEACHING YOUR CHILD TO READ
AND WRITE

Although some of the autobiographies in this book have

shown that some dyslexics have been taught to read and write by their parents, a large proportion of parents find that their attempts to teach their child generate resentment and are often ineffective. If there were enough specialist teachers available no parent would be obliged to teach their child, but currently a number of parents are forced to assume a teaching role.

If it is really impossible for you to obtain specialist help for your child, you should begin by reading a few of the books intended for teachers in order to understand the principles of the multi-sensory, cumulative, structured approach which is recommended for these children. If possible ask a specialist teacher to see you and your child. Have her help you to draw up a teaching programme and suggest the correct supplementary materials. If you can afford it, take the child to the specialist teacher at regular intervals, perhaps every three months, to have the child's progress evaluated and to be given more teaching directives.

TEACHING SESSIONS SHOULD BE ENJOYABLE AND PRODUCTIVE. IF YOUR HOUSE IS A BATTLE GROUND, STOP.

Your child needs a loving relationship with his parent more than anything else.

If teaching your own child is not successful continue asking for extra teaching at school. Many bursary funds have been set up in recent years which will pay a proportion of the teacher's fee at a private centre and most of the proceeds from this book will go to this type of fund. It is certainly worthwhile enquiring about bursary funds.

MAKE LEARNING FUN

All the activities I have mentioned including the more serious teaching are meant to be fun. If they are treated as unpleasant work the child will not enjoy them and will not wish to continue. Keep it light, amusing and not too long.

With specialist teaching for children with dyslexia or specific learning difficulties, consistent parental support and love, adequate motivation and the willingness to work hard, dyslexics *can* live up to their potential and be successful.

PART THREE

Appendix I
THEORIES AND PRACTICAL ADVICE

Many people say there is no short term answer to 'curing' dyslexia other than by proper specialist help, whereby the child is taught a multi-sensory approach in which all the senses are used at the same time, thus combining speech with hearing, vision and feel. In other words all the senses working simultaneously e.g. the child looks at an 'M', says 'M', hears 'M', sees 'M', feels the 'M' with his finger as he traces it and notices what his mouth does when he pronounces the 'M' sound.

But there are some experts who feel they have found another 'answer' to dyslexics' problems other than specialist help. I have put together a number of these theories which have helped some and which may give 'hope' to others. Nevertheless, it is very important that parents do not cling to the theories as the quick solution to a child's problem, as, unfortunately, so far there does not seem to be any really effective solution other than proper specialist teaching.

MORE ZINC

Some say that dyslexic children may be lacking in zinc. This is

367

backed up by recent research which suggests that children with *certain types* of dyslexia may indeed be zinc deficient. The tests revealed that these children have about a third less zinc in their sweat than non-dyslexic children, possibly because their parents were short of this vital mineral when the child was conceived. But unfortunately, this does not mean that if all children with learning difficulties started taking zinc, the condition would disappear, although it is the sort of simple solution of which the parent of a dyslexic dreams.

If a child is zinc deficient, zinc can be found in food such as steak, eggs, tuna fish, liver, potatoes and parsley. Alternatively, zinc tablets are available from health food shops.

EYE MOVEMENTS

Ron Grant, who has just published *What the Eye Doesn't See* (VTP Aids, 21 Crescenta Walk, Bognor Regis), also has a theory which concentrates on eye movement.

Dyslexics often find newspaper columns easier to read than books. Ron Grant believes that this has much to do with poor visual control. To try to prove this to me he persuaded me to do an eye test at a Dyslexia Conference some years back. The printout of the tests showed that each eye was running along the lines and reading words at different rates. According to Mr Grant, this makes the messages to the brain from each eye confusing, hence the difficulty in reading books.

With a newspaper there are only about five or six words to the line so the messages to the brain from each eye don't get time to bump into each other and confuse the mind at the end of each line or at the start of the new one.

Ron Grant is anxious to get as many people as possible interested in the causes of reading problems and the need to take a diagnostic approach to help dyslexics overcome their difficulties. He says:

It is hard to persuade both teachers and optometrists that there is a correlation between reading difficulty and visual control problems at the reading distance. They do not look to visual problems as a possible cause of a child's difficulty with interpreting the written word.

Research into the connection between ocular anomalies and reading problems suggests that between fifty and sixty per cent of children with literacy difficulties have visual control anomalies.

Whatever you may feel about Ron Grant's theories, teachers, academics and youngsters with learning difficulties still find specialist multi-sensory help the most reliable way to improve their skills.

FOOD ALLERGIES AND DIET

As we discussed in the Parents chapter, the child's whole life style is important. Everything from a calm supportive home environment to nutrition.

The concern about food additives, preservatives and colourings has existed for some time. It has been established that some children are allergic to certain foods and that some of the fast foods can make some children hyperactive. The difficulty is discovering these allergies and knowing whether or not they are related to a child's learning difficulties and behaviour problems.

Healthy eating, whether it resolves learning difficulties or not, is a sensible first step to good health and to be recommended in any case. But Val Kearney believes that her daughter's learning difficulties were resolved by a change of diet.

Val Kearney sent the following testament relating to her daughter's progress after a change in diet.

At nine and a half Jane was a charming, lively and

apparently intelligent little girl. Yet she had never read a book or even a story for pleasure. Her spelling was bizarre and so was her number work.

For the next two years a kind and devoted young teacher did all she could to encourage and cajole Jane, and Jane and I worked most evenings for perhaps an hour – it took forty-five minutes to read one page.

There was some improvement but the basic problem remained in spite of all the hard work and good motivation.

Just before her thirteenth birthday I became ill and consulted a local expert on diet and nutrition. He told me that if I would give up eating artificial additives and also refined foods such as white flour and white sugar I would get better and he also said that Jane's dyslexia would disappear.

For the next eight months we tried to adjust to these rules and we gradually became more and more fond of the natural foods and found we no longer enjoyed what Jane graphically called 'plastic food'. At the end of the eight months I was completely rejuvenated and although Jane no longer suffered from mouth ulcers I could see no particular change in her school work. But by this time we had all decided to really do the thing properly – even taking sandwiches for school lunch made from my own wholemeal bread and giving up shop biscuits in favour of home-made.

Now things really began to happen – two months later those brown eyes shone with happiness as Jane told me she could 'learn like the clever kids'. Another three months and she found she could learn and remember the alphabet – she was now fourteen. Soon, she found herself reading 'Fidelity' on the radio and 'Academy' on the piano – she said 'I thought they were just patterns before'.

With ever increasing delight she found herself reading anything and everything and able to write fast and accurately. When she was fourteen years and four months she told me 'Now I can learn, it isn't boring.'

P.S. At the appropriate times she passed seven O-levels and two A-levels – one of which was English. She was *very* poorly with glandular fever during both O and A exam sessions. She is now doing a Fine Art degree.

Val's story is an inspiring one and I do sincerely believe healthy eating improves one's ability to work well, concentrate and enjoy day-to-day life. I have tried to eat a sugar-free, non-additive and non-preservative diet for years, but regrettably my 'condition' has not really improved. All I can say is heaven knows what it would be like if I started living on fast food and chips!

A FEW TRICKS

Most dyslexics have little tricks that we feel work for us. For instance I find that it is much easier to write a first draft of a book on yellow paper. If I write on white paper it is more difficult to read my own writing. Yellow pages or yellow pads as I call them, only help me read what I have written, in no way does it improve my spelling!

PINK TINTED GLASS

Perhaps the same principle applies to pink tinted glasses which everyone was so excited about. Perhaps the pink tint reduces the glare between the black and white. But once again, pink glasses cannot teach you to spell or sequence correctly.

ORANGE PERSPEX

Another trick worth trying is laying a sheet of orange/yellow perspex on top of the page you are reading. Not only does this stop the letters 'jumping' but it also slightly magnifies the words.

BLACKBOARD

To help children develop their memory at home a blackboard on the wall, say in the kitchen, is invaluable. Then should a word or a number come to mind, you or your child can just write on the blackboard so it can be referred to easily.

SPELL CHECKERS

When I was talking to Jackie Stewart, I noticed that he has a little handheld Franklin Computer Dictionary/Spellcheck, which he keeps with him at all times. It was given to him by King Constantine. Not everyone will have a spell checker given to them by a king, but for dyslexics such gadgets are very useful.

Many people have written to me in praise of their spell checkers. Certainly their beautifully typed, perfectly spelt letters are impressive. There are now many electronic spell checking gadgets which can be bought to assist in spelling. These vary in accuracy so it is worth doing some research first. Word processors can also have a spell checking facility which can be programmed to suit your needs. Here is an example of some text written on an Amstrad PCW9512 personal computer word processor.

This is the original version:

Many years later I did return, but not to find a tranquil woodland but a monsterous block of concreate flats, were once had stood those noble beaches. Ironically, on their forecort stood an unrecagnizible skulpture, reeding the plaet at its base it said simply 'Hedgehog' by Hereward Smith.

This is the checked version with the codes beneath:

372

Many years later I did return, but not to find a tranquil woodland but a **monsterous** block of **concreate** flats, *were* once had stood those noble *beaches*. Ironically, on their **forecort** stood an **unrecagnizible skulpture**, **reeding** the **plaet** at its base it said simply 'Hedgehog' by Hereward Smith.

Words picked up and corrected by WCP dictionary
WORDS PICKED UP BUT NOT IN WCP DICTIONARY
Words in dictionary with two possible spellings that sound the same.

This is the final corrected version:

Many years later I did return, but not to find a tranquil woodland but a monstrous block of concrete flats, where once had stood those noble beeches. Ironically, on their forecourt stood an unrecognizable sculpture, reading the plate at its base it said simply 'Hedgehog' by Hereward Smith.

PENCIL HOLDER

And finally there is a pencil holder, a plastic gadget that can be slipped on to the pencil. It has a special finger rest for the first and second finger and thumb so as to help keep the pencil in the correct position when writing.

Appendix II

HANDWRITING AND SPELLING SAMPLES

DYSLEXIC SPELLING

This letter is a wonderful example of classic dyslexic spelling. To me and to most dyslexics it is logical spelling, but to a head teacher or future employer, the reaction would be to reach for the red correcting pen or write off its sender as illiterate.

It takes imagination and logic to write 'because' as 'becouise' and 'embarrassing' as 'embarosing'.

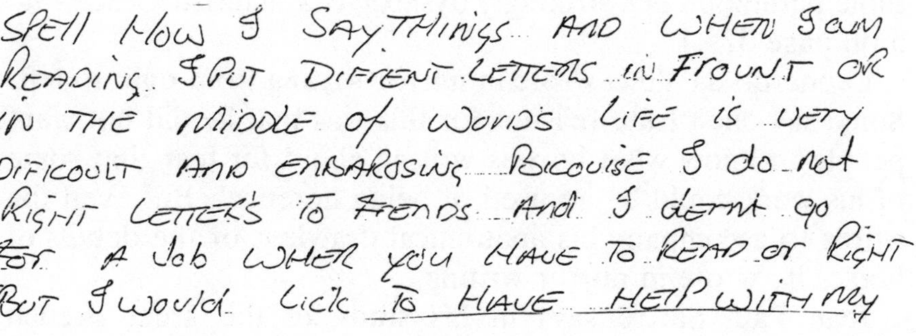

SPEll how I SAy THINGS AND WHEN I am
READING. I PUT DIFFENT LETTERS IN FROUNT OR
IN THE MIDDLE of WORDS LIFE IS VERY
DIFICOULT AND ENBAROSING. BICOUISE I do not
RIGHT LETTER'S TO FRENDS. AND I dernt go
FOR A Job WHER you HAVE TO READ or RIGHT
BUT I would LICK TO HAVE HELP WITH MY

Fig. 3 An example of dyslexic spelling

375

On page 377 is also an example of mirror writing in a letter sent to me by a dyslexic some time ago. To read it, hold it up to the mirror.

DOES EVERY LETTER COUNT?

Years ago everybody used spelling variances or alternative spelling. They enjoyed doing it and it was an asset rather than a liability. People didn't think of it as bad spelling, as content was all-important and that wasn't altered by the apparently eccentric spelling.

So to find examples of such spelling my cousin, Don Pavey, and I spent many hours in the British Museum going through manuscripts looking at the letters of such great writers as John Keats, Ben Jonson, Jonathan Swift, Alexander Pope and, perhaps the greatest of all literary men, who some think wrote Shakespeare's works, Sir Francis Bacon.

Dyslexics will be comforted to know that all these writers used varied spelling. But what was so exciting for someone who is trying to prove a point is that these writers often spelt words in several different ways on the same page. This does not necessarily mean these men were dyslexic. But, for Alexander Pope to spell 'easy', 'easy' and then 'easie' in the same paragraph is a strikingly dyslexic characteristic. (See Fig. 5 on page 379.)

Leonardo da Vinci wrote in mirror writing from right to left. Some say one of the reasons for this was that he did not want people to know what he was writing about for fear that some of his work could be accused of being heretical. But even the words to accompany his anatomical drawings or the details of horses he wrote in mirror writing.

Jean Paul Sartre says in his study of the great French writer Gustave Flaubert, who wrote *Madame Bovary*, that his mother was in despair as Gustave did not learn with

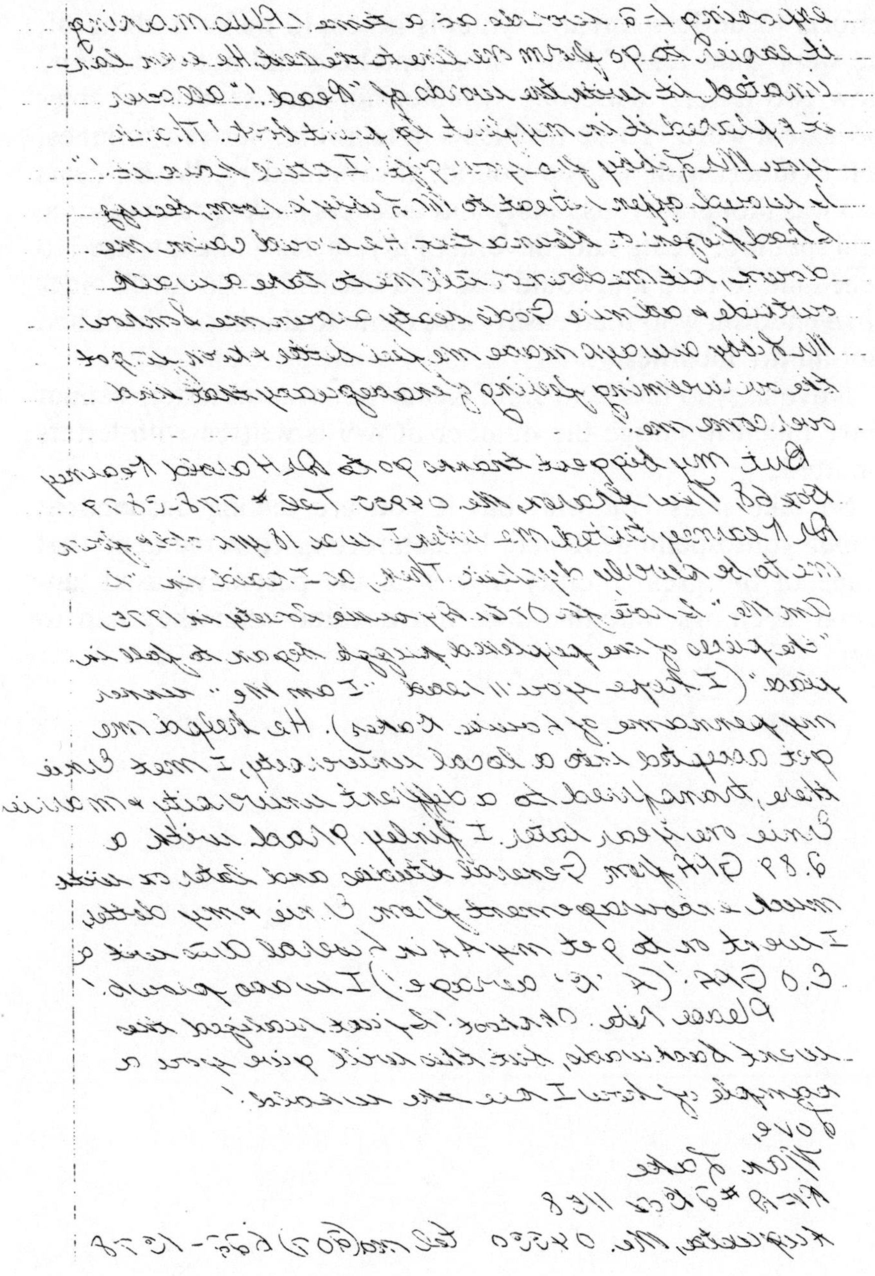

Fig. 4 An example of mirror writing

377

the same ease as her other children. 'Having made strenuous efforts to understand the symbols he could make nothing of, he wept giant tears.' For a long time he could not understand how two letters made one syllable, nor how several syllables became a word. These problems in learning, Sartre continues, left Flaubert with a 'deep wound, always hidden'. W. B. Yeats too was thought by his family and teachers backward in reading and spelling. Yeats said 'Several of my uncles and aunts used to teach me to read and could not, and because I was much older than children who read easily, had come to think . . . that I had not all my faculties.'

Anyone who has read John Keats' poems and letters cannot have failed to notice the number of words written with letters omitted.

So take it as you will, but if you are feeling despondent about your spelling, it may be comforting to remember that some of the great literary figures of the past have used 'unusual' spellings, but this does not devalue what they had to say.

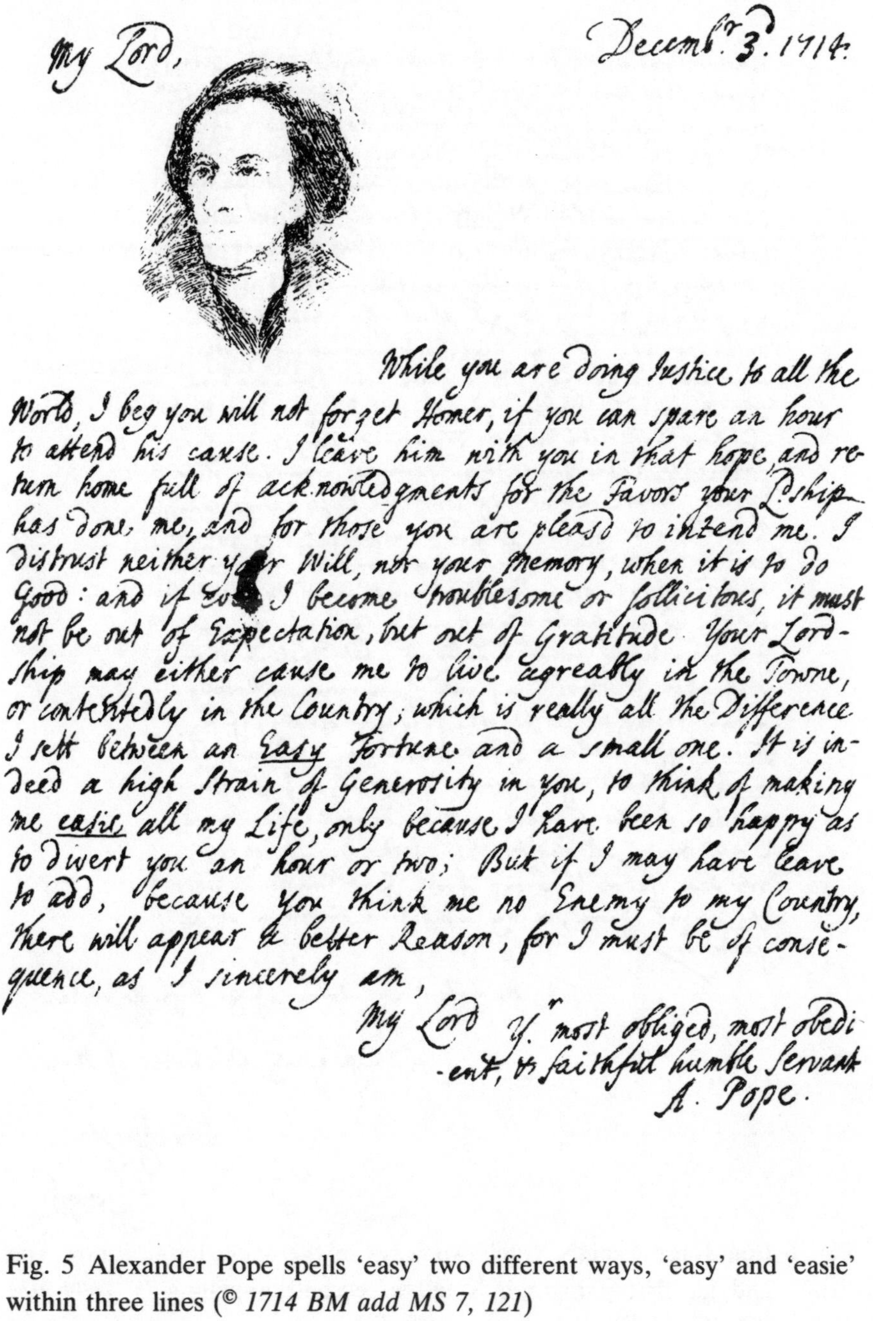

My Lord, December 3. 1714.

While you are doing Justice to all the World, I beg you will not forget Homer, if you can spare an hour to attend his cause. I leave him with you in that hope, and return home full of acknowledgments for the Favors your Lordship has done me, and for those you are pleas'd to intend me. I distrust neither your Will, nor your Memory, when it is to do Good: and if ever I become troublesome or follicitous, it must not be out of Expectation, but out of Gratitude. Your Lordship may either cause me to live agreably in the Towne, or contentedly in the Country; which is really all the Difference I sett between an Easy Fortune and a small one. It is indeed a high Strain of Generosity in you, to think of making me easie all my Life, only because I have been so happy as to divert you an hour or two; But if I may have leave to add, because you think me no Enemy to my Country, there will appear a better Reason, for I must be of consequence, as I sincerely am,

My Lord Y.r most obliged, most obedient, & faithful humble Servant A. Pope.

Fig. 5 Alexander Pope spells 'easy' two different ways, 'easy' and 'easie' within three lines (© *1714 BM add MS 7, 121*)

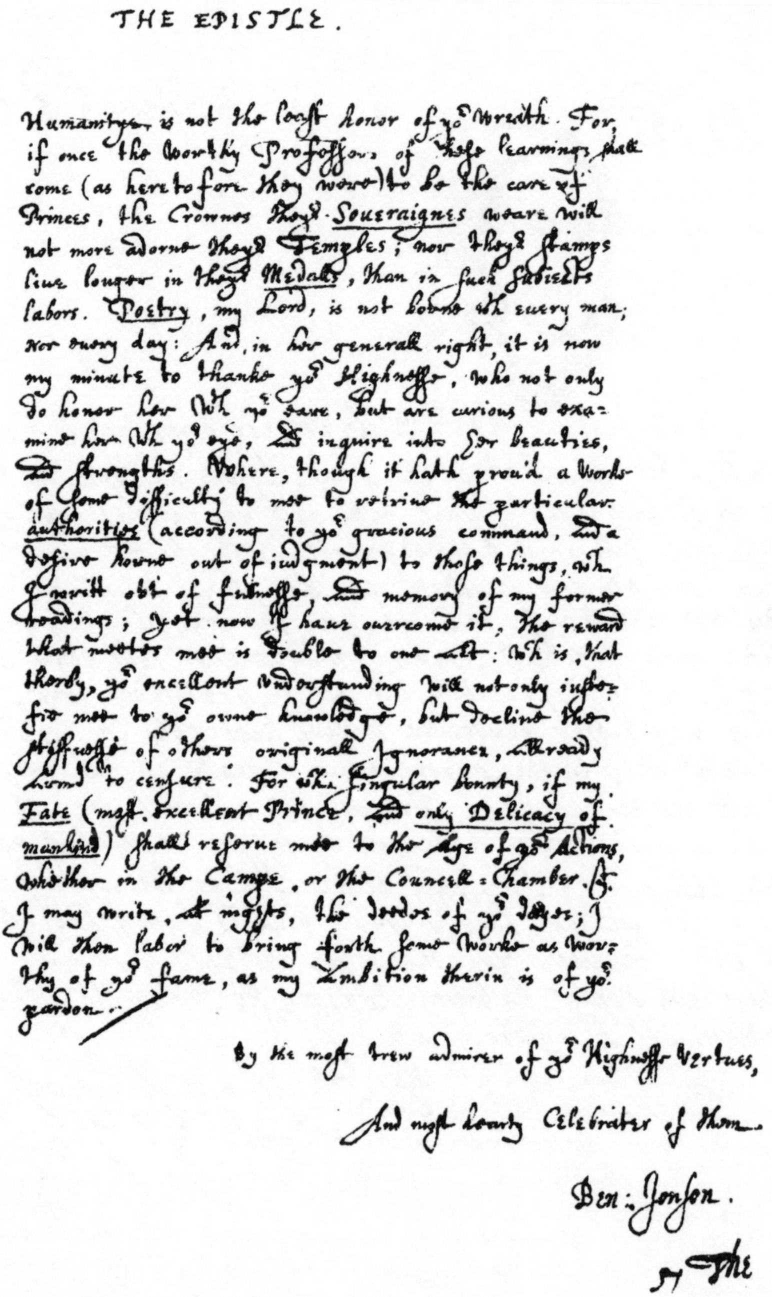

THE EPISTLE.

Humanitye is not the least honor of yor Wreath. For, if once the worthy Professors of these learnings shall come (as heretofore they were) to be the care of Princes, the Crownes theyr Soueraignes weare will not more adorne theyr Temples; nor theyr stamps liue longer in theyr Medalls, than in such Subiects labors. Poetry, my Lord, is not borne wth euery man; nor euery day: And, in her generall right, it is now my minute to thanke yor Highnesse, who not only do honor her wth yor eare, but are curious to examine her wth yor eye, & inquire into her beauties, & strengths. Where, though it hath prou'd a worke of some difficulty to mee to retriue the particular authorities (according to yor gracious command, & a desire borne out of iudgment) to those things, wch I writt out of fullnesse, & memory of my former readings; yet now I haue ouercome it, the reward that meetes mee is double to one act: wch is, that therby, yor excellent vnderstanding will not only iustifie mee to yor owne knowledge, but decline the stiffnesse of others originall Ignorance, allready arm'd to censure. For wch singular bounty, if my Fate (most excellent Prince, & only Delicacy of mankind) shall reserue mee to the Age of yor Actions, whether in the Campe, or the Councell-Chamber, I may write, at nights, the deedes of yor dayes; I will then labor to bring forth some worke as worthy of yor fame, as my Ambition therin is of yor pardon.

By the most trew admirer of yor Highnesse Vertues,

And most hearty Celebrater of them.

Ben: Jonson.

Fig. 6 Ben Jonson spells 'true' two ways in the same letter, 'trew' and 'true', and his first paragraph is full of eccentric spelling (© *1609 BM Royal MS, 18AXLV*)

THE MASQVE OF
QVEENES.

It encreasing, now, to the third time of my being vs'd
in these seruices to her Ma:tis personall presentacio's,
wth the Ladyes whome sho pleasd to honor; it was
my first, and speciall regaurd, to see that the Nobility
of the Inuention should bee answerable to the dig=
nity of theyr persons. For wch reason, I chose
the Argument, to be, A Celebration of honorable &
true Fame, bred out of Vertue: obseruing that rule
of the best Artist, to suffer no object of delight to
passe wthout his mixture of profit, & example.   "Hor. in Art.
And because her Ma:tie (best knowing, that a prin=   Poetic:
cipall part of life in these Spectacles lay in theyr
variety) had commaunded mee to thinke on some Daunce,
or Show, that might precede hers, and haue the place
of a foyle, or false Masque; I was carefull to
declino not only from others, but mine owne steppes   b.
in that kind, since the last yeares I had an Anti=Ma=   In the Masque
sque of Boyes: and therefore, now, deuisd that twelue   at my L: Haddintons
Women, in the habite of Haggs, or Witches, sustayning   wedding. /
the persons of Ignorance, Suspicion, Credulity, &c.
the opposites to good Fame, should fill that part; not
as a Masque, but a Spectacle of strangenesse, pro=
ducing multiplicity of Gesture, & not vnaptly
sorting wth the current, & whole fall of the Deuice.

First, then, his Ma:tie being set, and the whole Com=
pany in full expectation, that wch presented it selfe
was an ougly Hell: wch flaming beneath, smoakd vn=
to the top of the Roofe. And, in regard all Euills
are (morally) sayd to come from Hell; as also from
that obseruation of Torrentius vpon Horace his Cani=
dia.

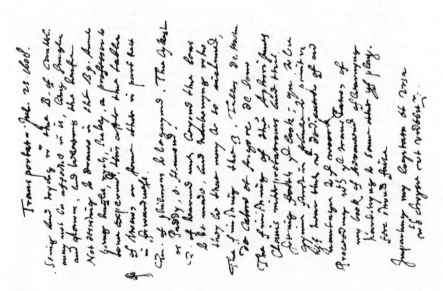

Fig. 7 Among the spelling mistakes, note Sir Francis Bacon's spelling of 'scornfully' as 'skornfully' (© *1608 BM add MS 27, 278*)

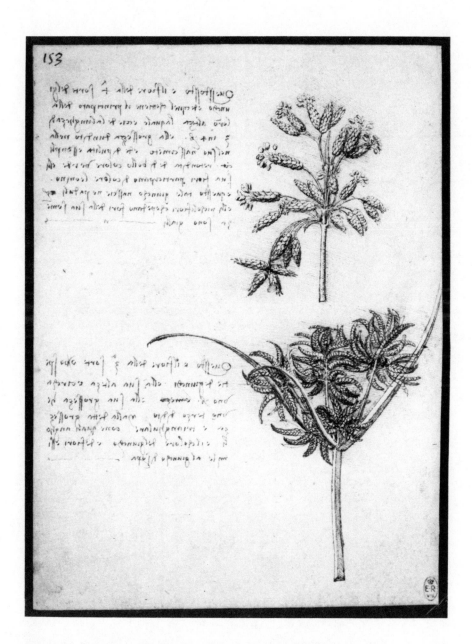

Fig. 8 A sample of Leonardo da Vinci's mirror writing
(Windsor Castle, Royal Library. © 1989 Her Majesty The Queen)

Appendix III
FURTHER READING AND USEFUL ADDRESSES

FURTHER READING

Susan's Story by Susan Hampshire (Corgi). An autobiographical account of her struggle with words.

Understanding Dyslexia, On Helping the Dyslexic Child, More Help for Dyslexic Children, The Dyslexic at College by T.R. Miles (Hodder & Stoughton 'Teach Yourself'). A series of guides written in easy-to-understand language.

This Book Doesn't Make Sens Cens Sns Scens Sense by Jean Augur (Bath Educational Publishing Ltd). Written for parents by a parent to offer support and practical advice.

The Child Under Stress – Dyslexia? by Zita M. Albes (Granary Press). A book linking stress with dyslexia. Of particular interest are pre-school tests which parents can follow to assess their child.

Overcoming Dyslexia by Dr Bevé Hornsby (Martin Dunitz). A guide for families and teachers.

Reversals – A Personal Account of Victory Over Dyslexia by Eileen Simpson (Gollancz). The problems of dyslexia written from personal experience.

Take Time by M. Nash Worthian (L.D.A./Living & Learning). Exercises for parents to help a young child with co-ordination, rhythm and timing.

Booklets available from the Dyslexia Institute:
Special Needs – Special Provision (£1.00). General information on dyslexia/specific learning difficulty.
A Different Way of Learning
> *Information for Parents* (75p)
> *Information for Teachers* (75p)
> *Information for Adult Dyslexics* (75p)
> *Information for Employers* (75p)
GCSE Examinations and Dyslexic Students 1988 (75p)

The following are one-sheet general information sheets available from the Dyslexia Institute free of charge (please send an S.A.E.).
What is Dyslexia?
General Assessment Information
Education Act 1981
Finding Funding for Special Teaching
General Reading List
Donation Leaflet
Area Information Sheet
National Fee Guideline Sheet

USEFUL ADDRESSES

The Dyslexia Institute, 133 Gresham Road, Staines TW18 2AJ (Tel: 0784 463851). Advice, assessments, 120 teaching centres around the country and teacher training
British Dyslexia Association, 98 London Road, Reading, Berkshire RG1 5AU (Tel: 0734 668271). Advice and counselling
Helen Arkell Dyslexia Centre, Frensham, Surrey

Hornsby Centre, 71 Wandsworth Common West Side, London SW18 2ED (Tel: 01 871 2846)

St Bartholomew's Hospital Dyslexia Clinic, West Wing, West Smithfield, London EC1A 7BE

The Centre for Complementary Change, 36 Greenhill Street, Stratford-upon-Avon, Warwickshire CV37 6LE

Bath Educational Publishing Ltd, 7 Walcot Buildings, London Road, Bath BA1 6AD

L.D.A./Living & Learning, Duke Street, Wisbech, Cambridgeshire

Scotland

The Dyslexia Institute Glasgow, 74 Victoria Crescent Road, Glasgow G12 9JU (Tel: 041 334 4549)

Scottish Dyslexia Association, Mrs G. Thomson, Cakemuir House, Nenthorn, Kelso, Roxburgshire TD5 7RY (Tel: 0753 24806)

Eire

The Dyslexia Association Ireland, 27 Upper Mount Street, Dublin 2

Wales

The Dyslexia Unit Wales, Department of Psychology, UCNW, Bangor, Gwynedd LL57 2D

USA

Orton Dyslexia Society, 724 York Road, Baltimore, Maryland 21204, USA

Canada

Association of Children and Adults with Learning Disabilities, Maison Kildare House, 323 Chapel Street, Suite 200, Ottawa, KLN 722, Canada

New Zealand

SPELD, PO Box 13391, Christchurch, New Zealand

387

Pakistan
Dyslexia Association of Pakistan, D-208 Shalamar Estates, Clifton 5, Karachi 6, Pakistan

My Dear Fellow Dyslexics,

If there is one sentence in this book that has given you courage, cling to it and put it to good use.

Much Love and Good Luck,

Susan Hampshire